The African American Experience
in Vietnam

The African American History Series

Series Editors:
Jacqueline M. Moore, Austin College
Nina Mjagkij, Ball State University

Traditionally, history books tend to fall into two categories: books academics write for each other and books written for popular audiences. Historians often claim that many of the popular authors do not have the proper training to interpret and evaluate the historical evidence. Yet, popular audiences complain that most historical monographs are inaccessible because they are too narrow in scope or lack an engaging style. This series, which will take both chronological and thematic approaches to topics and individuals crucial to an understanding of the African American experience, is an attempt to address that problem. The books in this series, in lively prose by established scholars, are aimed primarily at nonspecialists. They focus on topics in African American history that have broad significance and place them in their historical context. While presenting sophisticated interpretations based on primary sources and the latest scholarship, the authors tell their stories in a succinct manner, avoiding jargon and obscure language. They include selected documents that allow readers to judge the evidence for themselves and to evaluate the authors' conclusions. Bridging the gap between popular and academic history, these books bring the African American story to life.

Volumes Published

Booker T. Washington, W.E.B. Du Bois, and the Struggle for Racial Uplift
    Jacqueline M. Moore
Slavery in Colonial America, 1619–1776
    Betty Wood
African Americans in the Jazz Age: A Decade of Struggle and Promise
    Mark Robert Schneider
A. Philip Randolph: A Life in the Vanguard
    Andrew E. Kersten
The African American Experience in Vietnam
    James E. Westheider

The African American Experience in Vietnam

Brothers in Arms

James E. Westheider

ROWMAN & LITTLEFIELD PUBLISHERS, INC.
Lanham • Boulder • New York • Toronto • Plymouth, UK

ROWMAN & LITTLEFIELD PUBLISHERS, INC.

Published in the United States of America
by Rowman & Littlefield Publishers, Inc.
A wholly owned subsidiary of The Rowman & Littlefield Publishing Group, Inc.
4501 Forbes Boulevard, Suite 200, Lanham, Maryland 20706
www.rowmanlittlefield.com

Estover Road
Plymouth PL6 7PY
United Kingdom

British Library Cataloguing in Publication Information Available

Library of Congress Cataloging-in-Publication Data

Westheider, James E., 1956–
  The African American experience in Vietnam : brothers in arms /
James E. Westheider.
    p. cm. — (African American history)
  Includes bibliographical references and index.
  ISBN-13: 978-0-7425-4531-1 (cloth : alk. paper)
  ISBN-10: 0-7425-4531-8 (cloth : alk. paper)
  ISBN-13: 978-0-7425-4532-8 (pbk. : alk. paper)
  ISBN-10: 0-7425-4532-6 (pbk. : alk. paper)
  1. Vietnam War, 1961–1975—African Americans. I. Title.
  DS559.8.B55W46 2008
  959.704'308996073—dc22
                                                    2007008668
Printed in the United States of America

⊗™ The paper used in this publication meets the minimum requirements of
American National Standard for Information Sciences—Permanence of Paper
for Printed Library Materials, ANSI/NISO Z39.48-1992.

For my wife Virginia

Contents

Acknowledgments   ix

Chronology   xi

Introduction   xvii

Chapter 1   African Americans in the Armed Forces
before Vietnam   1

Chapter 2   American Involvement in Vietnam and the Draft   17

Chapter 3   The Black Military Experience in the
Vietnam Era   39

Chapter 4   Antiwar Sentiment and Black Disillusionment   63

Chapter 5   Racial Violence in the Military and the
Military Response   81

Chapter 6   Vietnamization and Going Home   105

Appendixes   115

Documents   121

Bibliographic Essay   161

Index   167

About the Author   177

~

Acknowledgments

Thanks to all the fine people at Rowman & Littlefield Publishers, but especially Laura Gottlieb, and to African American History Series editors Nina Mjagkij and Jackie Moore. I owe a debt of gratitude to my colleagues at the University of Cincinnati-Clermont College, but in particular Dan Goodman, Habtu Ghebre-Ab, Howard Todd, Michael Vislosky, and my division chair Patricia Friel, and to Terri Premo, Dan Beaver, Herb Shapiro, and John Brackett. Special thanks go to Fred Krome, managing editor of the *Journal of the Archives of Hebrew Union College*; Joe Fitzharris, St. Thomas University; Don Bittner, Marine Command School, Quantico; Selika Duckworth-Lawton, University of Wisconsin, Eau Claire; David Ullrich, Ball State; and Chris Dixon, University of Newcastle, Australia. I also owe a debt of gratitude to all the veterans who were willing to share their experiences in Vietnam with me, but especially to Alfonza Wright, and Allen Thomas Jr. Thanks to the National Archives, University of Cincinnati Libraries, U.S. Military History Institute at Carlisle Barracks, and Cornell University Archives.

Last but certainly not least I need to thank Bill Brungs, Mark Herbig, Mike Tojo, Tony Saupe, Paul "Cerbel" Justice, Mike Kruse, Jay Williams, and my sister Sandy Bains, all good friends who helped me keep a shred of sanity during the process. Most of all I need to thank my wife Virginia, for her patience, help, and advice. It is to her that this book is dedicated.

~

Chronology

Militia Act of 1792   Congress bars African Americans from serving in state militias.

1820   Blacks excluded from the U.S. Army.

September 20, 1861   Black service in the U.S. Navy authorized, about thirty thousand served in the Civil War.

July–August 1862   Congress authorizes the army to begin recruiting black soldiers, and 186,000 African Americans served the Union as "United States Colored Troops" during the Civil War.

1866   Congress authorizes the establishment of four black regiments in the army, the Twenty-fourth and Twenty-fifth Infantry, and the Ninth and Tenth Cavalry, better known as the "Buffalo Soldiers."

1870   James Webster Smith becomes the first African American to be appointed to the United States Military Academy at West Point.

1877   Henry O. Flipper becomes the first African American to graduate from West Point.

1889   Charles Young graduates from West Point, becoming only the third African American and last to do so in the nineteenth century.

August 13–14, 1906   The Brownsville Riot. Black troopers in Brownsville, Texas, exchange gunfire with white civilians leaving one civilian dead. One hundred sixty-seven black soldiers receive dishonorable discharges from the army without benefit of court martial.

May 1917   War Department establishes Fort Des Moines, the first black officers training camp, and 639 cadets graduate and are commissioned officers in the army during World War I.

August 23–24, 1917   The Houston Riot. The worst clash between black troops and white civilians in American history results in nineteen people killed. Seventy black soldiers were convicted of mutiny and murder; nineteen were executed and the rest given life in prison at hard labor.

June 1936   Benjamin O. Davis Jr., son of Colonel Benjamin O. Davis Sr., graduates from West Point, only the fourth African American to do so.

October 1940   The Selective Service Act of 1940 prohibits discrimination based on race or color.

October 1940   Benjamin O. Davis Sr. is promoted to brigadier general, becoming the first black general in American history.

June 1942   President Franklin D. Roosevelt orders the Marine Corps and U.S. Navy to enlist African Americans.

September 2, 1945   Ho Chi Minh declares Vietnam's independence.

November 1945   Frederick C. Branch becomes the first black commissioned officer (2nd Lt.) in Marine Corps history.

July 1948   President Harry Truman issues Executive Order no. 9981 mandating equal opportunity in the military regardless of race and effectively integrating the armed forces.

June 1950–1953   The Korean War.

1954   Benjamin Davis Jr. becomes the first black general in the U.S. Air Force.

1954   All American military units are now officially integrated.

July 1963   Secretary of Defense Robert McNamara established the office of the Deputy Assistant Secretary of Defense for Civil Rights.

1964   Over fifteen thousand Americans serving in Vietnam; blacks comprise 8.7 percent of the total.

July 2, 1964   President Lyndon Johnson signs the Civil Rights Act into law.

August 11, 1964   Congress passes the Gulf of Tonkin Resolution allowing for direct American participation in the Vietnam War.

March 8, 1965   First American combat troops arrive in Vietnam. Elements of the Third Battalion, Ninth Marines land at Red Beach Two in South Vietnam.

July 1–4, 1965   The Congress of Racial Equality (CORE) demands the withdrawal of U.S. forces from Vietnam and supports resistance to the draft.

August 6, 1965   President Lyndon Johnson signs the Voting Rights Act into law.

August 11, 1965   Riots erupt in the Watts section of Los Angeles.

December 1965   About 184,000 American combat troops in Vietnam, of which about 14.8 percent are African Americans.

1966   Bobby Seale (chairman) and Huey Newton (minister of defense) form the Black Panther Party for Self-Defense in Oakland, California.

January 6, 1966   The Student Nonviolent Coordinating Committee (SNCC) issues a statement condemning American participation in the Vietnam War and the use of the draft to raise the manpower needed in the conflict.

August 1966   The United States has 459,000 troops in Vietnam. African Americans make up 15 percent of American forces in Vietnam but have suffered 22 percent of the total casualties to date.

August 1966   Project 100,000 announced by Secretary of Defense Robert McNamara. Forty percent of the men recruited under this program are black.

April 28, 1967   Heavyweight boxing champion Muhammad Ali refuses induction into the armed forces.

May 1, 1967   Cleveland Sellers, national program director for SNCC, refuses induction into the armed forces.

May 1967   Dr. Martin Luther King Jr. publicly denounces the Vietnam War.

June 20, 1967   Ali convicted and sentenced to five years in prison for draft evasion.

1968   Gen. Frederic E. Davison becomes the first black officer to lead an active combat brigade in Vietnam, and Lt. Col. Frank E. Petersen Jr. becomes the first African American to command either a navy or Marine Corps fighter squadron.

1968 First Navy ROTC program at a predominately black college established at Prairie View A & M in Texas.

January 30, 1968 Beginning of the Tet Offensive. The Vietcong attack five major cities including Saigon and Hue, sixty-four district capitals, thirty-six provincial capitals, and fifty hamlets.

April 4, 1968 James Earl Ray assassinates Dr. King in Memphis, Tennessee. Riots erupt in more than one hundred American cities.

August 29, 1968 Black prisoners riot at Long Binh Stockade near Saigon.

Late 1968 The number of Americans in Vietnam totals 543,000, the height of American involvement. African Americans make up almost 10 percent of U.S. armed forces assigned to Vietnam.

January 1969 One of the first African American organizations established in the military, GIs United Against the War, is founded by Joseph Miles at Fort Jackson, South Carolina.

April 1969 Secretary of Defense Melvin R. Laird established the Domestic Action Council and charged it with developing major race relations programs for implementation throughout the armed forces.

July 20, 1969 First of several major racial gang fights at U.S. military establishments erupts at Camp Lejeune, North Carolina.

July 30, 1969 Racial gang fight at Millington Naval Air Station near Memphis, Tennessee.

August 1969 Racial gang fight at Kaneohe Marine Corps Air Station in Hawaii.

October 13, 1969 National Urban League Director Whitney M. Young condemns the war in Vietnam.

November 1969 Movement for a Democratic Military is organized by black marines at Camp Pendleton, California.

December 1969 The House Armed Services Committee Report on the racial violence at Lejeune released.

1970 The United States has 335,000 troops in Vietnam; about 10 percent are African American.

1970 Army commanders instructed to include "minority group representation" on all promotion boards.

1970 General Benjamin O. Davis Jr. retires from the air force.

January 1970 A barrack at Quantico, Virginia, is named after PFC. James Anderson Jr., the first black marine recipient of the Medal of Honor.

March 1970 Two black air force sergeants, Milton White and Mayanard Jordan III, organize the Malcolm X Society at Vandenberg Air Force Base, California.

1971 Navy, under Admiral Elmo R. Zumwalt Jr., chief of naval operations, announces a five-year plan to increase the percentage of minorities in the navy.

January 1971 Nathaniel Jones leads an NAACP investigative team to Germany to study the administration of military justice.

May 1971 Samuel Gravely becomes the first black admiral in the navy.

June 28, 1971 The Supreme Court overturns boxer Muhammad Ali's conviction for draft evasion on a technicality.

1972 Affirmative action instituted in the army.

1972 The Department of Defense releases the report by the Task Force on Military Justice, detailing widespread discrimination in many facets of military life.

1972 Gen. Daniel "Chappie" James is named deputy assistant secretary of defense for public affairs.

1972 African Americans make up 11.1 percent of U.S. armed forces assigned to Vietnam, but only 7.6 percent of the casualties.

May 1972 The Congressional Black Caucus issues its report on racism in the armed forces.

July 1, 1972 The Marine Corps Human Relations Institute formally established at the Marine Corps Recruiting Depot at San Diego, California.

October 11–12, 1972 Racial gang fight on the aircraft carrier *Kitty Hawk*.

November 1972 Racial violence on the aircraft carrier *Constellation*.

1973 The navy bans dapping and black power salutes during working hours.

January 23, 1973 Henry Kissinger and Le Duc Tho sign the Paris Peace Accords officially ending American participation in the Vietnam War.

March 29, 1973 The last American troops and POWs leave Vietnam. Only the marine embassy guards remain.

August 1974 A "racially mixed group" of fifty-five sailors refused to board the aircraft carrier *Midway* in Japan, claiming racism on board the ship.

April 1975 Saigon and South Vietnam fall to North Vietnamese forces.

~

Introduction

African Americans have served with distinction in all of America's wars from the American Revolution to the recent conflicts in the Middle East, and, like their white counterparts, they have served for a variety of reasons. Some, like Vietnam veteran General Colin Powell, did so out of a sense of duty and patriotism. Others signed up looking for adventure or for personal advancement. But for the black community as a whole, one of the ultimate goals of military service has always been full inclusion in American society and the gaining of full rights as citizens. During the Civil War the famous black abolitionist Frederick Douglass once wrote, "Let the black man get upon his person the brass letters U.S. Let him get an eagle on his button and a musket on his shoulder, and there is no power on Earth which can deny that he has earned the right to citizenship in the United States."[1]

Minorities have long been aware of the possible rewards for military service, and often they have fought for "the right to fight." Service by Irish Americans in the Civil War, Jewish Americans in World War I, and Japanese Americans in World War II, for example, helped convince a skeptical public of their patriotism and helped lead to greater acceptance of these groups in American society. More recently, women and gays have used military service to prove their prowess and capabilities to the skeptical and often bigoted elements of society. Since 1945, economic incentives, such as career training, better pay, and the GI Bill, have enticed many minorities and poor or working-class whites to join the armed forces.

But military service has not always guaranteed these rights. African Americans served with distinction in the Civil War and were admitted as a permanent part of the military in the postwar era. The problem facing blacks in the military was no longer primarily one of being excluded from the defense establishment, but of challenging its policy of segregation and expanding the limited role African Americans were permitted to play in the military. When the United States entered World War I in April 1917, African Americans and their white supporters seized this new opportunity to once again press authorities not only for "the right to fight," but also for a leadership role for qualified African Americans. The outcome was the establishment of the first Colored Officers' Training Camp at Fort Des Moines, Iowa. For the first time in American military history, large numbers of black officers led their fellow African Americans into war. Only one class of officers graduated from Des Moines during the war, yet the training of black officers at Fort Des Moines not only had lasting implications in the military but also a profound effect on the course of race relations and the black quest for civil rights in America in the decades following World War I.

Nearly 2.5 million African Americans served during the Second World War, and as they did during the Vietnam War, black leaders linked wartime service with the civil rights movement in the United States. On June 25, 1940, President Franklin D. Roosevelt, under pressure from labor leader and civil rights activist A. Philip Randolph, issued Executive Order no. 8802, mandating equal employment by any corporation holding a government defense contract and establishing the Fair Employment Practices Commission (FEPC) to oversee racial fairness in the workplace. In World War II, the "Double V" program, originated by the *Pittsburgh Courier* in early 1942 and eventually supported by most of America's 210 black newspapers, called for a victory over fascism abroad and over racism at home. The "Double V" was controversial and was criticized by some black leaders and most whites. The War Department in particular deemed the program to be less than patriotic. Assistant Secretary of War John McCloy complained that the emphasis on the "Double V" in "papers like the *Pittsburgh Courier* . . . serve to take the mind of the Negro soldier . . . off what you term the basic issues of the war. . . . I bespeak greater emphasis on the necessity for greater out-and-out support of the war, particularly by the Negro press."[2]

Ironically, both America's war in Vietnam as well as the racial problems that plagued the armed forces in that conflict had their origins largely in the latter stages of World War II. In 1944, the Office of Strategic Services (OSS), the wartime forerunner of the Central Intelligence Agency (CIA), established direct contact with Ho Chi Minh's followers, the Vietminh, who were fighting the Japanese occupation of Vietnam during World War II. Thus began America's involvement in what would become known as the Vietnam War. Meanwhile, the armed services at home faced growing racial problems, including fights between white and black soldiers. McCloy reported to Army Chief of Staff George Marshall: "Disaffection among Negro soldiers has spread to the extent that it constitutes an immediately serious problem."[3] Much of the dissatisfaction stemmed from a lack of opportunity in the armed forces. After the war, in July 1948, President Harry Truman made "equal opportunity" official military policy when he issued Executive Order no. 9981, ordering the desegregation of the armed forces.

Desegregation had many benefits for the military. It was more cost efficient than the duplication of many services needed in a segregated military, but just as importantly, it helped to lessen racial friction. After initially resisting mandatory desegregation, the military began to embrace it in the 1950s, and by the early 1960s the armed forces could truthfully claim to be one of the most racially integrated institutions in America. Although personal and institutional racism continued to exist within the armed forces, most African American military personnel saw the military as an "island of integration in a sea of Jim Crow."[4]

It was in this context that many blacks and whites viewed the war in Vietnam as an opportunity to demonstrate the merits of integration. Blacks competed with whites on a near-equal basis for the first time in Vietnam. Some African American soldiers even viewed the disproportionately high casualty rates in the early years of the war as a form of vindication. One high-ranking black officer remarked in 1966, "I feel good about it. Not that I like the bloodshed, but the performance of the Negro in Vietnam tends to offset the fact that the Negro wasn't considered worthy of being a front-line soldier in other wars."[5] Such optimism about integration persisted throughout the first half of the war in Vietnam.

By 1968, there were over five hundred thousand United States soldiers in country and tens of thousands more served throughout the rest of Southeast Asia in support roles. Over 2.5 million men, three hundred thousand of whom were black, served in Vietnam before the end of America's involvement in 1973. In 1968, however, several factors merged to prove that the military's highly vaunted success in race relations was somewhat of an illusion. The war in Vietnam reached a turning point in January with the Tet Offensive, involving simultaneous attacks by Vietcong supporters of Ho Chi Minh throughout South Vietnam, which shattered American hopes for a quick victory. The war was becoming increasingly unpopular in the United States, and for the first time many black leaders, including Dr. Martin Luther

King Jr., were openly counseling young black men to avoid military service. Far from having to "fight for the right to fight," as they had in previous conflicts, inequities in the selective service system meant that African Americans and poor whites assumed a disproportionate responsibility in fighting the war and a disproportionate share of the casualties. Most black recruits felt isolated and threatened in an institution controlled almost totally by whites. More importantly, the armed forces had failed to keep pace with the sweeping changes in civilian society. Despite the boasts of the Department of Defense, personal and institutional racism remained endemic to the system. Consequently, many blacks no longer viewed the military as a professional opportunity but rather an undue burden on the black community. Young black men no longer sought military service to prove their right to citizenship, but claimed exemption from service on the grounds that they were not equal citizens and therefore did not share the same obligations as whites. The front lines in the fight for equality were no longer in the military, but in the backwoods of the South and the urban ghettos of the North.

Many black soldiers reacted to changing race relations by promoting a sense of racial pride and solidarity, and they articulated this through cultural expressions such as the "dap," their ritualized handshake. They called themselves "brothers," wore "slave bracelets" made from bootlaces, or flew black power flags over their quarters.

But there were others, both black and white, who resorted to violence. Preoccupied with the quagmire in Southeast Asia, military authorities ignored growing signs of racial unrest, including several major incidents of racial gang fights such as one at Camp Lejeune, North Carolina, in July 1969. In the years following both the Tet Offensive and the assassination of Martin Luther King Jr., the armed forces were plagued by numerous morale, racial, and drug-related problems. Ironically, combat units in Vietnam, while divided along other lines, were seldom involved in the racial warfare.

Nonetheless, African American soldiers questioned inequities, and military officials reacted by branding them as militants and troublemakers, and sought to expel black activists from the armed forces. Many camp commanders banned dapping and other black cultural expressions. But military officials also sought to eliminate the institutional and personal racism that had caused many of the original problems. They banned symbols of white supremacy such as the confederate flag. Officers had to undergo race relations training, and their fitness and promotion reports now included how well they handled racial problems. The military started to administer racially neutral tests to incoming recruits and sought to ensure the enforcement of racially neutral disciplinary measures.

Toward the end of the Vietnam War, however, it seemed that the military's reputation as a model for racial equality had been irretrievably lost. One indication of this was the reenlistment rates of black veterans. In 1966, over two-thirds of black veterans chose to reenlist, but by 1972 only 20 percent did so. The armed forces also witnessed declining numbers of black first-time enlistments. The military eventually regained much of its former reputation as an institution that represented racial equality. In the early 1970s, the armed forces instituted reforms aimed at eliminating racism and ensuring equal opportunity. As the war in Vietnam ended and as the United States entered an economic recession, the armed forces once again became an attractive career option for many African Americans. As a result, the number of black officers and noncommissioned officers increased. African Americans accounted for only 2 percent of the officer corps throughout much of the Vietnam War, but by the early 1980s they made up over 6 percent. In addition, blacks accounted for nearly a third of all senior noncommissioned officers, and the black reenlistment rate was above 80 percent. A decade later, on the eve of the Persian Gulf War, blacks constituted 25 percent of the army's active duty strength.

Race, to a significant degree, shaped the experience of African Americans who served in Vietnam. Racial violence became a serious problem for the military in the latter half of America's involvement in Vietnam. But African American military service in Vietnam and the United States helped shape modern black culture and fostered a sense of black solidarity in the armed forces.

Notes

1. Quoted in Whitney Young Jr., "To Be Equal," *Baltimore Afro-American*, February 19, 1966, 1.

2. Lee Finkle, *Forum for Protest: The Black Press during World War Two* (Canbury, NJ: Associated University Press, 1975), 110.

3. Bernard C. Nalty and Morris MacGregor, eds., *Blacks in the Military: Essential Documents* (Wilmington, DE: Scholarly Resources, 1981), 121.

4. Charles C. Moskos, "The American Combat Soldier in Vietnam," *Journal of Social Issues* (1975) 31: 25–26.

5. Gene Grove, "The Army and the Negro," *New York Times Magazine*, July 24, 1966, 37.

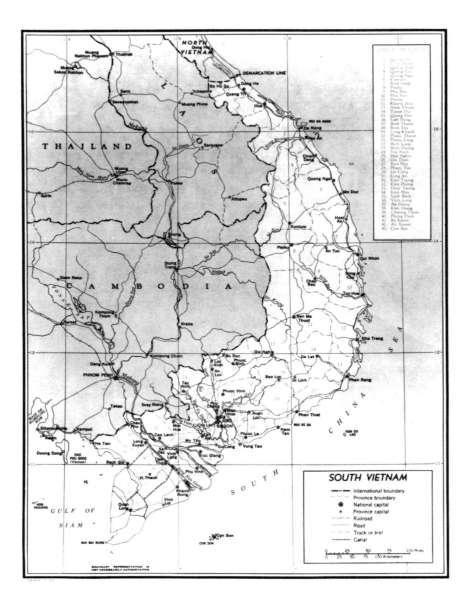

SOUTH VIETNAM

- - - International boundary
- - - Province boundary
⊚ National capital
• Province capital
+++ Railroad
— Road
- - - Track or trail
+++ Canal

CHAPTER ONE

African Americans in the Armed Forces before Vietnam

From the birth of the United States African Americans have played their part in the nation's armed forces, while struggling to gain acceptance, recognition, and opportunity. Vietnam was not the first war in which African Americans served, nor was it the first one involving integrated units. But it was the first war in which blacks served in an integrated military from the start of the conflict, and in a military that was committed to equality and equal opportunity.

African Americans first served in the armed forces in the American Revolution, when nearly five thousand blacks served in the Continental Army. Many of the black soldiers started the war as slaves but won their freedom through military service to the new nation. For most, however, the ideals of the Revolution proved to be hollow promises. After all, the new United States was established on the great Enlightenment principle that "all men are created equal, and endowed by their creator with certain inalienable rights," yet it was a nation constructed on chattel slavery and the belief that blacks were inferior to whites. As a result, the presence of African Americans in the army created a conundrum for whites. Allowing blacks to fight for independence would also give them a legitimate claim to the same rights and privileges that whites enjoyed. As a result, the new nation showed its gratitude toward African Americans by barring them from state militias, with the Militia Act of 1792, and from the army, by act of Congress in 1820.

When the Civil War began in 1861, African Americans eagerly volunteered for service, only to be told that it was a "white man's war" and turned

1

away. However, after the casualties began to mount and the initial enthusiasm wore off, the Lincoln administration began to rethink the long-standing prohibition against black troops. In July 1862, the War Department finally authorized the recruitment of black volunteers for state units and the Federal army. They would have to serve in segregated units, but black men were finally back in the army, and by war's end over 186,000 "United States Colored Troops," roughly 10 percent of the North's military strength, had helped preserve the Union and destroy the institution of slavery. It was also the first time black officers commanded black men in battle. By 1865 about 100 African Americans had served as commissioned officers and another 7,000 as noncommissioned officers. African Americans won sixteen Medals of Honor during the Civil War, but black soldiers paid a high price for participation and recognition. Thirty-eight thousand black troops gave their lives in the struggle, or roughly 18 percent of those who served—three times the death rate for whites.

Military service during the Civil War did help win a permanent place for African Americans in both American society and in the army. With the Reorganization Act of 1866, Congress established four segregated black regiments in the postwar army, the Twenty-fourth and Twenty-fifth Infantry and the Ninth and Tenth Cavalry. Two of these regiments, the Ninth and Tenth Cavalry, won fame and distinction as the "Buffalo Soldiers" on the western frontier and in the Spanish-American War in 1898.

But black participation in the regular army was limited to these four segregated regiments. African Americans were kept out of the more prestigious arms of the service, such as engineering and artillery, and they were seldom assigned to the more comfortable military bases east of the Mississippi River. The vast majority of officers serving in the black regiments were not African Americans; in fact, there were very few black officers in the army. Between 1870 and 1884, twenty-two African Americans were nominated to the United States Military Academy at West Point, New York, but only nine were admitted, and only four graduated and received commissions in the army. When Charles Young received his commission in 1889, he was the last African American to graduate from West Point until 1936. Four more black cadets won entrance to the academy by 1900, but none finished. In 1898, when the United States went to war against Spain, Young was one of a handful of black officers in the army. In the early 1900s, a few more black officers were added when the army allowed promising noncommissioned officers to take the exam to become commissioned officers. In 1901, Young helped successfully tutor one candidate, Benjamin O. Davis Sr.

Despite segregation and discrimination, black leaders believed it was essential for African Americans to serve in the armed forces to prove their capabilities to skeptical white Americans. Though the armed forces were just as segregated as civilian society, African Americans hoped to build on the black soldiers' record of excellent service and use the military as a catalyst for racial change. However, the reliability of black soldiers was called into question in August 1906. Racial tension between black troops and white civilians erupted into violence in Brownsville, Texas. The Brownsville riot left two whites dead and resulted in the dishonorable discharge of 167 black soldiers. The incident was a blow to those who hoped to use military service as a tool in gaining civil rights, and it once again called into question the reliability of African Americans in uniform.

When the United States entered World War I in April 1917, African American leaders took the opportunity to stress the profound patriotism in the black community. Robert R. Moton, president of Tuskegee Institute in Alabama, wrote to President Woodrow Wilson assuring him that the nation could "count absolutely" on the loyalty of blacks. The National Association for the Advancement of Colored People (NAACP) urged the army to include new African American units in their expansion plans. W. E. B. DuBois, a leading black spokesman, predicted that blacks would emerge from the war with new rights as a result of their loyal service in the military and on the home front. Yet in his famous 1918 "Close Ranks" editorial in the NAACP's journal, Crisis, DuBois begged black Americans to "forget our special grievances and close our ranks shoulder to shoulder with our own white fellow citizens" for the duration of the war.[1]

Despite the hopes of African Americans, white officials initially envisioned a very limited role for blacks in the military, and the army's policies reflected this view. The War Department established fourteen new Officer Training Camps (OTC) for whites, but none for blacks. In fact, the highest-ranking African American officer, Lt. Colonel Charles Young, who would have likely been promoted to brigadier general, was retired by the army because of "high blood pressure." In May 1917, Secretary of War Newton D. Baker finally agreed to open a Colored Officers' Training Camp at Fort Des Moines, Iowa, overruling the objections of numerous white officers, many of whom remained convinced that blacks were incapable of command duties. Black leaders were under no illusions and realized that the majority of white officers were hostile to the notion of black officers. To a great degree, the original class of 1,250 black candidates at Des Moines represented the hopes and aspirations of the black middle class. While 250 of the black candidates were regular army noncommissioned officers, the rest were primarily college students or faculty. Forty percent of the candidates held college degrees; four of them were Harvard graduates. Over 600 black men completed their training and were commissioned as officers in the United States Army.

Before Des Moines could graduate its first class of African American officers, however, another violent clash between black soldiers and white civilians once again raised questions about the reliability and loyalty of black troops. On August 23, 1917, between one and two hundred armed black soldiers, enraged over racist treatment by local authorities and civilians, marched into Houston, Texas, and exchanged gunfire with white police and civilians; by morning four black troopers and fifteen whites were dead. It was the worst clash between black troops and white civilians in American history. Seventy black soldiers were convicted of mutiny and murder; nineteen were executed and the rest given life in prison at hard labor.

Like the earlier incident in Brownsville, the Houston riot created a dilemma for many black leaders. How could they praise mutinous soldiers for resisting racism and still profess loyalty to a white government? Among whites, it again renewed questions about black loyalty and discipline under arms. But there was a crucial difference: This time, unlike the aftermath of Brownsville, no one seriously considered disbanding the black regiments; their place in the army was secure. Eventually, over 380,000 black men served in the army in World War I, and another 10,000 in the U.S. Navy. Despite serving in a conflict, ostensibly to "make the world safe for democracy," they did so in a segregated military and with constant reminders of their inferior status.

Though they served in every Military Occupational Specialty (MOS) except pilot, the vast majority of African Americans were assigned to labor battalions; only one in nine, or about 42,000, served in combat infantry units. Those who saw combat, however, garnered praise from their white compatriots. General John J. Pershing, commander in chief of the American Expeditionary Force (AEF) in Europe, referred to the all-black Ninety-second as a success and complimented the men on their discipline and morale. The all black Ninety-third Division, under French command for much of the war, also established an excellent record, especially its 369th regiment, nicknamed the "Harlem Hellfighters." The 369th served 191 continuous days in combat "[w]ithout losing a trench, giving an inch or surrendering a prisoner."[2] The French were impressed enough to award the entire regiment one of France's highest military decorations, the Croix de Guerre. But not all black soldiers or units performed as expected, and whites were quick to criticize and denigrate the record of African Americans. Despite his public praise for the Ninety-second, Pershing, like most white officers, privately thought the division had performed poorly in combat. He had originally wanted to use its troops for laborers, and it was one of the first divisions sent home after the war.

Ultimately, African Americans reaped no immediate benefits from wartime service in either civilian society or the military following World War I. In fact, racial conditions worsened in the years following the war, which witnessed the rebirth of the terrorist Ku Klux Klan, race riots in over two dozen cities, and a rise in the number of lynchings. At least ten of the victims were veterans, many still in uniform. As early as 1919, the army announced that except for rare "special cases," blacks would be restricted to service in segregated infantry units. In practice, the army used them primarily as service troops. The Marine Corps continued to reject black applicants, and the navy restricted blacks to messmen duties.

The Great Depression further worsened the situation. With defense budgets slashed to the bone in the early to mid-1930s, existing black units were often reduced in numbers to permit the retention of whites. By 1940, African American participation in the armed forces had reached a dangerous low. There were only 5,000 blacks in an army of 230,000 men, constituting a mere 1.5 percent of its total manpower. There were only five black officers, and only two of them served in combat units. Conditions in the navy were even worse. Only 4,000 African Americans served in the navy, all as messmen, and there were no black officers. The Marines Corps and Army Air Corps remained all white.

There were some bright spots. In 1936, Benjamin O. Davis Jr. overcame tremendous personal and institutional racism to become the first black to graduate from West Point since Charles Young in 1889. In 1938 the army addressed the issue of black underrepresentation by announcing that African Americans would be recruited in proportion to their percentage in the civilian population. In April 1939, Congress authorized the training of black Army Air Force pilots, fulfilling yet another long-term goal, and announced that all branches of the army would be open to African Americans. On June 25, 1940, President Franklin D. Roosevelt issued Executive Order no. 8802, mandating equal employment by any corporation holding a government defense contract and establishing the Fair Employment Practices Commission (FEPC) to oversee racial fairness in the workplace. On October 15, 1940, Roosevelt promoted Colonel Benjamin O. Davis Sr. to brigadier general, breaking down another symbolic, yet crucial barrier. The army now had its first black general. The pace of racial reform accelerated after the United States entered World War II, following the Japanese surprise attack on Pearl

Harbor on December 7, 1941. Roosevelt ordered that the enlistment barriers in both the navy and Marine Corps be dropped, and both services began accepting black recruits by the summer of 1942. As promising as these developments were, it was obvious that the president had no plans to desegregate the armed forces during the war. Roosevelt, Secretary of War Henry Stimson, and Army Chief of Staff General George C. Marshall supported increased opportunity for African Americans, but not integration. All shared the view that it could cause racial friction in the services and seriously impair the war effort.

Ironically, the official policy of providing greater opportunities to black service personnel, but in a segregated environment, probably contributed to the racial problems that did develop in the armed forces during the war. By mid-1943, riots and racial disturbances, reminiscent of what would occur during the Vietnam War, had erupted on numerous stateside bases, from Camp Breckinridge, Kentucky, to San Luis Obispo, California. Reports indicated great unrest among black soldiers at many bases due to incidents of discrimination and the military's official policy of segregation. The War Department concluded that the best remedy consisted of shipping black combat soldiers to an active theater as soon as possible to avoid another Brownsville or Houston riot. Moreover, the War Department insisted on much stricter enforcement of its policy of providing equal facilities.

Throughout World War II, segregation was the official policy of the War Department, even when evidence indicated that segregation, which greatly contributed to racial friction among American service personnel, hampered military efficiency. Ironically, at the same time that officials were clinging to Jim Crow, numerous facets of military life were being quietly integrated. In March 1943, the War Department ordered integrated recreational facilities, post exchanges, and transportation facilities on all stateside bases. The army also abandoned segregation at all of its Officer Candidate Schools (OCS), with the exception of those training pilots. By late 1944, the army was operating twenty desegregated OCS camps and had begun to desegregate its specialist training schools. The integrated camps were more efficient, were more cost effective, and reported far less racial friction than the segregated ones. During the German Ardennes offensive in December 1944, over 2,500 black service troops volunteered to be retrained as combat infantry men because officers promised them that they would fight in integrated units with white soldiers who were eager to fight side by side with them. When white officers objected, the army assigned the black troops to all-black platoons, although in previously all-white companies. However, there was no question about commissioning black officers as there had been in World War I. By August 1945, there were 7,768 black officers in the army and Army Air Corps. The majority were lower-ranking company-grade officers, mostly lieutenants and captains, and only eight held the rank of colonel or above. Of those, only Davis was a general. Few of them remained in the armed forces after the war.

The navy began training black officers in January 1944, and by 1945 the first fifty were commissioned ensigns. The navy also made quiet progress in other areas, especially after James Forrestal became secretary of the navy in May 1944. Forrestal was far more sympathetic to reform than his predecessor, Frank Knox, and by the end of the war he had integrated almost all navy training programs for both officers and enlisted men. On February 27, 1946, six months after the end of the war, the navy dropped all racial restrictions and announced a policy of nonsegregation, thus becoming the first branch of the service to do so.

While the armed forces displayed a willingness to integrate many facets of military life in the name of efficiency and cost-effectiveness, "separate but equal," which was endorsed and sanctioned by most military leaders, remained the operative doctrine in the immediate postwar years. The issue of military integration was further complicated by the death of President Roosevelt in April 1945. His successor, Harry S. Truman, was something of an enigma when it came to race relations. Truman, a Missouri farmer, used racial epithets freely, told racist jokes, and had once written his future wife Bess that he thought "one man is as good as another, as long as he is honest and decent and not a nigger or a Chinaman."[3] But as a United States senator, he had consistently supported legislation favored by the black community, including a federal antilynching law. As president, Truman proved to be even more supportive of civil rights, sometimes for political reasons. Truman needed to placate A. Philip Randolph and other black activists who were calling for an African American "boycott" of the draft if the armed forces were not desegregated. Moreover, Truman needed black support to win the presidential election that fall against his Republican rival Thomas Dewey. On July 26, 1948, Truman issued Executive Order no. 9981, calling for "equality of treatment and opportunity for all persons in the Armed Services without regard to race, color, religion or national order." Without stating it, Truman effectively ordered the desegregation of the armed forces.

Black leaders were initially elated. A major barrier was destroyed, and the president responsible for it was returned to office in the election that fall. Here was a long-awaited opportunity to use the military as a social laboratory, to demonstrate the merits of integration and equal opportunity to a segregated civilian society. But opposition to integration remained strong in the military. In 1949, the newly independent air force took immediate steps to comply with the directive, but it was obvious that the other services were reluctant to implement desegregation in any meaningful way. The marines, for example, had abolished segregated training but still maintained all-black units. The army agreed in March 1950 to comply with Truman's executive order, but an NAACP investigation of racial conditions in Korea and Japan in early 1951, led by Thurgood Marshall, found rigid patterns of segregation the norm in the army's Far East command. Marshall was convinced that most members of the senior command, General Douglas MacArthur in particular, were diehard segregationists. As late as 1953, there were only twenty-three thousand African Americans in the navy, and over half were still in the racially exclusive stewards' branch.

In both world wars, military officials had argued against attempting to integrate the armed forces during hostilities, but just the opposite occurred during the Korean War. In August 1950, two months after the start of hostilities, the army began integrating training units and implemented "battlefield integration" in Korea, which meant shipping replacements to combat units regardless of race. This practice drew hostility from ardent segregationists within the army and did not become official policy until General Matthew Ridgeway, who assumed supreme command of the UN forces in Korea in April 1951, personally requested it. In July 1951 the army officially approved Ridgeway's request, and by May 1952 the army in the Far East was effectively desegregated. Even the staunchly racist Marine Corps tentatively embraced integration, and the Korean War brought two important firsts for black marines: Lieutenant William K. Jenkins was the first to lead men into combat, and Lieutenant Frank E. Petersen became the first black marine aviator. Far from hampering military efficiency, the integrated units performed quite capably in the field, and a study conducted by Johns Hopkins University found that whites and blacks accepted integration and most believed that it increased military efficiency. The army now dropped its opposition to integration, and the Pentagon announced at the end of October 1954 that the last all-black units had been officially integrated.

The army's announcement came less than six months after the Supreme Court struck down the doctrine of "separate but equal" in *Brown v. Board of Education* in May 1954. After decades of resisting racial change, the armed forces now embraced their new role as a social laboratory, presenting the services as a shining example of racial cooperation and equal opportunity. Integration did increase efficiency and reduce costs, and it made wonderful Cold War propaganda, both at home and abroad. In addition, throughout the armed forces, younger, more racially conscious officers like General Matthew Ridgeway were replacing retiring segregationists like MacArthur.

African Americans may have found a more congenial and less racist environment in the military as compared to civilian society, but they also had financial considerations for choosing a career in the armed forces. The military provided economic and professional opportunities largely unmatched in the civilian sector. Despite the post–World War II economic boom and the advances of the civil rights movement, poverty and job discrimination among African Americans remained widespread problems throughout the 1960s. In 1964 black workers made only fifty-four cents for every dollar a white worker earned. The African American unemployment rate nationally was nearly twice that for whites, and for black men between the ages of eighteen and twenty-five it was five times higher.

The armed forces, in contrast, offered decent pay, job security, and a chance for professional advancement. By 1968, most recruits could expect to earn sixty dollars a week, with no housing, food, or medical expenses. Married soldiers received even higher food and off-base housing allowances. A tour of duty in Vietnam added yet another sixty-five dollars per month in "hostile fire" pay, and there were bonuses for staying in the military. Depending on rank and MOS, military personnel received an additional nine hundred to fourteen hundred dollars for reenlisting after their original three years were up. It was no wonder that 49.3 percent of eligible black servicemen "re-upped" for a second tour in 1964, compared to only 18.5 percent of their white counterparts. While there were still very few Americans in Vietnam that year and the casualty rate was still relatively low, even the escalation of the war in 1965 had no immediate impact on black reenlistment rates; in fact, the opposite was true. In 1966, 66 percent of all African Americans eligible to reenlist signed on for another "hitch," whereas only about 12 percent of eligible whites decided to remain in the service. Even someone as talented, intelligent, and ambitious as future Secretary of State Colin Powell believed that he had a much better chance to succeed in the army than in civilian society. "I was in a profession," Powell stated, "that would allow me to go as far as my talents would take me. And for a black, no other avenue in American society offered so much opportunity."[4]

Military life was also appealing to African American men because it gave them a sense of pride and manhood, as opposed to the often-demeaning situations they encountered in civilian society. Reginald Edwards, for example, was adamant about signing up because "the Marines built men."[5] Military service gave black men a sense of empowerment beyond their years in the armed forces. Sergeant Willie E. Burney Jr. believed his war experience strengthened him to fight racial injustice at home. Helicopter gunship pilot

Wesley C. Wilson agreed that "the thing that you leave with is a sense of assertiveness—a sense of self-esteem—that's very important."[6]

When it came to race relations, the armed forces were far from perfect, but in spite of their failures and shortcomings, life for African Americans on integrated military installations was preferable to the civilian alternative. On stateside bases at least, the military had made a strong commitment to equality. In many areas, such as housing and education, it was a model for civilian society. Since the mid-1950s, all on-base housing had been desegregated. By the early 1960s, military installations had truly become "islands of integration in a sea of Jim Crow." Black Master Sergeant William B. Tapp, recalling his first days in the military at Fort Campbell, Kentucky, remembered, "It was the first time I had ever been treated like an individual."[7]

Segregation and discrimination, however, were still the norm in many communities surrounding military bases. Sometimes attempting to get service in an establishment was humiliating and demeaning; many restaurants, for example, only sold African Americans carry-out food from a backdoor or window. In 1958, Allen Thomas Jr. and his wife were even thrown off a local bus near Fort Knox, Kentucky, for attempting to ride in the front. Confrontations between black servicemen and white civilians could become violent. In December 1962, William Miller was refused service at a white-owned restaurant in Tennessee. When Miller argued with the attendant, the white man shot him in the leg.

Presidents John F. Kennedy and Lyndon B. Johnson both supported the efforts of the Department of Defense (DOD) to ensure equal treatment of all service personnel by civilian establishments and institutions. In 1963, for example, following a presidential review of minority progress in the armed forces, Secretary of Defense Robert McNamara established DOD guidelines, urging base commanders to use their influence to help end the more egregious aspects of off-base racial discrimination. To help ensure compliance, he also created the post of assistant secretary of defense for civil rights. The most potent weapon in the Pentagon's arsenal against discrimination was the Civil Rights Act of 1964, which outlawed discrimination in any activity or program that received federal funding. The service secretaries also announced newer and stronger antidiscrimination initiatives based on the Civil Rights Act. Later that year the secretary of the navy, for example, issued a directive banning navy or Marine Corps participation in any event or organization that practiced racial segregation or discrimination.

These measures were important steps that demonstrated commitment by the armed forces to integration and equality, but black service personnel continued to face discrimination and racism off-base. A mid-1960s Department of Defense study found continued discrimination in restaurants, hotels, bars, bowling alleys, and other businesses, as well as at libraries, city parks, and sports stadiums. Most black soldiers had little recourse in fighting civilian discrimination and racism at off-base facilities, especially in the Deep South, where white base commanders often avoided confronting the issue. The most they could do was declare a place "off-limits" to base personnel. But the policy of declaring a recreational facility off-limits usually resulted in blacks being restricted and whites continuing to patronize the establishment.

One of the most troubling aspects of service personnel discrimination involved the education of military dependents. The military often contracted with local school systems to provide on- or off-base schooling for the children of military families. However, many Southern school districts defied the Supreme Court's 1954 *Brown v. Board of Education* decision and closed their schools, rather than integrate them. This often meant that there was no good on- or off-base schooling for the children of black military personnel. The Department of Defense took steps to remedy the problem. In 1955 the Hampton City school system, which had operated the public schools at Langley Air Force Base and Fort Monroe, Virginia, declined to desegregate. In response, the Department of Defense canceled its arrangement with the local school system, took over operation of the schools, and integrated them. In 1959, public schools in counties around Seymour Johnson Air Force Base and Cherry Point Marine Air Station, North Carolina, agreed to desegregate rather than lose students from the military bases. Sometimes an individual could make a difference. In the early 1960s, young black aviator Wesley C. Wilson fought successfully to enroll his children in Lee Hall Elementary School in Newport News, Virginia. His children became the first black students in the previously all-white system.

The Civil Rights Act of 1960 authorized the Department of Health, Education, and Welfare (HEW) to provide integrated education for military dependents in areas where public schools had been closed in defiance of the law. President Kennedy used this law to further integrate schooling for military dependents. In March 1962, Secretary of Health, Education, and Welfare Abraham Ribicoff threatened to cut off all federal aid if the military had to withdraw students from school districts that refused to integrate. In September, Attorney General Robert Kennedy filed suit in Richmond, Virginia, to withhold federal funds from Virginia's Prince George County school system, serving nearby Fort Lee, because it refused to desegregate. In January 1963, HEW threatened to build and operate integrated schools for military dependents in Alabama, Georgia, Mississippi, and South Carolina if officials in those states did not comply with federal directives to desegregate.

Pressure from HEW, the Attorney General's Office, and other government agencies, along with diplomatic and patient negotiations of many base commanders, produced some results. The commander of Fort Belvoir, Virginia, for example, negotiated a desegregation plan with the nearby Fairfax County School Board. The commandant of the Marine Corps Schools at Quantico got Stafford County, Virginia, school officials to admit all Marine Corps dependents on an integrated basis to their high school and two elementary schools. A similar agreement integrated schools in Albany, Georgia. The air force successfully reached agreements to integrate public schools near Eglin, Whiting, and MacDill Air Force Bases in Florida, and six installations in Texas, including Sheppard and Connally Air Force Bases. The navy claimed similar successes in school districts in Texas, Florida, and Tennessee.

Nonetheless, by the end of the 1964 school year, Pentagon officials could boast of relatively few victories. While 14,390 children attended on-base integrated schools at forty-nine different installations, over 76,300 students at these same bases, including 6,177 African Americans, attended segregated schools off-base. Although the military could withhold funds from segregated schools, many base commanders were reluctant to impose sanctions on local school systems. Some were sympathetic with segregation while others did not want the extra work of finding alternative schooling for the affected students. There was also a widespread belief that sanctions would antagonize local communities instead of solving the problem. In this matter base commanders often had either the overt or covert support of their superiors. As late as 1964, the uniformed leaders of every branch of the services officially opposed the policy of withholding federal funds from local school districts that still segregated military dependents in school.

As on the issue of integrated public schooling, the military often tried to avoid controversy with nearby civilian communities about off-base housing discrimination. Before 1962, for example, the Marine Corps claimed it did not assign black women to Camp Lejeune, North Carolina, because of the lack of acceptable off-base housing. Although the most blatant incidents of housing discrimination occurred in the South, the practice was prevalent from coast to coast. The Marine Corps did not assign African Americans to installations located in California, South Carolina, and Nevada because of housing problems. Even black officers had difficulty finding decent off-base housing for their families. The best housing Captain Colin Powell could find for his wife and children near Fort Benning, Georgia, was across the state line in a disreputable section of Phenix City, Alabama. His fellow white officers had no problem finding good housing in nearby Columbus, Georgia.[8]

The Pentagon tried to address the housing problem. In 1963, McNamara directed base commanders to declare all segregated housing near their installations off-limits to military personnel, and in 1964, he told them to work with local leaders to help eliminate off-base discrimination. However, these measures produced few results because most base commanders had no training in dealing with racial issues, and some were racist. To remedy the lack of training, Deputy Assistant Secretary of Defense for Civil Rights Alfred Fitt met with base commanders to help them formulate policies and tactics for dealing with local segregation and to provide them with legal advice. The Civil Rights Act of 1964 also gave Fitt and the Department of Defense a formidable weapon against housing discrimination.

The Pentagon had some initial success in dealing with off-base housing discrimination. Most of the success stories concerned installations in the North or the Pacific West, but in areas where segregation was still strong the efforts stalled. By 1967, the Pentagon's program was largely a failure. In most cases, it had made minimal progress in combating off-base housing discrimination. Only about 3 percent of twenty-three thousand housing units within commuting distance to Andrews Air Force Base, near Washington, D.C., for example, were listed as integrated. Likewise, African Americans stationed at Fort Meade, Maryland, had to commute as much as forty-eight miles one way just to find suitable housing.

In 1967, McNamara responded to the continuing problem and established a Housing Referral Office at stateside military bases with five hundred or more personnel, and, once again, he issued explicit orders declaring all segregated housing near any stateside military base "off-limits." That same year the Pentagon also established a Special Action Program in Washington, D.C., to deal with housing discrimination; however, it produced limited results. Like earlier initiatives, it relied too heavily on the diplomatic skills of base commanders and voluntary cooperation from local landlords, instead of legal action. In the same year Deputy Secretary of Defense Cyrus Vance argued against legal sanctions, claiming that they would worsen the problem rather than solve it.

Base commanders were just as reluctant to enforce sanctions against landlords and communities that practiced housing discrimination as they were to punish segregated school districts. Even those commanders who had successfully challenged other forms of discrimination found that it was harder to prove housing discrimination than other, often more overt, forms of discrimination. Base commanders had to negotiate with only a handful of school districts in dealing with school segregation, but in trying to ensure equal housing, a commanding officer would have to monitor the practices of literally hundreds of landlords and rental properties. Often base commanders could proceed against a landlord based on complaints they received from black service personnel, but proving housing discrimination was time consuming and difficult, especially in areas where housing was in short supply. Commanding officers had no legal authority outside the military compound, and though they worded directives very strongly, they had no real power to enforce them. At best, they could remove the rental property from the list of approved housing kept at the base Housing Referral Office. In response, many white landlords backdated the leases of their white military tenants to a date before the property was declared off-limits. Others hid their prejudices, acted cordially, and simply lied to prospective black tenants about the availability of housing.

The biggest breakthrough in fighting off-base housing discrimination came when Congress passed the Civil Rights Act of 1968, which outlawed any form of housing discrimination. The Department of Defense quickly issued a directive that enabled base commanders to report discrimination to federal authorities who could now prosecute violators, thus relieving commanders of the responsibility for taking legal action. Riding the coattails of the new housing act, military authorities announced that their antidiscrimination policies had been a success. By the end of 1968, the Pentagon declared that nearly 83 percent of all apartments and trailer courts located near defense installations were integrated.

But old habits die hard, and even with the force of law behind them, military and federal officials did not have the resources at their disposal to keep track of offenders and prosecute all of them. In the early 1970s, significant off-base housing discrimination still existed, largely because base commanders were not effectively dealing with the problem. In 1972, General William Westmoreland, chief of staff of the army, admitted that after years of attempts by military officials to end housing discrimination, they had accomplished little of substance. The Black Congressional Caucus concurred with Westmoreland, charging that local military commanders spent more time trying to circumvent housing regulations than enforcing them.

African Americans stationed overseas in the 1950s and 1960s also encountered racism and discrimination in their interaction with foreign civilians. Overseas base commanders were relatively powerless because they did not have the authority to declare rental properties that discriminated off-limits to service personnel until late in the Vietnam War era. West Germany was one of the worst countries, especially in the area of off-base housing. Many African American service personnel found that rental properties the military had officially approved still refused to rent to them. Wilfried Vollmerhaus, a real-estate agent in Frankfurt, estimated that about 80 percent of local landlords did not want black tenants. The United States military command in Europe did not have the power to declare housing that discriminated against African Americans off-limits until 1970. But, as in the

United States, many base commanders were reluctant to use even this modest sanction against German landlords. Many African Americans grew frustrated with what they viewed as a lack of determination by the armed forces to protect their civil rights in the civilian world, but they did not blame the military for the racism they encountered off-base.

The military had become arguably the most integrated institution in America, and African Americans deeply appreciated the opportunities the armed forces offered them in this era. This appreciation was widely shared by many black officers, enlisted personnel, and black civilians. A 1966 poll found that two-thirds of African Americans believed they had a better chance to get ahead in the armed forces than in civilian life. Many black soldiers praised the military for setting an example of racial fairness and cooperation, and white columnist Roscoe Drummond called it "the most completely integrated, successfully integrated segment of American society."[9]

Much of what Drummond said was true, but the military's highly vaunted success in race relations was also somewhat partial and temporary. The military did not keep pace with the progress of the civil rights movement in civilian society, and as the draft and the war came under attack, racial unrest would also rise again in the armed forces during the Vietnam War era.

Notes

1. W. E. B. DuBois, "Close Ranks," *Crisis*, July 1918, 1.

2. Lou Potter, William Miles, and Nina Rosenblum, *Liberators: Fighting on Two Fronts in World War Two* (New York: Harcourt Brace Jovanovich, 1992), 26.

3. William E. Leuchtenburg, "The Conversion of Harry Truman," *American Heritage*, November 1991, 55.

4. Colin Powell, with Joseph E. Persico, *My American Journey* (New York: Random House, 1995), 61.

5. Herman Graham III, *The Brothers' Vietnam War: Black Power, Manhood, and the Military Experience* (Gainesville: University Press of Florida, 2003), [x], 179.

6. Mark St. John Erickson, "Military Has Become Model for Race Reform, Experts Say," *Newport News-Hampton, Virginia Daily Press*, July 28, 1998, A5.

7. Gene Grove, "The Army and the Negro," *New York Times Magazine*, July 24, 1966, 50.

8. Powell, *My American Journey*, 107.

9. James E. Westheider, "African Americans and the Vietnam War," in Marilyn Young and Robert Buzzanco, eds., *The Blackwell Companion to the Vietnam War* (London: Blackwell Publishers, 2002), 333.

CHAPTER TWO

~

American Involvement in Vietnam and the Draft

At the time the armed forces were taking their first halting steps toward integration and equal opportunity, the United States was taking its first steps toward involvement in Vietnam. During World War II, the Japanese invaded Vietnam, which had been part of the French colonies of Indochina since 1886, proclaiming that Japan was liberating Asian countries from Western colonial powers. The Japanese, however, had no intention of allowing Vietnam's independence, but instead expected to set themselves up as the country's new colonial master.

Sometime in early 1945, a small American military mission parachuted into the rugged countryside of northern Vietnam. The men went to assist a band of Vietnamese guerrillas who called themselves the "Vietminh" and were fighting the Japanese occupation of Vietnam. "Vietminh," which loosely translated means "freedom fighters," was short for "Viet Nam Doc Lap Dong Minh," or "the Vietnamese League for Independence." It was organized in May 1941 by three men who would play a major role in America's war in that country, Pham Van Dong, Vo Nguyen Giap, and the leader of the movement, Ho Chi Minh. After World War II, Pham became one of the leading statesmen and diplomats of the Vietminh, and Giap their greatest general. But it was Ho who led and inspired the movement and commanded the allegiance and respect of the Vietnamese people.

Ho Chi Minh was born in 1890, the son of a minor official. His real name was either Nguyen Sinh Cung or Nguyen Tat Thanh but he later took the name Ho Chi Minh, which means "he who liberates" or "he who enlightens."

He was educated for the civil service but at age twenty-one decided to travel the world. He visited the United States, including the South, where he witnessed segregation firsthand, and he may have even briefly lived in Harlem. During America's war in Vietnam, the North Vietnamese used Ho's firsthand experiences as an important propaganda tool to appeal to African Americans. Ho expressed sympathy for the plight of black Americans, claiming that they and the Vietnamese people shared a common quest for independence and equality and that racism in the United States, rather than the Vietnamese people, was their true enemy.

During World War I, Ho moved to Paris, where he soon became involved in politics. He was one of the Vietnamese nationalists who unsuccessfully petitioned the French government to reform their rule over Vietnam at the World War I peace conference at Versailles. Although he gained fame for his dedication to the Vietnamese cause, Ho was disillusioned with moderate progressive reform and turned to revolutionary ideas. He became a devoted communist and was a founding member of the French Communist Party. Ho saw communism as the best vehicle for achieving his goals for Vietnam. For the next twenty years, he worked for Moscow's Comintern, in the world communist movement, using the name Nguyen Ai Quoc or "Nguyen the Patriot." During these years he traveled widely in the service of the party and organized the Indochinese Communist Party. Ho did not return to Vietnam until World War II.

In August 1940, Japanese troops occupied French Indochina, including Vietnam. France was in no position to resist the invasion of the Nazis' Pacific ally, having just been defeated by Germany and forced into a humbling surrender. The Japanese were brutal overlords, exploiting the Vietnamese people and seizing the rice, rubber, and coal that their empire needed. In resisting the Japanese, Vietnamese nationalist leaders saw an opportunity to strike a blow against yet another foreign invader and further the cause of independence. Ho returned to Vietnam in 1941 and helped organize the Vietminh. But the new Vietminh presented itself as a nationalist, not a communist movement, and since Nguyen Ai Quoc was a well-known communist, he changed his name to Ho Chi Minh to downplay his communist ties.

The Vietminh rescued American pilots shot down by the Japanese and provided the Americans with useful intelligence about enemy troop movements. In return, the American military began to provide the Vietminh with weapons. The Americans had already entered into an alliance with the Soviet Union to fight Nazi Germany, so the Vietminh's communist connections were not an issue during the war. Most of the Americans agreed that Ho, Giap, and their followers were Vietnamese nationalists first and communists second. The only stipulation the United States placed on the arms it supplied to the Vietminh was that they could not use them against the French. With American military support the Vietminh not only fought the Japanese but also slowly established political control over much of northern Vietnam and extended their reach southward for the first time.

By the summer of 1945 it was obvious that the Japanese were headed for defeat. Ho was determined to take advantage of the temporary power vacuum before the French had a chance to reassert colonial control. In August 1945, the Vietminh occupied and took control of Hanoi and the old imperial capital of Hue. On September 2, 1945, from a hotel balcony in Hanoi and with American intelligence officer Major Archimedes Patti at his side, Ho Chi Minh proclaimed an independent Vietnam. American military officers joined Giap to review marching Vietminh troops, and at least one American warplane flew over the crowd and dipped its wings in salute to the newly proclaimed republic. Ho hoped the United States would support an independent Vietnam, but American support of the Vietminh soon faltered.

As World War II ended, the economic, political, and military rivalry with the Soviet Union known as the Cold War was beginning. President Harry S. Truman and other American foreign-policy makers believed that the danger of an aggressive world communist movement was too great to ignore. In response they initiated a foreign policy that was based on two interconnected beliefs. The first was that of "containment," which argued that to defeat world communism it was necessary to contain it and keep it from spreading, and it would then collapse under its own weight. The second was the "domino theory," the belief that without containment, communist insurrections would spread gradually from one country to its neighbors, who would fall to communist domination like a row of dominoes, the ultimate "domino" being the United States. These beliefs were the cornerstones of America's post–World War II foreign policy that ultimately led the United States into its war in Vietnam.

When China became a communist country in 1949 and North Korean communists invaded South Korea in 1950, Americans believed the domino theory was in play and saw the Vietminh's war for independence against the French as part of a global communist plot to dominate Asia. Truman increased support for the French effort in Vietnam, and by 1950 the United States was paying 80 percent of France's cost for its war in Indochina. That year the first American military advisors arrived in southern Vietnam as part of the Military Assistance and Advisory Group (MAAG). American volunteer pilots, working for the CIA-owned Civil Air Transport, flew missions for the French, and U.S. Air Force ground crews serviced and maintained the planes.

The Geneva Accords of July 1954 ended the Franco-Vietminh War and awarded Ho and the Vietminh temporary control over the northern half of Vietnam, which they proclaimed as the Democratic Republic of Vietnam, while the South remained under French control. Vietnam was supposed to be reunified in a nationwide election in 1956, but the election did not take place. The Americans supported a separate Republic of Vietnam in the South, and provided financial and military support to its leader Ngo Dinh Diem. American military advisors began training, arming, and advising the Army of the Republic of Vietnam, or ARVN.

Not everyone in South Vietnam supported the Diem regime. In December 1960, one month before President John F. Kennedy took office, the Vietnamese communists established an umbrella organization, the National Liberation Front, to unite all of the rebellious factions in South Vietnam, and created a military force called the Peoples Liberation Armed Forces (PLAF). The PLAF included the communist Vietminh as well as noncommunist groups opposed to Diem's government in Saigon. In an attempt to portray all of the PLAF as communists, the Diem government dubbed them "Vietcong," which is short for "Vietnamese communists." Beginning in 1960, the Republic of Vietnam faced both military attacks by the North Vietnamese Army in the North and sabotage and assassination of officials from the Vietcong in the South.

By the late summer of 1963, the Kennedy administration had lost all faith in Diem and decided to back a coup against him led by his own senior generals. The coup began on the night of November 1, 1963, and by the following morning Diem and his brother Nhu had been assassinated by the rebellious generals. Far from creating a more efficient and less corrupt government, the coup severely destabilized the South Vietnamese government. Three weeks later President Kennedy was assassinated, and it was up to his successor, Lyndon B. Johnson, to find a solution. When Johnson inherited Vietnam, matters had reached crisis proportions. The situation in South Vietnam seemed grim, but leaving Vietnam would tarnish America's reputation in the Cold War. Johnson chose to escalate America's commitment to South Vietnam and increased the number of American military advisors serving in that country. Conflict was inevitable, and in August 1964, following two incidents, one in which North Vietnamese torpedo boats fired on American ships, Congress passed the Gulf of Tonkin Resolution, which gave President Johnson sweeping powers to conduct a war in Vietnam.

In the spring of 1965, President Johnson decided to commit ground combat troops and begin a bombing campaign of North Vietnam in the hopes of undermining their support for the Vietcong in the South. On March 2, 1965,

"Rolling Thunder," the air campaign against North Vietnam, began. It continued, with occasional pauses, for over three and a half years. On March 8, 1965, the first American combat troops arrived when U.S. Marines stormed ashore at Red Beach Two in South Vietnam. The marines were the first of 184,000 U.S. combat troops to arrive in Vietnam by the end of 1965. There were over 385,000 troops in Vietnam by the end of 1966, with African Americans making up roughly 15 percent of the total. Escalating the war also meant a rise in American casualties: 1,369 American soldiers died and 5,300 were wounded in 1965, and another 5,009 were killed and 30,093 wounded in the following year.

The dramatic increase in the number of casualties may have been the result of the growing number of draftees entering the military. The draft was one of the most controversial and contentious issues during the Vietnam War. For much of the war, the black community was just as bitterly divided over the morality and fairness of the selective service as was the rest of the nation, and this debate contributed to a growing antidraft and antiwar movement among African Americans.

The use of a draft in general has always been a controversial issue in American history. During the American Revolution the various states sometimes resorted to an unofficial draft or "press" to fill state regiments, but George Washington and the members of the Continental Congress believed that men should fight voluntarily for their liberty, and thus they did not institute a national draft. The first use of conscription occurred during the Civil War when in April 1862, the Confederate states made all white men between the ages of eighteen and thirty-five liable for military service. In March 1863, the Union followed suit with the Enrollment or Conscription Act, which made all able-bodied men between the ages of twenty and forty-five liable to conscription into the National Army.

Although opposition to the draft existed in all wars, the absence of a noticeable antidraft movement in World War I and World War II made protest against the draft in Vietnam seem abnormal and un-American. Many of the men who served on local draft boards during Vietnam were World War II or Korean War veterans, who believed that since they had fought "their" war, it was the duty of the young men coming before them to fight in Southeast Asia. Thus, they were reluctant to grant exemptions. Although the racial fairness of the draft was not a high-profile issue in either World War I or World War II, African Americans were overdrafted in the First World War. Blacks made up nearly 10 percent of the draft age population, but the 367,710 black draftees constituted 13.08 percent of all those conscripted between 1917 and 1919. This overrepresentation did not worry black leaders, however, because their main fear had been that African Americans would be excluded from the draft. The army in 1938 responded to black concerns about the fairness of the draft by establishing a quota and announcing that African Americans would be recruited into the army in proportion to their percentage in the civilian population. Two years later, Congress passed the Selective Service Act of 1940, which stipulated that all male citizens between twenty-one and thirty-six years of age were liable for conscription and outlawed discrimination based on race or color in both the selection and training of recruits. For political reasons President Franklin D. Roosevelt instructed the selective service to take measures to ensure that blacks were neither overdrafted nor underdrafted. The result was that in World War II African Americans made up nearly 11 percent of the general population, and comprised 10.7 percent of the draft calls, a near-perfect ratio.

The Selective Service Act of 1948 governed the Vietnam War era draft and was responsible for much of the controversy. Ironically, the law was designed to be as fair and racially unbiased as possible. Like the Selective Service Act of 1940, it did not allow racial discrimination, and it did not mandate racial quotas, which greatly pleased most black leaders. However, during the Korean and Vietnam wars, blacks were overrepresented in the draft calls. Between 1950 and 1954, African Americans made up 12.8 percent of the total number of draftees.

Theoretically the Selective Service Act of 1948 made all men who were older than age eighteen liable for military service, but after the Korean War ended in July 1953, the military did not need nor want all of the potential recruits. The Pentagon's problem was not getting enough men, it was limiting the manpower pool to a manageable level. Military officials solved the problem by granting virtually automatic occupational and educational deferments. Draft-eligible men between the ages of eighteen and twenty-five were in the primary draft pool, but once registrants reached twenty-six, they were placed in a secondary category, further reducing the number of potential draftees. To limit the pool and get better-qualified recruits, the military raised the minimum mental and physical standards for induction. Under this system the military got enough recruits to fill the ranks each year and the civilian economy suffered less disruption because those considered more productive and valuable were generally exempted from service. The Pentagon referred to this policy as "manpower channeling," arguing that it was in the interest of the nation to exempt students, professionals, and skilled workers. This deferment system benefited middle- and upper-class whites and created much of the contention in the Vietnam-era draft. Whites with potential for success in civilian life could normally avoid the draft, while African Americans were drafted in disproportionate numbers. With the exception of a few African Americans who could afford college, the draft took the intelligent and most physically fit from the community.

In 1965, following the Gulf of Tonkin Resolution, the American troop commitment to Vietnam began to increase rapidly and the Johnson administration was faced with the difficult task of finding enough manpower. The first problem was the sheer number of men necessary to fight the war. The manpower problem was compounded by the military's rotation policy. Instead of serving for the duration of hostilities as was the case in World War II, the army set a standard tour of duty in Vietnam at twelve months, and the marines at thirteen months. This rotation policy was implemented to help distribute the burden of the war more evenly and help prevent "combat fatigue," known more commonly today as post-traumatic stress disorder (PTSD). It was a well-intentioned policy, but it also meant that the armed forces would need constant replacements for the men whose tours were up. Moreover, the United States still feared a possible confrontation with the Soviet Union and had to keep considerable military forces stationed in Europe. Activating the reserves and National Guard was an option, and the government had done so in all the previous wars of the twentieth century, but mobilizing members of the reserves and Guard would likely disrupt the economy. The Johnson administration settled on the draft; it was already an established and efficient system, which would be less intrusive to the economy, since most of the draftees were young and had yet to establish families or careers.

From the beginning, African Americans were drafted in disproportionate numbers. According to Department of Defense figures, black Americans comprised about 12 percent of the nation's population during the war. Yet in 1966, they made up 13.4 percent of the inductees, and in 1967 and 1970 more than 16 percent. Between 1965 and 1970, during the height of American involvement in Vietnam, blacks accounted for 14.3 percent of all draftees. Despite the fact that African Americans bore an undue burden, they supported and trusted the selective service more than whites did, at least in the early years of the war.

By the mid-1960s, the successes of the civil rights movement, as well as its failures, had made African Americans more keenly aware of discrimination within American institutions like the military and the police. While some disaffected African Americans continued to seek change through the system, others looked to revolutionary doctrines. More than a few took their anger into the streets. During the summers of 1963 and 1964, racial unrest erupted in Cambridge, Maryland; Philadelphia, Pennsylvania; Jacksonville, Florida; Brooklyn, New York; Cleveland, Ohio; and elsewhere. The biggest riot occurred in the summer of 1965 in the Watts section of Los Angeles. On August 11, Watts exploded with some of the worst rioting in modern American history, following an incident of white police brutality against a black man. The California National Guard, with help from the army, finally suppressed the riot but only after thirty-four deaths, four thousand arrests, and millions of dollars worth of property damage.

In October 1966, two community college students in Oakland, California, Bobby Seale and Huey Newton, announced the formation of the Black Panther Party for Self-Defense (BPP). Members of the BPP used black nationalist rhetoric, Marxist ideas, and guns to defend themselves against white racism in the police force and elsewhere. Their fame and notoriety spread quickly. In 1972, the House Committee on Internal Security called the Black Panther Party a threat to the internal security of the United States.[1]

The leaders of the civil rights movement all lived and preached a doctrine of nonviolence, but the riots and the rise of black self-defense groups were a stunning indication that many young African Americans had rejected peaceful protest. Ironically, even members of the Student Nonviolent Coordinating Committee (SNCC), despite their name, were considering selected use of force. Although the organization did not endorse mindless violence or rioting, its members understood the underlying frustration and desire to employ more aggressive tactics. Like many young blacks in this era, they were attracted to the rhetoric and bold tactics of black nationalists like Malcolm X, the national spokesperson for the Nation of Islam. Malcolm was defiant and aggressive, but also charismatic, brilliant, and articulate. His message to blacks, to distance themselves from whites and take pride in their heritage, appealed greatly to young, urban African Americans. Unlike the leaders of the civil rights movement, Malcolm X saw no reason to work with or show any respect for the white power establishment. In 1964, after he had broken with the Nation of Islam, Malcolm X denounced both the war and the United States government as hypocritical for drafting African Americans and sending them to fight in Vietnam when blacks could not even register to vote without fear of being murdered. In January 1965, he argued in a speech at Oxford University that Africans and African Americans should be on the same side as "those little rice farmers" who had defeated French colonialism, and he predicted that the Vietnamese would beat the United States.[2] One month later, on February 21, three men connected to the Nation of Islam assassinated Malcolm X as he gave an address at the Audubon Ballroom in Harlem.

Although Malcolm was gone, his ideas and those of other black nationalists gained ground among the younger civil rights organizations. Five months after the assassination, the Congress of Racial Equality (CORE) rejected the doctrine of nonviolence and officially endorsed the objective of black power. It also became the first of the civil rights organizations to break with Johnson over the war by demanding the withdrawal of U.S. forces from Vietnam and supporting resistance to the draft. In July 1965, the Mississippi Freedom Democratic Party advocated that African Americans from Mississippi should not "fight in Vietnam for the white man's freedom, until all the Negro people are free in Mississippi."[3] In 1966, Stokely Carmichael took over as chairman of SNCC and began to steer the organization toward a black nationalist philosophy based on economic and political power for black people. "The only way we gonna stop them white men from whippin' us is to take over," he announced to a jubilant audience in Jackson, Mississippi. "We been saying 'freedom now' for six years and we ain't got nothing. What we got to start saying is black power."[4] He fired all of the remaining whites in the organization and in June 1966 publicly broke with Dr. King and the civil rights movement. "Why should black folks fight a war against yellow folks so that white folks can keep a land they stole from red folks?" he argued. "We're not going to Vietnam. Ain't no Vietcong ever called me nigger."[5]

Most of the militants and nationalists vehemently denounced African American participation in the Vietnam War. Stokely Carmichael referred to black GIs as mercenaries. Ultimately, black nationalists held a far different view of military service than did the moderate integrationists. Since World War II, black leaders had praised the military as a shining example of integration and equal opportunity, but the black nationalists believed that the armed forces were just as racist as the rest of white America. To them, Vietnam was not an opportunity to start a career; it was a place to get killed while fighting for the white power structure. Malcolm X, SNCC, and other black militant groups and individuals exerted a profound influence on many young African Americans who entered the armed forces after 1965. African Americans, both in and out of the military, began to question all aspects of military service, beginning with the draft.

Many blacks may have opposed the draft on principle, but they also had specific racial grievances. Some argued that because African Americans did not fully enjoy the rights and privileges of American citizenship, they were not obligated to fight, and possibly die, for the United States. Even the most moderate of African Americans agreed that the draft inherently favored whites, and many condemned it as just another racist institution in a racist nation. Some militants, such as SNCC members Stokely Carmichael, Cleveland Sellers, and Walter Collins, as well as former-criminal-turned-black radical Eldridge Cleaver, even charged that the draft was part of an insidious plot to eliminate young black males by conscripting them and sending them to their death in Vietnam. It was a charge that persisted throughout the war. As African Americans became more fully aware of the racial disparities in the draft, and as the number of black casualties mounted, their support for the selective service system eroded. By June 1969, a public opinion poll conducted for *Newsweek* revealed that most African Americans believed the draft was racially biased.[6]

No single aspect of the draft was as acrimonious or associated with white privilege as the granting of college deferments. By the time the United States began committing ground troops in 1965, the exemption from military service for college students had become automatic and college campuses had become safe havens from the draft and the war. The problem was that few African Americans at that time qualified for or could afford to go to college. Only about 5 percent of black males attended college during the war. Most African Americans, especially in the South, had attended segregated and second-rate public schools. As a result they often lacked the skills necessary to meet college entrance requirements. Those who did meet the requirements often could not afford college tuition. The average black family did not have the economic resources to pay for four or more years of college. In 1967, over 30 percent of all African American families lived at or below the poverty line. The median annual income of an average white family was $8,274, while that of an African American family was $5,141, and only one in five urban black families earned more than $10,000 a year. There were few government loans or scholarships available that would have allowed qualified but poor black students to attend college.[7]

Thus, class and economic discrimination contributed to the disproportionate number of black draftees. Black congressmen, such as Detroit representatives John Conyers and Charles Diggs and New York City's Adam Clayton Powell Jr., questioned the fairness of the exemptions, especially college deferments, claiming that they benefited middle-class whites at the expense of African Americans. As the war progressed and more people, including a large number of African Americans, became critical of the draft, the government instituted reforms to make the system fairer both racially and socioeconomically. In March 1966, a presidential advisory commission recommended initiating an impartial random selection of draftees, such as a lottery.

In late 1969, the government established a lottery system, based on birthdays. Each day of the year was chosen at random and assigned a number from 1 to 365. The lower the number of a draftee's birthday, the greater the likelihood that he would be called up. On December 1, 1969, the selective service held its first draft lottery. By then, however, the process of "Vietnamization," or ending America's role in the war, had begun. As a result, the draft calls for 1971 and 1972 were relatively light compared to preceding years. Graduate student deferments finally ended in the spring of 1968, but the law protected those already in graduate school until 1970. Undergraduate exemptions did not end until after 1971.

In addition to their access to education, whites also had an advantage in obtaining medical deferments. Whites almost always had greater access to medical care than most blacks, thus, they were either already aware of a particular ailment or could afford the expensive tests to find a deferrable condition. A host of non-life-threatening physical ailments, ranging from flat feet to bad allergies, qualified individuals for deferments. Even if no verifiable condition existed, many doctors were allegedly willing to fake one, in exchange for money or because they opposed the war and the draft. Every potential draftee had to undergo a physical examination by a military doctor, but the physicians were generally overworked and often lacked the expertise to challenge the diagnosis of a specialist. Thus, they usually deferred to the civilian doctor's diagnosis rather than spend time reexamining the inductees. Many registrants from Harvard, for example, arrived for their preinduction physicals armed with letters from doctors and psychiatrists testifying to their inability to serve in the military. In 1966, a mentally qualified white inductee was 50 percent more likely than a mentally qualified African American to fail his preinduction physical. By 1970, more than 33 percent of white recruits but only 25 percent of African Americans were exempted from service for medical reasons.

The composition of the local draft boards was yet another reason why African Americans were drafted in disproportionate numbers. Educational exemptions were fairly routine and automatic, but some of the exemptions, such as obtaining status as a conscientious objector (CO) or a hardship deferment, needed the approval of the applicant's local draft board. There were over 4,080 local draft boards operating during the war and they wielded great discretionary power in determining who would be drafted. The composition of draft boards was supposed to be representative of the residents of a community, and therefore impartial, but throughout much of the war blacks were greatly underrepresented on the boards, especially in the South. In 1966, when African Americans made up 13.4 percent of the draft calls, blacks comprised only 1.3 percent of total draft board membership. There were no black board members in Alabama, Arkansas, Georgia, Louisiana, Mississippi, and South Carolina—all states with large black populations.

Black antidraft activists argued that the boards were not truly representative and therefore had no right to draft African Americans. When state officials refused requests to appoint additional African Americans to local boards, the NAACP and other civil rights organizations sued to halt the conscription of blacks in those states. In March 1967, the NAACP, along with the American Civil Liberties Union, (ACLU), filed a class-action suit to halt the drafting of African Americans in South Carolina because no blacks served on that state's local boards. In 1968, Charles Evers, executive secretary of the NAACP in Mississippi, sued in federal court to force Governor John Bell Williams to appoint African Americans to the state draft boards.

The argument was successful in a handful of individual cases, most notably that of SNCC official Cleveland Sellers. In May 1967, he reported to the Atlanta Induction Center but refused to take the standard lie detector test, delaying his processing. Sellers did swear, however, that he was not a communist or fascist, nor did he belong to any organization considered "subversive" by the Attorney General's Office. Sellers and ten other inductees, five black and five white, were ushered into the induction ceremony at around 3:30 p.m. Sellers was the only one who did not take the step forward indicating acceptance of induction into the armed forces. Sellers was then advised that he could face charges of felony draft evasion and was given a second chance to step forward. When he again refused, the authorities proceeded to charge him with draft evasion. The SNCC official and his ACLU attorneys claimed that the Selective Service System systematically excluded African Americans from serving on draft boards and was thus discriminatory. Sellers avoided induction when a federal judge agreed that the absence of African Americans on state boards in Georgia constituted an impermissible bias.

The number of black representatives on local draft boards more than doubled in 1968. That year, about 600 African Americans were serving on local draft boards compared to 284 in 1967. In 1968, the first three African Americans served on Alabama draft boards—one each on local boards in Birmingham, Huntsville, and Mobile—and black representation was up in most other Southern states. Arkansas appointed thirty-five African Americans to local boards, and fifteen blacks served in Georgia. In the next two years Louisiana appointed thirty-three African Americans to local draft boards. Despite this increase, blacks were still grossly underrepresented. Only six African Americans served on draft boards in South Carolina, and none served in Mississippi, making it the last state without black representation on its draft boards. In addition, all of the fifty state directors were white, although two African Americans served in the equivalent post of territorial director, in the Virgin Islands and in the District of Columbia.

By 1970, the number of blacks serving on draft boards increased to 6.6 percent of the total board membership. The rest of the members were usually white, middle-aged men with military experience, some of whom were avowed racists. The Grand Dragon of the Louisiana Ku Klux Klan, for example, was head of the state's largest draft board from 1957 until 1966, when he was removed in response to NAACP protests. Others may not have worn white sheets in their spare time but were equally racist. In 1966, for example, the chairman of the Atlanta draft board referred to Georgia State Representative Julian Bond as "this nigger" and regretted that the board had been unable to draft him.

Most board members, however, were not overt racists and thought they were doing their civic duty in an impartial manner. Nonetheless, many harbored racial stereotypes and racist attitudes that influenced their decisions about African American requests for deferments. This was particularly true when it came to granting conscientious objector status and hardship exemptions. During the Vietnam War potential draftees could apply for conscientious objector (CO) status if they had a "sincere and meaningful" revulsion to killing and war. The United States government had granted CO status in World War I and II, largely to members of pacifistic denominations like the Mennonites, Amish, or Quakers. During Vietnam, however, a CO deferment did not necessarily have to be based on religious beliefs. In 1965, in *United States v. Seeger*, the Supreme Court broadened the definition to include individuals with strong moral objections to war and killing. Those who received conscientious objector deferments did not have to fight in the armed forces but were obligated to perform two years of alternative public service, such as providing medical care in Veterans Administration hospitals.

Many African Americans applied for and were granted conscientious objector status, even by all-white boards in the South. Most black applicants had a difficult time, however, because few knew their rights. Many received bad or confusing advice. A white woman at a selective service office told James Daly that he could not apply for conscientious objector status when he applied for a deferment based on his religious beliefs. In 1968, a member of a Chicago draft board expressed doubt that African Americans were capable of deep religious and pacifist beliefs, proclaiming, "They say they object to going because of religious reasons . . . they pretend to believe in God and say I don't want to kill anybody, then right afterwards they go out in the streets and cut some person's throat."[8]

Many white board members shared this skepticism, particularly when members of the Nation of Islam (NOI) applied for CO status. During the Vietnam War, members of the NOI routinely applied for and were routinely denied religious deferments, even though they did meet some of the basic criteria for the exemption. The NOI had established a tradition of draft and war resistance since its inception in 1929 and prohibited its members from serving in the armed forces. During World War II, for example, over eighty members of the NOI, including its leader, the Honorable Elijah Muhammad, went to federal prison on charges of draft evasion and interfering with the draft. In 1942, Muhammad was sentenced to six years in a federal prison for interfering with the draft by disrupting an induction center. However, the NOI was not pacifist and allowed members to fight if religious leaders declared a jihad, or holy war. The draft boards and federal courts agreed that individuals could not pick and choose conflicts, and the aversion to war and killing had to be total to receive a deferment.

The most famous member of the Nation of Islam to defy the selective service during the war was boxer Muhammad Ali. Born Cassius Clay in Louisville, Kentucky, in 1942, his battle with the Selective Service Administration began when Clay turned eighteen in April 1960. He went to the local draft board and in compliance with the law registered for the draft. In the same year Clay won a gold medal in boxing at the Rome Olympics. In March 1962, he was classified I-A, eligible for conscription, but the war in Vietnam had yet to heat up and draft calls were low, thus the rising young boxer faced little chance of being called up. His chances of getting drafted were further reduced when he failed the armed forces mental aptitude test in January 1964. A second exam proved that Ali had not purposely failed the first one and he was reclassified as mentally unfit for service. Shortly thereafter, Ali defeated Sonny Liston for the world heavyweight championship, and then shocked the world by announcing that he had joined the Nation of Islam and intended to change his name to Muhammad Ali.

As Ali rose in fame and in controversy the war in Vietnam began to escalate and the armed forces needed more draftees to help meet its manpower requirements. In April 1965, they lowered the aptitude exam score necessary for induction. Ali was now eligible for conscription, and on February 17, 1966, his Louisville draft board informed the heavyweight champion that he had been reclassified and would be drafted. Ali knew that he would not have to fight in Vietnam if inducted. The army planned to send him on tour to entertain the troops as heavyweight champion Joe Louis had done in World War II. But Ali was deeply religious and convinced that supporting the war would violate his principles. He therefore decided to resist the draft on moral grounds. In March, he applied for conscientious objector status, citing his membership in the NOI. Ali told reporters that he had no personal quarrel with the Vietcong and that he could not serve in Vietnam because it was not a declared holy war. Subsequently, the Louisville draft board rejected Ali's petition for CO status. His lawyers then tried several different tactics. They filed for CO deferment claiming that Ali was a minister of the NOI. They filed for another deferment insisting that his conscience and not his affiliation with the Nation of Islam would not allow him to serve in the armed forces. They also requested a hardship deferment, citing his alimony payments to ex-wife Sonji Clay. Finally, they petitioned on the grounds that African Americans were not represented on the local draft board. None of the appeals succeeded and the draft board ordered Ali to report for induction in April 1967. At this point, one of Ali's lawyers who was a colonel in the Illinois National Guard offered to reserve a spot for him. The position in the National Guard would have been an easy way out for Ali, but his fight with the Selective Service System was based on principle and not convenience, thus Ali turned it down.

In April 1967, Ali reported to the Houston Induction Center. At the ceremony, although the officer called out both names Ali and Clay to make sure there was no confusion, Ali refused to step forward to indicate his acceptance of the induction. Retribution came quickly. Later that month the World Boxing Association stripped Ali of his heavyweight title, and on June 20, 1967, he was convicted of draft evasion, sentenced to five years in prison, and fined ten thousand dollars.

Critics of the draft praised Ali as a hero and a champion of the cause. The Brooklyn chapter of CORE vowed to protest the government's denial of Ali's ministerial exemption. Julian Bond was ecstatic that a public figure had spoken out against the war. And civil rights leaders such as Dr. Martin Luther King Jr. and SNCC's Stokely Carmichael praised Ali's actions. From his pulpit at Ebenezer Baptist Church in Atlanta, King praised Muhammad Ali for refusing induction and pleaded with other draft-eligible men to follow the heavyweight's example and declare themselves conscientious objectors. Carmichael likewise praised Ali as his hero for refusing induction and urged other young blacks to follow the boxer's example.

While many Americans praised Ali, he also had his detractors. Among them were black soldiers in Vietnam, most of whom disapproved of the antidraft movement. Fellow athletes also criticized Ali, including former heavyweight champion Floyd Patterson and retired baseball legend Jackie Robinson, who had supported Ali in his conversion to the NOI. On the floor of the House of Representatives white Pennsylvania Congressman Frank Clark denounced Ali as a "complete and total disgrace," and chided the boxer for failing to do his duty for a nation that made him famous and gave him the opportunity to make millions of dollars. Clark also questioned Ali's manhood for refusing to fight.[9] Ali's spiritual mentor, the Honorable Elijah Muhammad, abandoned him temporarily during the crisis. Muhammad had originally supported Ali, but he had his own problems with the white power structure and did not like the negative publicity his organization was getting as a result of Ali's actions. In 1969, in order to put some distance between the NOI and the controversial heavyweight, the black Muslim leader blasted Ali for putting money above God and suspended the boxer from the Nation of Islam for one year.

It was not until June 28, 1971, that the Supreme Court overturned Ali's conviction based on a legal technicality. Although black Americans viewed the Court's decision as a victory over racism, the ruling did not set a precedent and thus was of no help to other draft resisters. Most members of the NOI lacked Ali's allies and resources and could not obtain exemptions. Stanley L. Garland, for example, cited his Muslim religious beliefs when he refused to take his preinduction physical exam in 1965. After two years of court battles, Garland lost and was sentenced to three years in a federal prison. Garland was one of almost one hundred NOI members who served prison sentences for resisting the draft during the Vietnam War.

Government authorities tried to use the draft as a weapon against militant African Americans and civil rights activists. Former Attorney General Ramsey Clark claimed that General Lewis Hershey proposed drafting antiwar activists and thereby crushing the protests. The chair of the House Armed Services Committee, L. Mendel Rivers, advocated immediate prosecution of draft evaders and wanted charges brought against the "Kings and Carmichaels" for advocating draft resistance. Mississippi civil rights activist Robert James was successful in securing a CO deferment, but when authorities in that state found out about his civil rights activities they tried to get rid of him by ordering him to perform his two-year alternative service in a remote town. Hubert Davis claims that he received his draft notice right after he declared his candidacy for mayor in a small Mississippi town. New Orleans activist Jeanette Crawford refused to testify before the Louisiana House Committee on Un-American Activities, and within one week her three sons received draft notices. When her oldest son James did not report for duty, he was indicted for failure to register for the draft. The charges were dropped when authorities discovered that James was already in the army; indeed, he was a thirteen-year veteran serving in Germany.

SNCC members were particularly vulnerable. They were of draft age, and few of them received college deferments because hostile local draft boards in the South, where most of them resided, were unlikely to grant them exemptions. In January 1966, for example, the selective service announced that it was going to review the conscientious objector status of former SNCC chairman John Lewis because of his outspoken opposition to the draft and the war.

Apparently they were particularly agitated over his professed "admiration" for those who burned their draft cards. Between January and May 1967, fifteen members of SNCC, including Chairman Stokely Carmichael and National Program Director Cleveland Sellers, received orders to report for induction. SNCC had between eighty and one hundred staff workers at that time; losing fifteen of them, including two top officials, could have crippled the organization.

Unlike many leading, vocal white resisters, African American draft resisters often faced criminal charges for draft evasion. Only a few white draft evaders and several prominent activists in the antiwar movement were prosecuted. The government, for example, never brought charges against white folk singer Joan Baez and others who refused to pay part of their income tax as protest against the war. Likewise, Alex Jack, a white founding member of the New England Resistance Movement, turned in his draft card and refused induction, but was never arrested or prosecuted. His draft board simply granted him a deferment and reclassified him.

A few prominent African American draft resisters received better treatment. Stokely Carmichael had an easier time with his local draft board than did most of his SNCC colleagues. Carmichael had stated he would not go to Vietnam if drafted, but, unlike Sellers, he did not have to fight the Selective Service System; he failed his physical and was declared unfit for service in March 1967. Carmichael may well have deserved a medical deferment, but it may have been helpful that his local board was in the North, where board members generally exercised more leniency than in the South. It is also possible that his local board granted him a medical deferment in order to avoid controversy. For all of the trouble SNCC members had in battling the Selective Service System, many of them avoided induction or prison.

Failure to get an exemption from a local draft board did not necessarily mean service in Vietnam. A good lawyer could delay induction, thus many draft resisters continued to fight their status in court. A potential draftee could appeal to the state board and, if that failed, to the federal courts, which tended to be fairer in their treatment of draft resisters than most local boards. This was especially true for African Americans, who often faced a racially based double standard in dealing with the local selective service boards. Some men convicted of draft resistance were given extremely light sentences by sympathetic judges. One judge, who was known for giving draft resisters one day's probation, sentenced a young man to one hour's probation. However, win or lose, the process took years and effectively kept an individual out of the service.

Enforcement of the draft law varied greatly, and prosecutors often declined to bring draft evasion cases to trial in areas where antiwar sentiments prevailed. In San Francisco, for example, the nation's first African American U.S. Attorney, Cecil Poole, only prosecuted about one out of every ten draft evasion cases referred to his office because of the strong antiwar sentiment prevalent in the Bay Area. Many U.S. Attorneys were reluctant to bring draft evasion cases to trial because prosecution was difficult and time consuming. In 1967, those active in the resistance movement began to demand a court trial for each case, thereby slowing down the legal system with thousands of cases and wearing down the will of federal officials to prosecute. Toward the end of the war, many prosecutors did find it more convenient to drop a case based on a technicality rather than go to court. Lawyer's fees usually ran around twenty-five hundred dollars, or about half the yearly income of most black families, preventing many from pursuing legal action.

Joining either the National Guard or the Armed Forces Reserve was a popular strategy to avoid service in Vietnam, particularly for those who found legal maneuverings and fake deferments distasteful. The National Guard and the reserves had been employed in both world wars and Korea, but President Johnson's desire to avoid disrupting the civilian economy meant that neither would be used extensively in Vietnam. More than seven hundred thousand guardsmen were called up for federal service during the Korean War, but only about thirty-eight thousand were called up for Vietnam. Of those, only fifteen thousand went to Vietnam, all of them during the height of American involvement in 1968. Only ninety-seven National Guardsmen, twenty-eight of them commissioned officers, were killed in Vietnam, and all of them were volunteers.

Like the regular armed forces, both the National Guard and reserves were open to all races, but the number of African Americans in either branch was extremely small. In 1965, there were only 5,590 African Americans among the 411,533 National Guardsmen, comprising less than 2 percent of its total strength. In most states, the Guard was composed largely of white middle-class college graduates seeking to avoid the draft. In 1966, the National Guard Association estimated that 71 percent of those applying to the National Guard hoped to avoid the draft. That number increased to 90 percent by 1970. As the draft calls increased, the number of African Americans in the National Guard declined. The problem was especially bad in the South where racism and white favoritism virtually excluded blacks from the Guard. In 1965, Alabama had only fourteen black guardsmen and Georgia only three. As late as 1969, only one of the 10,365 guardsmen in Mississippi was black, despite the fact that African Americans made up 42 percent of that state's population. As the war progressed, it became more and more difficult for anyone without personal connections to gain admission to the Guard. By

1970, the Guard's national waiting list contained over one hundred thousand names, the vast majority of whom were white.

Federal officials may have mandated equal treatment in the selection of guardsmen, but money and political influence opened doors for middle- and upper-class whites that the vast majority of African Americans did not have. The problem was that each state controlled the selection process for its Guard units, and in many areas corruption and favoritism allowed those who were politically connected and wealthy to get onto, or move ahead of, others on the lengthy waiting lists. The group that entered the Texas Air National Guard with George W. Bush, for example, included the son of a congressman, the sons of two U.S. senators, and seven members of the Dallas Cowboys football team.

Even when African Americans managed to get into the Guard, they often lost out in promotions and choice assignments. In early 1966, for instance, there were no black officers in the entire Maryland National Guard, even though there were many qualified African Americans languishing on the state's waiting list.

As in the National Guard, competition for a spot in the reserves was intense. Applicants took the same entrance exam as for the regular army. While a high score on the test was a prerequisite for admission, money and political favoritism also helped. A lot of draft-eligible men, desperately seeking acceptance to the Guard or reserves, were literally willing to pay the price. Just as a few local draft board members sold deferments, some reserve commanders were willing to guarantee a spot in their unit for a fee, sometimes as high as twelve hundred dollars.

The Department of Defense did take steps to curb the abuses. In February 1967, it ordered all reserve vacancies to be filled strictly in order of application; however, these measures had little effect until late in the war. The Department of Defense's attempts to increase the number of African Americans in the reserves, and especially in the National Guard, were more successful. Military officials were especially interested in raising the number of black guardsmen following the urban uprisings of the mid- to late 1960s. In April 1968, the President's National Advisory Council on Civil Disorders predicted renewed rioting that summer and argued that black guardsmen might discourage uprisings and looting and have a "sobering effect" on rioters. The council advised the Pentagon to initiate a three-year recruiting effort to increase the number of African Americans in the National Guard. Meanwhile, President Johnson ordered Secretary of Defense Robert McNamara to give the matter his immediate attention. The Pentagon responded by creating an experimental "over-strength" program, which subsidized a 5 percent increase in manpower for state formations that attempted to recruit African Americans. The New Jersey National Guard, for example, recruited 527 African Americans under this program.

The "over-strength" program did help increase black participation in the National Guard. By June 1971, there were 16,792 African Americans in the Guard, and 28,472 by September 30, 1972. African Americans still made up only 3.1 percent of the total Guard and reserve manpower, but the number slowly rose in the following years. The war and the threat of the draft was almost over, thus the long waiting list evaporated. In fact, many of the whites who had originally sought positions in the Guard were now trying to get out. In addition to college deferments, the abuse of the selection process for the Guard and reserves angered African Americans more than any other aspect of the Vietnam draft.

African Americans not only had a tough time fighting the draft: If convicted of draft evasion, they also received stiffer prison sentences than whites. The penalty for conviction on a single count of draft evasion could be as much as five years in jail and a ten-thousand-dollar fine. African Americans often got the maximum penalty. Robert James, for example, was convicted of draft evasion and sentenced to five years in a federal prison after refusing to perform alternative service as required by his conscientious objector status. SNCC official David Bell spent two years in the Danbury Federal Correctional Institute for resisting the draft, a light sentence compared to that of his coworker Walter Collins, who refused five straight notices from his Louisiana draft board and was sentenced to five concurrent five-year sentences in July 1969. Warren Crawford, son of New Orleans civil rights leader Jeanette Crawford, received the harshest penalty for draft evasion during the Vietnam War. He was sentenced to six concurrent five-year sentences, the most severe sentence imposed on any of the Vietnam resisters.

Young African Americans facing induction during the Vietnam War faced a dilemma similar to that of their white comrades in the draft. They were asked to fight, and possibly die, in a war that an increasing number of Americans deemed unnecessary and immoral. But African Americans faced additional problems. They realized that blacks were drafted in disproportionate numbers, and they knew that since African Americans were unlikely to obtain positions in the Guards or reserves, most of the black draftees would serve in Vietnam. Yet, many draft-eligible black men were deeply patriotic. Most believed that the United States was protecting the freedom of both America and South Vietnam and went willingly into the armed forces. Despite the moral ambiguity of the war and an influential antidraft movement, most young men took that one step forward and accepted their induction into the armed forces.

Notes

1. U.S. House, *Investigation of Attempts to Subvert the United States Armed Forces*, hearings before the Committee of Internal Security, 92nd Congress (Washington: U.S. Government Printing Office, 1972), 6545, 6616, and 7058.

2. H. Bruce Franklin, "The Antiwar Movement We Are Supposed to Forget," *Touchstone* 10, no. 5 (November/December 2000) (online edition).

3. Carson Clayborne, *In Struggle: SNCC and the Black Awakening of the 1960s* (Cambridge: Harvard University Press, 1981), 185–86.

4. Darlene Clark Hine, *The African American Odyssey*, vol. 1 (Upper Saddle River, NJ: Prentice Hall, 2003), 545.

5. Howard L. Bingham and Max Wallace, *Muhammad Ali's Greatest Fight* (New York: M. Evans and Company, 2000), 119.

6. Richard M. Scammon, "Report from Black America," *Newsweek*, June 30, 1969, 19.

7. Scammon, "Report from Black America," 19.

8. L. Deckel McLean, "The Black Man and the Draft," *Ebony*, August 1968, 64.

9. Herman Graham III, *The Brothers' Vietnam War: Black Power, Manhood, and the Military Experience* (Gainesville: University Press of Florida, 2003), 74.

~

CHAPTER THREE

The Black Military Experience in the Vietnam Era

Despite all of their progress, the armed forces still had significant racial problems, problems that an expanded draft and the war exposed and magnified. America was also changing rapidly in the early years of the war, and gains in civil rights and economic opportunity, coupled with the chance of getting killed or maimed in Vietnam, made military service a far less attractive option. Finally, many of the younger recruits were more militant than their predecessors and viewed all American institutions, including the armed forces, as inherently racist. They expected to face both racists and racism in the military, and far too often their suspicions were confirmed.

Personal racism was the most obvious. Those in command or supervisory positions could use the system to engage in racist practices against minority service personnel, and they often did so with serious consequences. Company commander Major Michael F. Colacicco relieved a white platoon sergeant from duty because he had set up black soldiers for disciplinary action. In the course of his investigations, Colacicco discovered that the sergeant was waking up white soldiers but not black soldiers, so that the black men were often late for duty. Personal racism was also a factor in promotions and assignments. One white sergeant bluntly told a black private, "If you're white, you're all right, but if you're soul, there ain't no hope."[1]

There were many ways bigoted individuals could sabotage a soldier's chance to be promoted. Many racist officers never recommended black soldiers for promotion or they wrote biased efficiency reports. In 1966, after fourteen years of serving in the air force, African American Sergeant Crispus

Bosworth was positive that such biased reports were one of the main reasons blacks did not receive their fair share of promotions. Black seaman Ron Carter claimed that whites in the navy were given exceptional evaluations whereas African Americans usually were rated only as adequate. Racist officers often failed to notify blacks of an impending promotion board meeting or exam. Allen Thomas, for example, was at a remote firebase when he learned at 11 p.m. of a promotion board hearing the following morning. He risked attack during an all-night truck ride on dangerous and hostile roads but still could not make it back to the base in time for the hearing. It could have been a simple oversight, but Thomas and other blacks were convinced that racism was the main factor. Nearly 64 percent of African Americans interviewed thought that racism contributed to a slower promotion rate for blacks.

Compounding the problem was the fact that many whites, even those who did not consider themselves particularly racist, often harbored preconceptions or stereotypes that inadvertently contributed to a racist environment. White recruit John "Jackie" Breedlove apparently liked and respected his black roommate Tom Cummings, describing him to his parents as a nice guy. Breedlove's idea of a joke, however, was to tell Cummings that if he did not shape up the white men in his unit would get the Ku Klux Klan after him. African American James Daly was a prisoner of war in 1968, an experience he shared with white Army doctor Captain Floyd Kushner. Daly was convinced that Kushner was a racist, despite the physician's denials. In a long conversation Kushner stated he had nothing against African Americans, but "he wouldn't want to live next door to one." Apparently some of the other white prisoners agreed with the doctor. Daly wrote in disgust that "when a couple of the guys started to side with Kushner, I really got stirred up."[2] The doctor's views reflected those of many Americans.

A second form of discrimination that African Americans faced was institutional racism, which the Department of Defense defined as "policies or practices which appear to be neutral in their effect on minority individuals or groups but which have the effect of disproportionately impacting upon them in harmful or negative ways."[3] Institutional racism differed from the legal racism that governed race relations in the military prior to Truman's 1948 executive order, in that it was usually unintentional and definitely more subtle and harder to detect and prove. Much like personal racism, it was often built on false preconceptions.

The biggest problem with institutional racism was that the Pentagon refused to admit that it still existed. In 1968, the Department of Defense proudly announced that it had officially eliminated racial discrimination in the military services and that it now gave promotions solely based on merit.

Civilian officials and commissioned officers thus convinced themselves that any racial problems in the armed forces were not due to military policies. General William Westmoreland was convinced that a handful of radicals were responsible for the army's racial problems during Vietnam, claiming in his memoirs that dissent in the army was "usually fanned by outsiders."[4] Vice Admiral Samuel L. Gravely Jr., the first black admiral in the navy, also believed that racial problems in that branch of the service were caused primarily by outside militants. As late as 1971, when the DOD was investigating institutional racism in the military justice system, Assistant Secretary of Defense Roger T. Kelley was largely blaming outside factors. "I think we have to admit that some of the same racial tensions that explode in the civilian sector also explode in the military," he explained.[5] Many of the racial problems plaguing the armed forces were in fact imported from the civilian sector, but most military officials failed to see that the defense establishment was also responsible for many of the racial troubles that erupted within the ranks.

Racial tension in the military was especially problematic in wartime. Of all the factors on the battlefield, none are more important than teamwork and cohesion. No one wants to let a buddy down in combat and no one wants to be out there alone. Modern military training is geared to instill those feelings of comradeship with, and reliance on, one's fellow recruits, on the one hand, and loyalty and a sense of pride and belonging in one's unit and branch of service, on the other. To this end the military needed conformity. It worked to eliminate civilian individuality from recruits and promoted unit cohesion among new soldiers. Shaving a recruit's head was partially a hygiene measure, but it also made each recruit look alike. "There were no black marines, and no white marines," the saying went, "only green marines."

One of the universal experiences of all military recruits during the Vietnam War was basic training, or "boot camp," a six- to eight-week course designed to convert civilians into soldiers. Physical training is an important aspect of boot camp, but the real conditioning is largely psychological, in that successfully completing basic training builds up the recruits' confidence and sense of manhood, and gives them a feeling of true accomplishment. The vaunted marine obstacle course, for instance, was reputed to be one of the most grueling and difficult in the world, but someone in reasonably good shape and health had little real trouble in earning a passing grade. It was also in boot camp that the military instilled the all-important principles of teamwork and unit cohesion. One popular method for converting individuals into a cohesive unit was to provide them with a common enemy to hate. In boot camp that often was the training company's drill instructor, or DI.

Many black trainees were happy when they learned that they had been assigned to a black drill instructor, expecting him to be kinder and more understanding than a white instructor. Yet they proved just as tough and usually more demanding than their white counterparts. In truth, all drill
instructors were mean and demanding, but only because they knew that one
small mistake on the battlefield could mean the difference between life and
death. Better to despise the DI in boot camp than get blown into a thousand
pieces in Vietnam. For their part, many of the DIs went out of their way to
antagonize particular trainees, either to motivate them to do better or to
unite the training company to get them through the ordeal. It was not unusual for a DI to verbally abuse a trainee by questioning his manhood or sex-
ual orientation, or by using racial insults or pejoratives. Some of the DIs were
bigots, but often racial insults were designed to get the most out of a recruit,
and most instructors did not do it out of hatred or animosity. Many recruits
understood this and had few racial problems in boot camp.

But for many African Americans, basic training was their introduction
not only to military life but also to the dominant white power structure.
Many black recruits had had little interaction with whites in civilian society,
but now in the military they were required to work and get along with them.
The civil rights and black power movements had made African Americans
more sensitive to racism and less likely to tolerate it than in previous generations. Moreover, changes in the law and American society meant that they
had a greater ability to challenge racism than did their military forefathers.
Many of them were also reluctant draftees and had little desire to serve in the
military or in a war they did not support. They did not see the drill instructor's tactics as motivational, but racist. Instead of instilling unit cohesion, the
tactics confirmed an opinion that many of them already held, that the military was just as racist as any other white institution in the United States.
"They say I am just a Marine," Private Allen E. Jones told a reporter from the
Baltimore Afro-American, but "how can I forget eighteen years of being black
and all that being black means in this country?"[6] By the late 1960s the stage
was set for a major confrontation between the military and militant African
Americans who denounced the armed forces as a racist institution.

Institutional racism plagued African Americans in virtually every aspect
of their service careers, beginning with their first assignments after boot
camp. At the time of their induction, recruits took a series of exams and tests
to gauge their general intelligence and aptitudes. Everyone took the Armed
Forces Qualification Test (AFQT), which was similar to a standard civilian
intelligence quotient test. In addition, each branch of the service employed

other devices for rating the recruits' mental abilities. The scores on these exams were extremely important because they largely determined a recruit's career path in the armed forces. A high score meant that the inductee would have a much wider choice of job options, or Military Occupational Specialties (MOS), including the prestigious and rewarding "hard-core" specialties, such as military intelligence and the more advanced technical fields. A recruit needed to score forty on the air force entrance exam to qualify for enlistment, but he needed at least a sixty to qualify for advanced electronics training. The army tests placed recruits into five categories, the highest of which were I and II. A recruit who tested in these categories could choose any MOS. Those who tested in III or IV were assigned to a "soft-core" area, meaning service and supply, or combat training. Those who tested in category V were considered mentally unfit for service.

African Americans often did not do well on these exams. In 1965 and 1966, for example, 40 percent of African American recruits tested fell into category IV, a trend that persisted throughout the Vietnam War era. As late as 1971, the Defense Department admitted that black scores were still "markedly lower" than whites. The Pentagon found that only about 25 percent of whites with between nineteen and twenty-four months' service fell into category IV, but for African Americans the figure neared 75 percent.

There were several reasons for the low scores; one of the most important was the lack of proper education. The same substandard schooling that prevented many African Americans from securing a college deferment also kept them from securing a good job in the armed forces instead of a combat assignment in Vietnam. The schools most blacks attended were often segregated, almost always underfunded, and, unlike most schools for whites, did not stress the science and advanced mathematics courses needed to score well on the technical exams. One black sergeant told an investigator from the Department of Defense that a poor education relegated many African Americans to the "soft-core" specialties, such as transportation and supply. The Pentagon should have been well aware of the problem because the military had conducted numerous studies over the preceding three decades.

Some black critics, however, cited a second and more controversial reason for the low test scores. The battery of exams that recruits took was supposed to be objective, but critics charged that they contained a Eurocentric bias because they tested knowledge of white culture and values. The Pentagon instituted reforms to address the disparities, but initially without much success or enthusiasm. With a war going on, reform was low on their priority list, and besides, they needed more combat soldiers than technical

experts. Many military officials, including most black senior officers, believed that the armed forces would have to lower their standards to increase
the number of African Americans in the hard-core MOS.

Consequently, African Americans were often excluded from the advanced technical fields and assigned to combat and "soft-core" MOS. Many
became combat infantrymen. Blacks made up over 12 percent of the enlisted strength of the armed forces but were less than 5 percent of the military's electronics equipment technicians and only 7 percent of the personnel in communications and intelligence specialties. The air force was the
most technically oriented branch of the armed forces and there African
Americans were largely assigned to "soft-core" MOS in administration, air
police, food service, supply, and transportation. One witness told a congressional hearing late in the war that blacks, Chicanos, and Puerto Ricans
got the jobs nobody else wanted.

Conditions did improve as the war progressed. Between 1968 and 1972,
the number of African Americans in the army's military police increased
from 8 to 15 percent, and black representation improved in other specialties.
Moreover, the military implemented these changes without lowering the
standards. In 1973, the army began using a new exam, the Army Classification Battery (ACB), in place of the AFQT. Black scores improved remark-
ably while white scores remained the same, supporting the earlier charge that
the AFQT exams had been racially biased. In 1972, over 42 percent of
African Americans tested into the top categories under the new test, compared to only 33 percent under the old.

Most of the military reforms came late in the war and did not affect the
majority of African Americans who served. The military did offer "lateral" or
cross-training for another MOS, but it was difficult to do so and often led to
another dead-end soft-core specialty. Throughout the war, blacks remained
concentrated in the combat arms and in the soft-core specialties. As late as
1972, for example, African Americans in the air force made up 25 percent of
the air personnel assigned to administration and 37.7 percent of those assigned to service and supply units.

Black service personnel discovered that assignment to a soft-core area
hurt their chances for promotion and advancement. Ron Carter joined the
navy in 1962 and rose to the rank of master chief petty officer of the Atlantic
Fleet, before retiring in 1994. He remembered the menial tasks and assignments African Americans performed at Oceana Naval Air Station during the
war and concluded that they were an obstacle to promotions. "If you were assigned to washing airplanes or cleaning the barracks, and other people were
allowed to work with the airplanes, they had an edge," he explained.[7] Blacks

were also concentrated in specialties that required fewer noncommissioned officers than did the technical fields, such as the infantry and administrative and service and supply units. Often there were too many qualified African Americans competing for a handful of promotions in their field. A black serviceman stationed in Germany explained to an NAACP committee that to earn promotion in his current MOS he would have to get a near-perfect score. Many African Americans were also convinced that racism hurt their chances for promotion. In some cases it was the racist preconception that African Americans were not as capable as whites, meaning blacks usually had to prove themselves far more than whites to be considered for advancement.

Many deserving African Americans did receive promotions and had successful careers in the military. In addition, not all African Americans subscribed to the belief that white racism affected their chances for promotion. Some believed it was a poor excuse for those who just could not make the grade. Lt. Colonel Hurdle L. Maxwell, the first African American to command a marine combat battalion, believed the slow promotion rate had more to do with lack of seniority than racism. Simply put, he did not believe blacks had been in the armed forces long enough to win promotion to the senior ranks. Other black veteran officers shared his views.

But it is clear that institutional practices contributed to the disparity in the number of black and white officers in the top ranks. Seniority was certainly a factor. Segregation had only ended in the armed forces in 1948, and prior to that time blacks were limited in both numbers and opportunities in all of the service branches. By 1965, when the United States escalated the war in Vietnam, African Americans had only served in an integrated military for about seventeen years, which is usually not enough time to have advanced into the most senior ranks. Therefore, blacks were the most underrepresented in the highest pay grades. In 1972, African Americans constituted over 17 percent of the army's enlisted strength, but only 7 percent of the two highest pay grades. In all of the services, African Americans served in disproportionate numbers in the lowest pay grades.

The lack of black representation in the higher pay grades and in the commissioned officer corps hurt black soldiers' chances for promotion in two ways. Promotion depended not only on merit but also to a certain degree on personal connections. It helped greatly to have a champion or mentor in the form of a senior NCO or officer who could provide help and guidance and promote one's career. Colin Powell had Major George B. Price as a mentor and role model in Vietnam, and he in turn helped advance the careers of other young black officers. But there were not enough Prices and Powells to go around, and many promising black NCOs or junior officers never got the same kind of help available to most whites. In his early years in the navy, Ron Carter did not have the benefit of advice from seasoned black sailors who could have told him which jobs or assignments led to advancement. Lack of seniority also meant that fewer blacks served on promotion boards; thus, many African Americans appeared in front of all-white boards. The problem diminished as more African Americans advanced to senior ranks, and in 1970, the army mandated minority representation on all promotion boards. It was a worthwhile reform, but came too late in the war to help most black service personnel.

Racism was also a factor when it came to assignments. A tour of duty in Vietnam almost always led to swifter promotion to at least one and sometimes two ranks higher than what was normal for peacetime duty both for blacks and whites. But in Vietnam, whites were often rotated to noncombat duties when they reached E-4 or higher, whereas African Americans were given greater responsibility but kept in the field. Many African Americans were thoroughly convinced that racism was the reason. S.Sgt. Lawrence Holloman, for example, complained he was stationed at a remote place that was surrounded by Vietcong. Infantryman John R. White was certain that whites "don't like to see the Black man out of the woods," and he believed whites kept all of the good assignments for themselves.[8]

Some African Americans had a good service or support job, only to find themselves reassigned to a combat unit. Sp/4 Joe Roberson Jr. started his tour of duty in Vietnam as a supply clerk, one of the easiest jobs in the military. But since he was a combat infantryman, he found himself reassigned within a few months to the dangerous job of door gunner on a helicopter. Even in combat blacks got the worst assignments. David Parks had a job as a fire direction control operator but was reassigned as a forward observer (FO) for a mortar platoon. It was dangerous and not a particularly popular assignment. Parks said that FO stood for "fucked over" because it meant carrying a telephone with an antenna, which made him an easy target for the enemy. Parks believed that the company sergeant always picked either blacks or Puerto Ricans for the worst and most dangerous assignments. Many African Americans believed that the only way to avoid the wrath of the white officers was to avoid confrontation and to humor them.

Many whites recognized the injustice and agreed that their black comrades in arms got the worst details. Occasionally some whites did do something about it. Parks remembered that some of the whites in his unit complained to their commanding officer about the discriminatory assignments, but little came of it. Many Vietnam-era veterans claimed that the chain of command was apathetic toward racism and largely ignored it. They believed that problems were rarely corrected because military leaders seldom paid any attention to complaints of discrimination.

Many white and black officers and NCOs disputed the notion that African Americans and other minorities were given the more dangerous or demeaning assignments. They claimed that men were chosen for certain duties because they had more aptitude for them than others in their unit. It was ability, and not racism, that often determined who was chosen for a particular job, including some of the more dangerous ones. Walking point, for example, was considered one of the risky tasks. The point was the lead man for the formation, scouting slightly ahead of the rest, in search of possible danger. African Americans believed they were often singled out to take their turn at the front of the line because they were black. To be a good point man, and not just to be the lead target, did require certain skills, and a lot of officers and NCOs believed that African Americans were generally better at it. After all, it made no sense to let someone lead who was not good at it, or did not want to be there, because it would endanger the individual and the entire unit.

Survival depended partly on skill and experience, and often on sheer luck. Arthur Westbrook earned a Bronze Star and five meritorious commendations in the war and returned without a scratch. Allen Thomas "got blowed up twice" by road mines while riding in a truck. His head hurt and his ears rang for days, but he suffered no serious injuries during his three tours. He remembers putting on his helmet, "and I never wore my helmet," seconds before the two-and-a-half-ton truck he was riding struck a mine. "Blew the whole front of the truck off," but Thomas escaped with only minor injuries.[9] He also defied the odds in another way; no one died under his command in all three tours of duty.

Not all black soldiers were as lucky. Casualties are normal in wartime, but African Americans suffered casualties far exceeding their percentage of American military forces in Southeast Asia. Between 1961 and the end of 1965, the death rate for African Americans in the army was 18.3 percent. In 1965 one out of every four American soldiers killed or wounded was black. By late July 1966, basically the first full year of U.S. combat, African Americans accounted for 22 percent of all American casualties. In 1967, black Americans still comprised over 14 percent of American deaths in Vietnam.

Some African Americans interpreted the high casualty rates as proof that they were finally erasing the negative stereotype of black soldiers as cowardly and inferior to whites. "I feel good about it," commented one of the highest-ranking black officers in the army, Lt. Colonel George Shoffer, in 1968. "Not that I like the bloodshed," he cautioned, "but the performance of the Negro in Vietnam tends to offset the fact that the Negro wasn't considered worthy of being a front-line soldier in other wars."[10] Even members of the Defense Department occasionally used this argument. One unnamed Pentagon spokesperson told newspaper reporters in March 1966 that if the figures demonstrated anything, "it is the valor of the Negro in combat."[11]

African Americans were proud of the accomplishments of black troops in Vietnam, but many were beginning to question the high price in lives the black community appeared to be paying in the war. Even moderate black publications that supported the war questioned the casualty figures and wondered if they were the product of racism. In 1966, the *Baltimore Afro-American* called the high African American death rate disturbing and hinted that racism was a factor. Some black civilians wrote letters to black publications, appalled at the losses and expressing anger about blacks in the military who defended them. Some black critics, such as former SNCC chairman Stokely Carmichael, claimed that it was black "genocide" and that the Pentagon was purposely sending large numbers of African Americans to Vietnam as "cannon fodder," to get them killed and reduce the civilian black population.

The Pentagon initially denied there was any discrimination in combat assignments. In February 1966, Senator Richard B. Russell, a Democrat from Georgia, raised the issue with the Chairman of the Joint Chiefs of Staff General Earle G. Wheeler and with Secretary of Defense Robert S. McNamara. Russell told them that some of his constituents had complained that African Americans were assigned to the most dangerous areas in Vietnam in disproportionate numbers. Wheeler denied the charges and later addressed a group of Southern senators, assuring them that whites and blacks shared the dangers proportionately. Pentagon officials also insisted that it would be premature to draw conclusions yet based on these figures.

Within a month the Pentagon had changed its story. On March 9, 1966, the Department of Defense released figures showing that African Americans did in fact comprise a disproportionate percentage of American casualties in Vietnam, largely due to their high representation in combat units. In 1965, African Americans made up 31 percent of U.S. combat infantry personnel. Pentagon figures indicated that African Americans comprised 18 percent of some airborne units, compared to the 13 to 14 percent average for other army units, and that the percentages were usually higher for elite units. African American reporter Thomas Johnson referred to one of these elite units, the 173rd Airborne, which was considered by many to be the best in the war, as "heavily Negro." One black veteran of the unit remembered that his company was over 40 percent black. In 1968, the black magazine *Ebony* reported that African Americans made up 60 to 70 percent of some combat units. It was a problem that continued throughout the war. Captain Henry L. Parker, who commanded a company in Vietnam from November 1969 to November 1970, remembered that 60 percent of his company, and 95 percent of its NCOs, were African Americans.[12]

Westmoreland tried to explain the disparity, claiming that if more African Americans served in combat units, it was because of their proficiency in battle. Ironically, black pride and military prowess might have inadvertently contributed to the high death rate. Army combat units as well as many of the marine units engaged in the early heavy fighting were composed of volunteers, and a high percentage of them were black. Moreover, African Americans enlisted and reenlisted in higher rates than whites. National Urban League President Whitney Young concluded that the high death rate among black troops was due to the high enlistment and reenlistment rates by blacks, as well as black soldiers' willingness to volunteer for elite units such as the special forces or airborne.

Whatever the reason, the high death rates alarmed Pentagon officials and they initiated steps to reduce black participation on the front lines and to spread black soldiers evenly between units. The percentage of blacks in the combat units did decline from 31 percent to a little more than 20 percent of the combat infantry personnel assigned to Vietnam in 1967. The changing emphasis of American military involvement in Vietnam, from ground combat early in the war to air power and support services in the last years, was also a factor that contributed to the lowering of casualty rates among black soldiers, since ground units were disproportionately black while the technical units were overwhelmingly white. The death rate for blacks began to drop after 1967, although the rate continued to be slightly higher than the percentage of African Americans in the general population. African Americans accounted for 13 percent of those killed in action in 1968, but only 9 percent in 1970. In 1972, the last year of active fighting, African Americans made up only 7.6 percent of American losses. As a result, the overall death toll average for the war was comparable to the percentage of blacks in the United States population. Of the 58,022 Americans who died in Vietnam between January 1, 1961, and April 30, 1975, about 12.6 percent were African Americans.

Despite the high casualty rates, not all assignments were bad ones. Since assignments rotate roughly every year in the military, many men who had been stuck in combat in Vietnam found themselves reassigned to something much better, or at least safer. Career officers and noncommissioned officers, in particular, understood that they would have to serve in the war. In fact, many of them volunteered for it, but they also got good and rewarding assignments before and after service in Southeast Asia. Lt. Colonel Maurice L. Adams was a veteran of Korea who served two tours of duty in Vietnam. In between assignments to war zones, he also worked with college ROTC units, including a stint as an instructor of military science at the University of Cincinnati. Major James C. Warren flew 117 combat missions in Vietnam, but his next assignment was to fly C-141s out of Travis Air Force Base in California. Even in Southeast Asia, many African Americans enjoyed good, relatively comfortable assignments. Airman Richard W. Harper was a self-styled "Saigon Warrior," meaning he did not have to go out into the field and thus was relatively safe, but it was not an easy assignment. Nonetheless, Harper claimed that he had experienced no discrimination during his ten months in Vietnam. The military also started doing a better job of recognizing and grooming talented minority officers for higher positions during the Vietnam War. Major Colin Powell finished second in his class at Command and General Staff College at Leavenworth, which contributed to his growing reputation as a brilliant young officer. In 1968 and 1969, during his second tour of duty in Vietnam, he served as a battalion executive officer before becoming the Americal division's G-3 operations and planning officer, a job normally held by a lieutenant colonel.

The military gave black men a chance to prove themselves, and Vietnam was the place to prove it. Black Army Major Beauregard Brown believed service in Vietnam represented the best chance for advancement for a black career officer. Corporal Lawrence E. Waggoner told a black reporter that there were no color lines in Vietnam; he was just a marine. It was an opinion General William C. Westmoreland shared. He believed that Vietnam was the first war in which the military did not condone racial inequality. Visiting civilians also commented on the apparent racial equality in Vietnam. Whitney Young of the National Urban League observed that in Vietnam, for "all intents and purposes race is irrelevant . . . in spite of dangers and loneliness. [In] the muck and mire of a war torn land, colored soldiers fight and die courageously as representatives of all America."[13]

Consequently, many African Americans volunteered for duty in Vietnam, and some even volunteered to go back. Women generally did not have to serve in Vietnam, but seventeen-year army veteran Doris "Lucki" Allen volunteered for duty in 1967. Many volunteered despite the personal sacrifices entailed. Sergeant Pinkie Hauser, like Allen, would not normally have been assigned to Vietnam, but she wanted to go so much that she turned down a choice public relations job at the Pentagon and declined four different opportunities to go to Germany, as well as a comfortable assignment at Fort Knox, Kentucky. Major General Frederic E. Davison not only had to convince army officials to send him to Vietnam, but he then had to contend with hostility from his own family who did not understand why he had volunteered. Even those who did not seek assignment to Vietnam accepted it as part of their patriotic duty.

As they had in previous wars, African Americans in Vietnam once again demonstrated their abilities as warriors. They compiled an impressive record in the early years of the war, and the military noticed it. In 1967, Westmoreland went out of his way to praise the valor and skill of African Americans under his command. His appraisal of black fighting prowess may have surprised and even irritated some of his audience, but it was the opinion of most officers in Vietnam, black or white.

African Americans at home were also hearing about the achievements of black soldiers. The black press praised them and some civil rights organizations used them to promote their own agenda. In 1966, the National Urban League expressed pride in the role of African American soldiers in Vietnam, comparing the battlefield there with the struggle against injustice at home. The Urban League was not alone in its observations. Many other commentators noted the connection between valor on the battlefield and the goals of the civil rights movement. African American military prowess was a staple feature not only in black publications: Even the mainstream press, such as *Life* magazine, increasingly covered the black combat experience in Vietnam.

Many black soldiers were developing national reputations for their military skills, including Brigadier General "Chappie" James, who by 1968 had already served in three wars. The highly decorated combat pilot flew 101 missions in Korea and earned the nickname, the "Black Panther," somewhat ironic given his disdain for the organization that bore that name. James flew 78 combat missions over North Vietnam as a member of the elite "Wolfpack." President Johnson personally debriefed the self-described "unabashed patriot" on his return from Vietnam. Colonel Frank E. Petersen, another black fighter pilot who made a name for himself, became the first black marine aviator to command a tactical air squadron. Petersen distinguished himself as commander of fighter attack squadron VMFA-314. In 1968, Petersen's unit earned the U.S. Marines' Hanson Award for the best fighter squadron. That same year General Frederic Davison became the first black man to lead an active combat brigade when he assumed command of the 199th Light Infantry Brigade in Vietnam.

Colin Powell was awarded eleven medals including a Bronze Star and a Purple Heart during his two tours of duty in Vietnam. Sergeant Allen Thomas Jr. earned a total of three Bronze Stars, several army commendations, a meritorious service medal, and a Civil Action Award for work with

Vietnamese villagers. Twenty African Americans also earned the Medal of Honor, the highest military tribute the nation awards, generally bestowed for conspicuous gallantry at the risk of life above and beyond the call of duty, often entailing that the recipient make the ultimate sacrifice. In 1965, Milton Lee Olive III became the first African American to win the medal for service in the Vietnam War but gave his life to earn it. In 1967, Private James Anderson became the first black marine to earn a Medal of Honor. In total, five black marines and fifteen black soldiers won the medal during the war.

Despite their outstanding performances, African Americans were becoming increasingly frustrated with racism in the military as the war progressed. The days when blacks viewed the military as the most integrated institution in America were beginning to fade. Many African Americans felt that the military was a white-dominated institution that catered largely to the needs of the majority and often neglected the personal and cultural needs of minorities. In their daily life in the military, blacks often faced unintentional discrimination that made them feel marginalized. For example, African Americans felt that base recreational facilities were geared to the interests of whites in general, and officers in particular. "You don't see many of the brothers out on the skeet range," mused one black marine.[14] Every large base had separate club facilities for officers, noncommissioned officers, and enlisted men, and these also tended to reflect the dominant white culture. Many blacks viewed base clubs as alien and often hostile places.

African Americans were especially upset about the music played in these clubs and on the Armed Forces Radio. There was a variety of music, including pop, jazz, rock and roll, soul, and country and western, but African Americans complained that music whites favored took preference over black-oriented music. They charged that there was too little soul music and too much country and western. One black serviceman complained to the NAACP investigators that the service clubs played country music during the popular weekend and off-duty hours, but played soul mainly during the workweek. To most young service personnel of that era, music was of vital importance culturally and socially. This was especially true for those serving in Vietnam, where popular music was often a pleasant reminder of home. The music played in the clubs and on the Armed Forces Radio was not a trivial matter. Many of the racial fights that erupted in the NCO and EM clubs were sparked by music. The lack of black live entertainment was another source of conflict. James Brown and other black stars, including at least one Miss Black America, performed for the men and women stationed in Southeast Asia, but all too often the USO tours featured predominantly white acts. Of course many African Americans enjoyed talented white comedians like Bob

Hope, and almost all appreciated the rare but treasured visit by several *Play-boy* "Playmates," which included a few black women, but almost all wanted to see more black entertainers come to Vietnam. Many black soldiers blamed the military for a lack of cultural sensitivity, yet others believed it was the fault of black celebrities who were too busy protesting the war to think of the "brothers" who were fighting it.

As they often had to, African Americans in Vietnam took matters into their own hands. Priscilla Mosby, for example, was a twenty-year-old military stenographer and a gifted singer. She joined a group of military personnel who entertained the troops. The group toured throughout Vietnam, including the demilitarized zone between the North and South, and other places where the USO tours did not go. The conditions under which she and her band performed were almost always short of optimal. Performing on firebases, which were smaller bases located in the war zone and designed to provide artillery support for units in the area, obviously had its hazards. Mosby survived her stint in Vietnam, but on one occasion, playing a gig at Bihn Thuy in the Mekong Delta, a mortar round hit the bunker, killing all of her bandmates who were seeking shelter there.

In addition to the lack of black-oriented entertainment, on-base shopping facilities were yet another source of discontent. Many African Americans complained that the post exchanges, or PXs, which were stores on military installations that generally sold products cheaper than civilian establishments, did not carry many black-oriented products. Clothing was a particular point of concern. There was a renewed interest among African Americans in their African roots, and a loose-fitting robe known as a "dashiki" was becoming increasingly popular, but it was seldom available in the PX. At times the PX might stock a black-oriented product but carry too few in its inventory. Airmen First Class Phillip D. West, for example, could get the black magazine *Sepia* regularly at his base PX in Japan, but since the store only got a few issues, it usually sold out early in the month.

One of the few advantages of serving in a war zone, however, was that the military often took pains to make sure that little reminders of home were available, including beer in the chow halls or service clubs, as well as magazines and American cigarettes at the local PX. Lance Corporal Rinell R. Glenn could get black magazines at the PX in Vietnam, as could Sergeant J. M. Wright, although they were usually a month old and in short supply. In a tradition that long predated Vietnam, soldiers lucky enough to get their hands on such a valuable commodity shared it and passed it around to other members of their unit. For the men and women stationed overseas, these items were particularly important because most of the service personnel in

Vietnam often felt vulnerable and alone, and needed that tangible connection with life back in the United States, or what they called the "real world."

African Americans stationed in the United States could shop off-base for black magazines, hair-care products, and other necessities that were not available on-base, but for blacks posted outside the United States, especially in South Vietnam, this option was seldom available. Allen Thomas, for example, tried to get the PX to stock more black-oriented products when he was stationed in Vietnam, and, when that failed, he wrote to church and civic groups appealing for their help. Corporations also were receptive to requests from service personnel. Companies such as Motown Records sent copies of the newest soul music to African Americans stationed in Southeast Asia. In 1968, Kraft Foods shipped a free supply of Kool-Aid for the entire base at Kontum after Sgt. Thomas wrote to the manufacturers and told them that the GIs stationed there missed the soft drink. Friends and relatives in the United States were also happy to send their loved ones cherished items, like Sergeant J. M. Wright's friend who mailed him his favorite black magazines when he could not find them in Vietnam.

Black magazines like *Jet*, *Ebony*, and *Sepia* were very popular because they provided welcome news and information about the black community. African Americans also loved these magazines because they ran regular features on the black experience in Vietnam. The magazines filled a critical need for many of the men in the war. The average enlisted man in Vietnam was young, usually in his early twenties, single, and lonely, and there were often very few women around. The magazines offered a reminder of the opposite sex. Pornography was extremely popular among the men, but many of them merely missed interaction with women who reminded them of their girlfriends and wives. Sometimes they formed a personal attachment to the wholesome looking young women in the magazines and on occasion wrote to them, requesting photographs or other small favors of appreciation.

The lack of black-oriented products was an inconvenience for African American service personnel, but institutional racism affected blacks in every facet of their military lives, sometimes with serious consequences. By the late 1960s, most African Americans considered the racism and abuse inherent in the military justice system to be the worst form of institutional racism that affected both their military and civilian careers. The armed forces administer justice and punishment at two different and distinct levels: courts-martial and nonjudicial punishment. Serious criminal infractions, such as theft, rape, assault, or murder, and military crimes, including striking a superior officer, desertion, or aiding and abetting the enemy, are judged by courts-martial. As in a civilian court, the defendants are entitled to legal representation, the prosecution presents the charges against them, and both sides have the right to present and cross-examine witnesses and introduce evidence. The defendant also has the option of being tried by a judge and jury, or a trial board of military judges. Nonjudicial punishment, also known as an "Article Fifteen" in the army and the air force, and a "Captain's Mast" in the navy and Marine Corps, is administered for relatively minor offences, such as being late for duty or a violation of the uniform code.

African Americans considered no single aspect of military life as unfair as the use of nonjudicial punishment. Independent studies from the Congressional Black Caucus, the Department of Defense, and the NAACP found that African Americans received nonjudicial punishment out of proportion to their representation among the enlisted personnel. There were problems with the wide discretionary power afforded the commanding officer in the process. Any officer or senior NCO could charge an enlisted person with an alleged infraction, which then led to a hearing by the company's commanding officer or ship's captain, who then unilaterally determined either guilt or innocence and meted out a punishment. There was no jury. The accused could speak in his own defense and have a personal representative present at the hearing, but this person was seldom a trained lawyer. Most of the men disciplined escaped with relatively minor punishments such as placement of an official letter of reprimand in their file. But punishment could also be severe, the maximum being thirty days in the stockade, forty-five days of extra duty, or sixty days restriction, and forfeiture of a half month's pay for two months. Punishment could also include loss of rank.

Nonjudicial punishment was supposed to instill discipline and help make the individual a better soldier. Good officers used Article 15 hearings or Captain's Masts judiciously. It was very important that the defendant understood why he was being disciplined and what was expected of him afterward. The officers who followed this procedure seldom had major complaints about their handling of these cases.

There were many officers, both black and white, who treated their commands with a commitment to fairness and equality, but there were also many who did not. African Americans complained with some justification that many white officers abused their wide discretionary powers when dispensing nonjudicial punishment. This led to a racially based double standard under which officers wrote up and punished blacks for infractions for which whites escaped punishment. For example, officers and enlisted personnel alike were prohibited from wearing or displaying anything that was not part of their official military uniform. The only sanctioned exceptions were wedding and service academy rings. Anything else was a "uniform code violation" and could lead to an Article 15 or Captain's Mast. In Vietnam, however, many commanding officers ignored these "Mickey Mouse" regulations, as they were derisively known, and allowed their men a certain amount of individuality, especially in combat units out in the field, or "Indian country," where officers put a premium on combat performance over passing uniform inspection. It was not uncommon for soldiers to wear fraternity rings, peace symbols, or other jewelry, and many chalked slogans on their helmets or flak jackets. Good officers were evenhanded and tolerated such behavior, when and if they allowed it, regardless of race, but many used it as an excuse to harass and persecute African Americans. In some units whites were permitted to write something as insubordinate and unmilitary as "fuck the war" on their helmets, but African Americans were given an Article 15 in the same command for chalking "black power" on theirs. Blacks also faced discipline for wearing a small bracelet, known as a "slave bracelet," usually woven out of bootlaces, or other symbols of black solidarity. One African American veteran testified to Congress that he was given fourteen days restriction and fourteen days extra duty by his commanding officer for wearing one.

Another issue was hair length and hairstyles. During the 1960s long hair among whites and "Afro" haircuts among blacks were symbols of defiance and the wearer's refusal to conform to the prevailing societal norms. Vanity and style aside, it meant a lot to the young men to be able to express themselves. The military shaved all recruits' heads upon induction, and military regulations decreed that hair be kept very short, but the regulations were often relaxed under certain circumstances. Submariners in the navy for instance, sometimes held beard-growing contests while on duty at sea, and in Vietnam commanding officers occasionally permitted troops to let their hair grow. The privilege was always considered temporary, and soldiers and sailors were required to conform to regulations when their submarine returned to port or their unit returned from duty in the bush. However, many commanders tended to favor whites over blacks when enforcing hair length regulations. One African American in Vietnam complained that whites in his unit could wear their hair as long as the Beatles but blacks were routinely written up for even a moderate Afro. Minority cadets petitioned for equal treatment at the Air Force Academy in 1970, for instance, pointing out that whites were allowed to display Confederate flags in their dormitory windows and on bathrobes, but black cultural expressions were largely suppressed by the administration.

Sometimes a lack of understanding contributed to the problem, especially when religious beliefs were involved. Representatives from the all-black "Fort Hood United Front" claimed that numerous Article 15s were given to one soldier who was a member of the Nation of Islam and refused to eat mess hall food because of religious reasons. The Department of Defense admitted to at least one case in which a Muslim African American military prisoner was denied a copy of the Koran, though it was standard practice to allow Christian and Jewish inmates copies of their religious texts in prison.

If an enlisted person did not want to submit to nonjudicial punishment, he could request a court-martial instead. A court-martial allows the accused an opportunity to defend himself in front of a more neutral body than one's commanding officer, though the boards are often made up of officers. Moreover, a defendant can normally appeal the decision to a higher court. Demanding a court-martial can help clear a defendant's name, but it also has some serious drawbacks. Authorities can hold the accused for up to thirty days in "pretrial confinement" without filing formal charges, and even longer if the presiding officer believes it necessary. Unlike civilian courts there is no bail, no appeal, and the military does not even have to inform the defendant of his continuing incarceration or the reason for it. The provost marshal or the defendant's commanding officer determines the use and length of pretrial confinement.

Many African Americans believed that pretrial confinement was far more common for blacks than it was for whites. The evidence seems to confirm the allegations. A Department of Defense study determined that for serious crimes such as rape or murder, the pretrial confinement rates for blacks and whites were similar, but the numbers were out of proportion for lesser offenses. Only 15 percent of whites charged with going "absent without leave" (AWOL) went to the stockade, compared to nearly 40 percent of blacks who faced the same charges. African Americans made up less than 10 percent of the army's enlisted personnel in West Germany but almost 50 percent of their pretrial confinements.

African Americans were not only more likely to receive pretrial confinement, they usually spent more time in it than did white defendants. Whites spent an average of twenty-nine days before they were either released or charged and tried, while blacks were confined on average for thirty-four and a half days. A few spent a considerable amount of time in jail awaiting their fate. Black militant Billy Dean Smith spent eighteen months in pretrial confinement before he was charged and court-martialed for the murder of two lieutenants in March 1971. Like many of the defendants who spent an inordinate amount of time in pretrial confinement, Smith was eventually found not guilty on both counts.

Authorities sometimes used pretrial confinement to eliminate those blacks whom the chain of command considered to be militants or bad influences.

African Americans stationed at Da Nang in Vietnam told the Congressional Black Caucus that they had spent fifteen to thirty days in pretrial confinement for having long hair, but no formal charges were ever filed against them. It was not an unusual practice. In 1970, the NAACP found that nearly a third of all black defendants held in pretrial confinement in military stockades in West Germany were released without formal charges ever being brought against them. Blacks were also court-martialed in disproportionate numbers. African Americans made up over 34 percent of the 1,441 court-martials in 1971 and 1972. In some cases African Americans made up the majority of those facing a military trial. At Camp Casey, Vietnam, for instance, 57 percent of the men facing a general court-martial were black. In another incident, whites and blacks were both responsible for a race riot that occurred at Goose Bay Air Force Base in Labrador in 1970, but the air force chose to court-martial five of the black airmen involved and none of the whites.

Education or, more specifically, the lack of it seems to have been a determining factor in who received a court-martial. Regardless of race, a serviceperson who did not have a high school diploma had a much greater chance of being court-martialed than one who did. Roughly 16.5 percent of the enlisted personnel in the army had not graduated from high school, but they made up over two-thirds of those court-martialed. The same substandard education that hurt African Americans when it came to draft deferments, testing, training, and assignments also appears to have greatly raised their chances of running afoul of the military justice system.

The double standard in the dispensation of military justice became obvious at trial. African Americans, while more likely to be charged with offenses, were also more likely to be acquitted than white defendants. Nearly 10 percent of all black defendants who contested the charges against them won acquittals, compared to less than 6 percent of whites. Given the high acquittal rate, it appears that the charges against African Americans were either exaggerated or fabricated.

One factor that led blacks to distrust the military courts was that during the Vietnam War only 2 percent of the commissioned officers assigned to the Judge Advocate General's Office were African American. From the judge to the jury, to the prosecuting and defense attorneys, a black defendant was likely to see only white faces. With few exceptions, all of the full- and part-time military judges were white. The problem was so acute that the Pentagon redoubled its efforts to recruit black lawyers and considered the possibility of hiring minority law firms to help make up for the shortage. The trial board was usually all white as well. A defendant could request that enlisted personnel be appointed to the trial board, but the typical jury in a court-martial was composed almost exclusively of commissioned officers. Enlisted soldiers often had a healthy distrust of those who outranked them, and many did not think that commissioned officers understood them or had any sympathy for their plight. Black enlisted personnel and black officers had an additional factor dividing them. The average black defendant was young and likely to be more militant, whereas black officers were generally just as conservative and career oriented as their white comrades, and they seldom shared the same values as the accused. Many of the more radical black enlisted men believed that African American officers had "sold out" their black brothers to curry favor and rewards from the white power structure, and they derisively labeled the officers "Uncle Toms."

For those convicted at a court-martial the penalties could be severe, including reduction to the lowest rank, forfeiture of pay, or long prison terms, often at hard labor. In the case of rape, murder, treason, mutiny, or cowardice or battlefield desertion, they could face the death penalty. Militant or subversive behavior usually resulted in unduly long prison sentences. In 1969, for example, Nation of Islam members Lance Corporal William Harvey Jr. and Private First Class George Daniels of the Marine Corps were sentenced to six and ten years, respectively, at hard labor for holding a spontaneous "rap session" with other blacks in their stateside unit and urging them not to go to Vietnam to fight the white man's war. Blacks convicted at court-martial were generally more likely to receive harsher sentences than white convicts. The average sentence handed down to a white was two and a half years in prison, but for blacks it was a full three years.

As a consequence of disproportionate charges and sentencing rates, African Americans were overrepresented in military stockades and brigs during the war. In 1968, 40 percent of the military prisoners in the seven military stockades in Europe were African American. The percentage was even higher at Long Binh Stockade, the largest military prison in South Vietnam, where 50 percent of the population was black in 1969. African Americans made up on average between 30 and 40 percent of the prisoners at the Da Nang Brig, the main confinement facility in Vietnam for the navy and marines, and up to 95 percent of the inmates held in maximum security. The numbers for stateside prisons were similar.

Fighting the military justice system was a daunting task, and most defendants, regardless of race, simply accepted whatever punishment was meted out to them. Some of the men did not understand how the system worked and were unaware of their basic rights. Many innocent defendants chose to accept nonjudicial punishment rather than submit to a court-martial because they did not believe they could get a fair trial in a military justice system that was dominated by whites. Others submitted to a court-martial in the hopes of receiving a fair hearing, only to be sentenced to long prison terms.

In addition to receiving longer sentences or harsher punishments than white offenders, African Americans were more likely to get a "less-than-honorable discharge" from the military. The discharge system in use during Vietnam dated from 1947 and provided for five different types of discharges. The first, and most desirable, was an "honorable discharge," which was given to personnel who had faithfully executed their duties and completed their enlistment, or had been wounded and medically discharged. The next type was a "general discharge," which the military issued under honorable conditions to individuals who could not complete their terms of enlistment for medical, personal, or emotional reasons, but had committed no infraction of military law. During the Vietnam War era the vast majority of individuals, regardless of race, received discharges that were either honorable or general under honorable conditions.

While it was possible for someone who had been convicted at court-martial to complete his or her enlistment and leave the armed forces with either an honorable or general discharge, it was far more common for someone convicted of more serious offenses to receive one of the other three types of discharges: "undesirable," "bad conduct," and "dishonorable." The armed forces used "undesirable" discharges to remove those who were not temperamentally suited to military life or could not adjust to the disciplined and ordered lifestyle. They also used the "undesirable" discharge to eliminate radicals, drug addicts, and "deviants," usually meaning homosexuals, from the ranks. Normally someone had to request a "general" or "undesirable" discharge, but many African Americans claimed they were threatened with prison time or otherwise pressured into requesting one. Soldiers also had the right to request a special hearing, but most defendants were either unaware of this right or chose not to contest their separation from the armed forces. Ninety-five percent of the soldiers who received some sort of administrative discharge waived their rights to either a review board or a court-martial.

Those who received "bad conduct" discharges had accumulated minor infractions, had committed a felony offense, or made a serious breach of the military code of conduct. Soldiers earned "dishonorable" discharges for serious crimes, such as murder, aiding and abetting the enemy, desertion, or cowardice in the face of the enemy. Both "bad conduct" and "dishonorable" discharges were "punitive" discharges that could only be imposed by court-martial, and they were given along with or in place of a prison sentence. "Dishonorable" discharges were relatively uncommon. In 1968, of nearly 860,000 individuals leaving military service that year, only 34 did so with "dishonorable" discharges. As with every other negative aspect of the military justice system, African Americans received more than their fair share of "undesirable" and punitive discharges.

Many African Americans believed less-than-honorable discharges were used to rid the armed forces of real or perceived black militants. In many instances the armed forces apparently did use such discharges for this purpose. Billy Dean Smith was busted to the rank of private and given a bad-conduct discharge even though he was found not guilty in his murder trial. Thomas Tuck was given a less-than-honorable discharge after he tried to organize a black antiwar organization at Fort Knox, Kentucky. Many of the militants were defiant and proud of their undesirable or punitive discharges.

Most of the African Americans who accepted less-than-honorable discharges were not militants, but many were willing to agree to anything to get out of the military. Some agreed to accept a less-than-honorable discharge after racist white junior officers told them that it would be easy to get it upgraded to "honorable" status at a later date. While it was possible to get a less-than-honorable discharge upgraded to an honorable one, the procedure was lengthy, often taking years to accomplish, and the applicant was seldom successful. In 1970, for example, the service review boards turned down 95 percent of all applications for an upgrade of a less-than-honorable discharge to honorable status.

An "undesirable" or punitive discharge was a "bad-paper" discharge and it carried serious consequences. Those who received them were ineligible for most veterans' benefits, and most did not qualify for either unemployment compensation or welfare. A bad-paper discharge often hurt their chances of finding good jobs at home, and many ended up in civilian prisons. In 1973, veterans accounted for 25 percent of the total U.S. prison population, with African Americans making up half of that total. For many black veterans, "bad-paper" discharges were just another example of how the military used African Americans to fight the war and then sent them back to poverty and unemployment in an uncaring civilian society.

In spite of the military's shortcomings, most black career soldiers trusted the system and believed that they could effect change by going through the proper channels without resorting to violence or militant action. African Americans often helped solve racial problems by either alerting or pressuring base authorities about it, and in return many did respond positively. For example, black sailors at the navy's Groton, Connecticut, submarine base convinced their commanding officer to pay more attention to their cultural needs, and the result was an increase in black products at the PX, and more soul music was played at the Enlisted Men's and Noncommissioned Officers Clubs. Groton was not an isolated example.

African Americans were indeed making a name for themselves as courageous and patriotic warriors in Vietnam in spite of the personal and institutional racism they encountered in training, assignments, military justice, and other aspects of their military careers. But there was a growing dissatisfaction in the black community with both the war and the treatment accorded black service personnel by the military, and this discontent would manifest itself both within the armed forces and in the growing antiwar movement.

Notes

1. PFC Donnel Jones, "Racism in Vietnam," Letters to the Editor, *Sepia*, August 1968, 6.

2. James A. Daly and Lee Bergman, *Black Prisoner of War: A Conscientious Objector's Vietnam Memoir* (Lawrence: University Press of Kansas, 2000), 133.

3. Department of Defense, *Task Force on the Administration of Military Justice in the Armed Forces*, vol. 1 (Washington: U.S. Government Printing Office, 1972), 19.

4. General William C. Westmoreland, *A Soldier Reports* (Garden City, NY: Doubleday and Company, 1976), 371.

5. Colonel Robert D. Heinl Jr., "The Collapse of the Armed Forces," *Armed Forces Journal*, June 7, 1971, 30.

6. "Poor Communication Seen As Cause of Marine Trouble," *Baltimore Afro-American*, January 10, 1970, 18.

7. William H. McMichael, "A War on Two Fronts," *Newport News-Hampton, Virginia Daily Press*, Williamsburg Edition, July 27, 1998, 1, A4-A6.

8. John R. White, "Letter from Vietnam," *Black Panther*, August 16, 1969, 9.

9. Allen Thomas Jr., Interview with the author, Erlanger, Kentucky, July 25, 2000.

10. Gene Grove, "The Army and the Negro," *New York Times Magazine*, July 24, 1966, 37.

11. "Casualties among Negro GIs High—'Valor,' Says Pentagon," *Cincinnati Enquirer*, March 10, 1966, 1.

12. Major Henry L. Parker Interview, Senior Officer Oral History Project, 1982.

13. Whitney Young Jr., "To Be Equal," *Baltimore Afro-American*, February 19, 1966, 1.

14. Steven Morris, "How Blacks Upset the Marine Corps," *Ebony*, December 1969, 60.

CHAPTER FOUR

~

Antiwar Sentiment and
Black Disillusionment

In the early years of troop involvement, despite growing concerns about the draft, there was overwhelming black support for the Vietnam War, partly because President Lyndon B. Johnson was a strong ally of the civil rights movement. In 1964, he secured passage of the Civil Rights Act, and he pushed through the Voting Rights Act in 1965. Black leaders were grateful for presidential support and, in return, either supported the war in Vietnam or remained quiet about it. For example, although Martin Luther King Jr. believed that the war was unjust, the Southern Christian Leadership Conference (SCLC) board would not let him speak against it for fear of alienating Johnson.

After 1965, however, the militant and nationalist organizations such as the Black Panthers openly condemned the war in Vietnam. Rule 6 of the Black Panther Party's by-laws, for example, prohibited its members from serving in any armed force except the Panther's Black Liberation Army and from participating in any colonial wars of aggression, including Vietnam. But the decision to oppose the war publicly could be contentious within civil rights organizations. By April 1965, a few members of SNCC, such as James Forman and Robert Moses, had opposed the war as individuals, but the organization as a whole remained divided over the issue. Moses decided to take a leave of absence from the organization to speak at a large antiwar rally in Washington, D.C., rather than antagonize other SNCC members who believed his priority should be the civil rights movement and not the war in Vietnam. By the end of the year, however, the organization had reached a consensus. SNCC drew up an antiwar statement condemning American participation in the Vietnam War. The group's opposition to the war was virtually preordained due to its members' pacifism, growing distrust of the government, and support of Third World nations who sought independence from imperial powers.

African Americans were involved in organizing and leading the antiwar movement from its very beginning. Several black organizations, including the Black Panther Party, SNCC, and the National Black Anti-War Anti-Draft Union, founded in February 1968, played a significant role. Black and white antiwar protesters cooperated, and black activists were often featured speakers at demonstrations. Robert Moses spoke at the Washington, D.C., rally in April 1965; Stokely Carmichael addressed the first group demonstrating against napalm in 1966; and Lincoln Lynch, associate national director of CORE, was one of the keynote speakers at the New York demonstrations in 1966. SNCC was involved in the antiwar protests staged at the wedding of President Johnson's daughter Luci as well as numerous other antiwar events. Some African Americans held leadership positions in the wider movement. Noted civil rights activist Reverend James Bevel led the biracial Spring Mobilization for Peace, which among other activities staged a protest and sit-in at Selective Service headquarters in Washington, D.C., at the end of March 1967. On April 15, the Spring Mobilization Committee staged massive demonstrations in New York and San Francisco.

Black nationalist groups, such as the Nation of Islam, Maulana Karenga's US movement in San Francisco, and the Black Panthers, were in near-universal agreement in their opposition to the war. The Honorable Elijah Muhammad denounced the war, predicting it would be the death of America, although he did not stage any protests. The religious leader wanted to avoid antagonizing the authorities. Other black militant groups, however, were very active in the antiwar movement, particularly the heavily armed and belligerent Black Panthers.

The Panthers considered their war against racism part of a greater revolutionary struggle against the oppressive capitalist ruling class, which happened to be overwhelmingly white. There could be black "pigs," traitors to the race, as well as progressive whites who were friends and allies in the war against class oppression. The Panthers' alliance with the radical left and their mutual admiration was genuine, and they often worked together. At a Berkeley demonstration, Black Panther John Turner, for example, expressed the Panthers' solidarity with white radicals. In July 1969, the Panthers invited white radicals to speak at their conference, "A United Front against Fascism," and in January 1970, the Black Panther Party cosponsored an antiwar rally at St.

Thomas Episcopal Church in Philadelphia. Panthers often proved to be effective allies in the struggle against the war in that they could provide the threat of armed rebellion normally lacking from most of the predominantly white groups. It was largely the presence of numerous Black Panthers and the Weathermen, a violent faction of the Students for a Democratic Society, a leftist organization with a strong presence on many college campuses, that convinced state authorities to prepare for a May Day demonstration at Yale University in 1970 by mobilizing four thousand marines and paratroopers to respond quickly to any violence. The Yale demonstration was symbolic of the alliance between the black nationalists and the antiwar movement. Roughly twelve thousand people protested both unfair police and judicial treatment of the Black Panthers and the U.S. invasion of Cambodia. In general, the vast majority of participants were both nonradical and nonviolent. Ironically, at Yale the Panthers were not the rioters, but the peacemakers. At one point several Black Panthers interceded to stop police from throwing tear gas at protesters, and protesters from throwing bottles at the police.

Though they worked with whites in the antiwar movement, the black nationalists often staged their own demonstrations. Like the radical white antiwar groups, they tended to prefer direct action tactics, such as raids on draft offices, mass demonstrations, and confrontations with authorities. At times, they paid the price for them. In August 1966, SNCC began daily picketing of the Army Induction Center in Atlanta, Georgia, and the authorities retaliated by arresting a dozen members of the organization. The twelve defendants, ten men and two women, were held in the Atlanta Stockade, where the males were frequently consigned to "the hole," an area only four feet square and seven feet high, for yelling out "black power" and other slogans. Six of the protestors were sentenced to three and a half year prison sentences for "interfering with the Selective Service Act," and a seventh, John Wilson, received three years on a Georgia chain gang for "insurrection."

Despite the shared dangers, blacks and whites in the movement sometimes had different priorities and did not always see each other as comrades in the struggle. Some militant black activists did not believe in cooperating with whites for any reason and were hostile to their involvement in what they considered to be exclusively black concerns. In one instance, black militants warned whites to stay away from Virginia Union University, a historically black college in Richmond, in July 1968, when over three hundred students gave black power advocate Stokely Carmichael an enthusiastic welcome and then took over the administration building. Many blacks were reluctant to take part in an antiwar movement they viewed as led by whites and reflective of white priorities. Even though the Black Panthers helped sponsor and provide speakers for the Philadelphia antiwar demonstration in January 1970, for example, only four African Americans showed up.

Historically black colleges, such as Virginia Union, had their share of antiwar activities. Nine hundred students demonstrated at Howard University in 1968, demanding both a more Afrocentric curriculum and an end to the Vietnam War. On April 17 that same year Tuskegee University abolished compulsory military training for all but freshmen, after students "captured" twelve prominent school trustees, including retired general Lucius Clay, and held them for thirteen hours. Sometimes the confrontations could turn deadly. In May 1970, Mississippi state troopers shot and killed two black students and wounded at least twelve others during an antiwar and civil rights demonstration at Jackson State College on the same day that four white students were gunned down by Ohio National Guardsmen at Kent State University.

Many members of the black caucus in the House of Representatives were particularly vocal in their opposition to the Vietnam War, especially Democrat Shirley Chisholm from Brooklyn, who denounced the war and the Pentagon in her maiden speech in Congress in 1969, and Democrat Ron Dellums, a fiery newcomer from Berkeley, California.

Those African Americans who publicly opposed the war often faced harassment. Julian Bond of SNCC was denied his elected seat in the Georgia State Legislature due to his own antiwar stance and that of his organization. Bond eventually won his case in the Supreme Court and his seat in the legislature, but that effort took up most of his time in 1966. In December 1967, the ever-flamboyant Stokely Carmichael was briefly detained by French police at Orly Airport in Paris as an "undesirable" and kept for fourteen hours in the airport. He was to be immediately deported, but at the last moment high-ranking French authorities intervened and gave him a three-month visa. There was often economic retaliation for opposing the war. Sociologist Dr. Nathan Hare claimed he was not renewed to teach at Howard University in 1967 in part because of his advocacy of black power and his antiwar activities, which included attending antiwar demonstrations on campus. He was also very critical of what he considered to be an emphasis on white culture and history in the university's curriculum.

Vietnam was one of the issues that helped divide, and then destroy, the civil rights coalition. SNCC and CORE openly opposed the war, but other more moderate civil rights groups, like the NAACP, the Urban League, and the SCLC, continued to support Johnson or at least remained silent. Few moderate civil rights leaders wanted to risk offending President Johnson, who was an important ally of the civil rights movement, especially because he could turn on people who opposed him politically. Martin Luther King Jr.

had personally opposed the war from the beginning. However, he had muted his criticism on the advice of the governing board of the SCLC in order to avoid antagonizing Johnson. Early in the war, King believed that the president was trying to negotiate a peaceful solution. In private meetings, King urged Johnson and other officials to seek peace, and for a time he left it to his wife Coretta Scott King to carry the public antiwar banner.

King was well aware that if the civil rights movement denounced the war it would appear unpatriotic. Yet, he also realized that the coalition was fracturing over a host of issues and that Vietnam was a critical one. In some respects he had been trying to bridge the chasm that the war had helped widen, walking a fine line between the radical antiwar stance of SNCC and the mainstream NAACP. He had never been entirely silent on the war, especially about his opposition to the draft, and he had often encouraged and empathized with the antiwar movement, but he had always stopped short of an outright denunciation of the war or the president. As an ordained minister and a deeply religious person, King believed that the war was morally wrong and a terrible mistake. He was a pacifist and passionately devoted to the principles of nonviolence. It also threatened to destroy everything he and all of the other dedicated activists had worked so long and hard to achieve. Early in the war many civil rights activists preferred to see Vietnam as a separate issue from the fight for equality at home, but King and others had always been aware of the link between the two. He knew that the war in Southeast Asia hurt the black community and the civil rights movement in two ways: First, the draft threatened to take from the black community the best and the brightest young men who were needed in the struggle for equality, and second, wars were expensive and took money away from social programs that could further civil rights causes.

On April 7, 1967, Dr. King officially and publicly denounced the war in an impassioned speech at the famous Riverside Church in New York. Following this speech, he brought all of the passion and commitment he had used in the fight for civil rights to the crusade against the war in Southeast Asia. White supporters of the civil rights movement felt betrayed by King and believed he needed to focus his attention on racial and not military issues. The black press also attacked King for his antiwar stand, claiming it portrayed African Americans as unpatriotic and damaged his credibility as a leader of the civil rights movement. The NAACP condemned King, which was symptomatic of the disastrous impact the war had on the civil rights coalition and its eventual breakup. The war had caused a bitter rift in the movement. In the summer of 1966, Whitney Young, for example, had announced that the Urban League would dissociate itself from any civil rights organizations—meaning, in essence, SNCC and CORE—that advocated black power or linked the war in Vietnam to the civil rights movement. Young later concluded that the war was damaging the movement and finally opposed it in 1969.

The NAACP remained rigid in its stand. Its annual convention issued statements "deploring the war" and hoping for a speedy settlement, but its official position was to keep the civil rights and peace movements separate. However, many members of the NAACP firmly believed that integration entailed black participation in all major national events, even if it meant involvement in an unpopular war. This position reflected the views of many African Americans, and support for Vietnam remained strong in many segments of the black community, including among blacks currently in the war. S.Sgt. Lawrence Holloman, for instance, did not care if other African Americans thought he was an Uncle Tom because he considered it an honor to serve in Vietnam.

The divisions in the civil rights movement over the Vietnam War were reflected among blacks in the military. Many African Americans in the armed forces were staunch supporters of both the war in Vietnam and the civil rights movement. Colin Powell was typical in this respect. While Powell was proud to serve in Vietnam, he was equally glad that others were waging the war for equality back home. During his tour in Vietnam eighteen bombings of black neighborhoods occurred in Birmingham, and his father-in-law sat up nights with a shotgun across his lap in case of an attack by white racists.

Black officers, such as Powell, continued to support the civil rights movement even late in Vietnam when black nationalism was a far more popular ideology among younger African Americans and many of them had turned against the war. Major Robert E. Jones, home on leave from Vietnam in July 1970, said that as a career officer it was his duty to support the war, even if it was not ideal. Roberts also supported the nonviolent civil rights movement. Support for the moderate wing of the civil rights movement was also prevalent among many enlisted men and noncommissioned officers. Sergeant Allen Thomas Jr. had been active in the civil rights movement since he was fourteen years old, so it was no wonder that his heroes were men like Dr. Martin Luther King Jr. and black labor leader Asa Philip Randolph. He was also representative of the black career soldiers who expressed concern about radical black leaders. "You've got to understand where I came from," he recalled. "Malcolm X scared the hell out of me, just like he scared a lot of white folks, he scared the hell out of a lot of black people too."[1]

Some black soldiers were extremely critical of the antiwar movement. Dr. King and Stokely Carmichael were wrong for protesting the war, according to James H. Scott, because "[t]hey live in a free country, and somebody has to pay for it."[2] Private First Class Tommy Burden heaped scorn on all of the protesters and hippies who did not fight. Corporal Lawrence E. Waggoner was not the least bit sorry the Marine Corps had sent him to Vietnam. He believed African Americans were Americans first and should support the war.

But many of the young black recruits who entered the armed forces after 1965 had a different attitude than did the vast majority of their predecessors. By 1970, the majority of black soldiers opposed the war. Malcolm X became even more revered and influential in death than he had been in life, particularly to a new generation of black activists, both civilian and military. He was the inspiration for one of the first black radical organizations established in the armed forces, GIs United Against the War, founded in January 1969 at Fort Jackson, South Carolina, by army private Joseph Miles; a second group was established at Fort Bragg the following April. Andrew Pulley, one of the leaders of GIs United, recalled that "it started when Joe Miles suggested to some of us in the barracks . . . that we listen to some Malcolm X tapes."[3] A little over a year later, in March 1970, Air Force Sergeants Milton White and Mayanard Jordan III founded the Malcolm X Society at Vandenberg Air Force Base, California, because African Americans at the installation "wanted a militant organization of persons interested in promoting awareness." They named it after the assassinated black nationalist because of all the black leaders they saw, "Malcolm X was the most appropriate symbol . . . of the continuing struggle for change" within the armed services.[4] Malcolm X was certainly a popular figure among young black men serving in Vietnam. Over 70 percent of the black soldiers that African American journalist Wallace Terry interviewed in Vietnam in 1970 expressed admiration for Malcolm X, and he was a potent symbol for African Americans in the armed forces who sought racial justice. On May 19, 1971, African Americans stationed at Youngsen Military Reservation in South Korea, for example, held a demonstration in his honor where five hundred enlisted personnel protested discrimination and racism in the military.

Although civilian and military authorities had legitimate concerns about the activities of radical black organizations and their members in the armed forces, they doubted that the militants had much influence on other soldiers. In 1972, Under Secretary of the Army Kenneth E. Belieu asserted that radical activity in that branch had been overestimated and overrated. The Marine Corps had no record of any individual who was affiliated with a subversive or extremist organization refusing to obey orders. Moreover, there was no evidence that organized militants were responsible for any of the racial incidents in the corps. Although dissidents organized demonstrations protesting racism and discrimination at Fort McClellan and at Fort Hood, attendance at these events was often low, and similar rallies at other installations attracted an average of only sixty to eighty spectators.

One reason for the lack of influence of black radicals among black soldiers was the radicals' praise of the Vietcong, whom they viewed as comrades in the struggle against racism and Western imperialism. Most editions of the *Black Panther Newspaper*, for example, carried an article or editorial lauding the North Vietnamese and Vietcong and stressing the Panthers' solidarity with them. When Ho Chi Minh died in September 1969, the Panthers extended their sympathy to the Vietnamese people and praised him for his leadership in the world socialist struggle. In return the North Vietnamese expressed their solidarity and support for the black nationalists in their struggle against white Western racism. In November 1969, the North Vietnamese even offered to release some Americans prisoners of war if the U.S. government agreed to drop felony charges against Black Panther leaders Bobby Seale and Huey Newton. They also invited delegations of African Americans to North Vietnam. While many of their fellow countrymen may have seen visiting the enemy in wartime as an act of treason, since there was never an official declaration of war against the North Vietnamese government, it was not illegal for Americans to visit North Vietnam, and many did. In 1966, Julius Lester of SNCC visited Hanoi to gather evidence of American war crimes. In December of that year, Diane Nash-Bevel, a prominent civil rights activist and founding member of SNCC, and three female companions spent eleven days in North Vietnam. In September 1970, the Reverend Phillip Lawson, an ally of the Black Panther Party and organizer of the New Mobilization Committee to End the War in Vietnam, visited the Democratic Republic of Vietnam and received a cordial welcome.

The North Vietnamese often invited visiting black radicals to give radio addresses, which were broadcast by Radio Hanoi in the North and the Vietcong's clandestine "Liberation Radio" in the South. As early as 1965, the stations aired audiotapes recorded in Beijing, China, by Clarence Adams, an African American who had deserted during the Korean War. Nash-Bevel took to the airwaves during her trip to tell her "black brothers" that the Vietnam War was a colonialist war. In 1967, Stokely Carmichael visited North Vietnam and informed his Communist Party hosts that he had warm support for the struggle against the common enemy and called the United States the greatest destroyer of humanity. Eldridge Cleaver of the Black Panther Party also made an appeal to African Americans fighting in South Vietnam, proclaiming black support for the Vietcong.

The North Vietnamese may have made their strongest overtures toward the black nationalists, but they also attempted to appeal to other members of the black community. For example, they stressed that Ho Chi Minh, the leader of North Vietnam, had visited Harlem and the Deep South and thus had heartfelt sympathy for and understanding of the plight of black Americans. When Dr. Martin Luther King Jr. was assassinated, North Vietnamese Premier Pham Van Dong sent the Southern Christian Leadership Conference his government's condolences, stating that the Vietnamese people share with "our Afro-American brothers this deep grief" over the civil rights leader's demise.[5]

More importantly, Vietnamese communist officials talked about alleged special treatment of black soldiers, indicating that the North Vietnamese and Vietcong preferred to kill whites and not African Americans. Whether it was true or not, many African Americans believed that the enemy would rather kill a white soldier than a black one. Terry Whitmore believed that the Vietcong waited for him to pass before they ambushed his unit near Con Tien and claimed that they shot all of the white marines before taking him prisoner. African Americans James Daly and his friend Willie Watkins were among six survivors of a North Vietnamese surprise attack on their company in 1968, and they were also taken captive. The Vietcong treated Daly and Watkins quite well, reassuring them that they would not be harmed and offering their captives cigarettes and food. Daly and the others were taken to a prisoner-of-war camp in South Vietnam, where they received special treatment, in an effort to exploit America's racial woes for propaganda purposes. Their Vietcong captors placed the black POWs in a hootch separate from the white prisoners. It was common for the North Vietnamese and Vietcong to force prisoners of war to attend political education classes, but they separated Daly and the other four African Americans at the camp from the white prisoners and gave them lectures emphasizing the racist nature of American society and communist sympathy for the oppressed minorities in the United States.

The prisoners who received favorable treatment often cooperated to some degree with their captors. Daly eventually concluded that the American war in Vietnam was wrong and joined the POW antiwar "Peace Committee." Along with other black and white POWs, he wrote letters protesting U.S. involvement in Southeast Asia and calling for an end to the war. In April 1972, after massive American B-52 raids on Hanoi, Daly even signed a letter volunteering to join the North Vietnamese Army. Special treatment also included the occasional release of American prisoners of war, many of whom were black. In January 1966, for instance, the Vietcong freed two black

Green Berets as a goodwill gesture, and in 1968, the North Vietnamese re-leased two black and one white prisoners of war. Daly and several other POWs, including some of those released as a goodwill gesture, were later charged with collaborating with the enemy. Black service personnel who re-sisted their captors, however, received no special treatment. While Daly and other collaborators had so much food that they could not eat it all, the North Vietnamese fed those who did not cooperate the "worst garbage" they could find. African American Air Force Captain Norman A. McDaniel refused to cooperate and was tortured, and his diet and living conditions were vile. Vietcong propaganda efforts and radical rhetoric thus did not seem realistic to most black soldiers, who still supported the war.

Although radicals did not make significant inroads among black soldiers in the first few years of active troop involvement in Vietnam, the balance tipped in their favor after 1968. That year, the United States faced a major turning point. The year began with the most decisive campaign of the war, the Tet Offensive, and ended with the election of Richard Nixon. Tet shat-tered the illusion that the United States could win, support for the war de-clined, and the government looked for ways to disengage from South Viet-nam with our reputation and honor still intact. For African Americans, the disillusionment with the war was compounded by the assassination of Dr. Martin Luther King Jr., which led to riots in major cities and caused many African Americans to lose faith in the system altogether.

Young recruits who entered the armed forces were now more likely to em-brace the militant black power movement, shunning the nonviolent civil rights movement's emphasis on peaceful integration in favor of separation and racial solidarity. The founder of the Malcolm X Society in the air force, Chief Master Sergeant Milton White, wrote glowingly of the "younger black airmen just entering the military system, fresh from the revolutionary civil-ian society outside." A white officer, Army Lieutenant Joseph H. Hall, testi-fied before Congress in 1972 that "the current nineteen year olds have less patience and interest in waiting, and this is true of both blacks and whites."[6] Black soldiers expressed their disillusionment in many ways, ranging from racial pride to racial violence.

After nearly three years of direct American involvement in Vietnam, pub-lic support for the war was eroding. In October 1967, a Gallup poll found that for the first time, more Americans opposed the war than supported it. There were massive antiwar protests throughout the nation. President John-son reacted by launching a public relations campaign to shore up support for the war, and he sent numerous officials, including Secretary of Defense Mc-

Namara and General Westmoreland, on a speaking tour throughout the United States. Both men were convinced that the attrition strategy of attempting to kill as many enemy soldiers as possible was producing results, and they argued that more time and patience would produce a victory in Southeast Asia. We had not yet won the war, according to McNamara, but in words that would come back to haunt him, he said we could see light at the end of the tunnel.

Despite the official show of optimism, the New Year began with some troubling signs. In late January 1968, around forty thousand North Vietnamese and Vietcong forces surrounded and began a siege of Khe Sahn, a Marine Corps base in South Vietnam. The White House and the Pentagon quickly became preoccupied with the defense of the base. Then, in the early morning hours of January 30, 1968, on Tet, the Vietnamese New Year, the Vietcong and North Vietnamese launched the Tet Offensive, attacking the five biggest cities in South Vietnam, as well as sixty-four district capitals, thirty-six provincial capitals, and fifty hamlets. Even the very symbol of America's presence in Vietnam, the United States embassy, became a target. The fighting was brutal, and in some cases protracted. Ultimately, the American and South Vietnamese forces successfully turned back the Tet Offensive, but the costs were high. There were sixteen hundred Americans killed and another eight thousand wounded. The Tet attack undercut the Johnson administration's pronouncements of imminent victory; far from seeing light at the end of the tunnel, there was no real end in sight. The American public felt that the government had lied and deceived them about the course and cost of the war.

The Tet Offensive, and Johnson's announcement that the United States would seek a negotiated settlement rather than victory, had a profoundly negative effect on morale and discipline among the over five hundred thousand men and women serving in Vietnam; few people want to die for a lost cause. For African Americans, the shock was compounded on April 4 when an assassin gunned down Dr. Martin Luther King Jr. as he stood on the second floor balcony of the Lorraine Motel in Memphis, Tennessee.

African Americans serving in Vietnam reacted to the assassination with a variety of emotions, ranging from grief to outrage. Many were saddened that King's legacy of peace and understanding would be marred by violence. The vast majority of black soldiers were shocked and numbed by the news. Not everyone felt it was a time for peace. Sergeant Allen Thomas remembered that although most of the men were just in shock, "some of the younger guys were angry and just wanted to hurt someone."[7] Thomas and the other noncommissioned officers convinced their commanding officer to "back off and let blacks in the company work through their emotions, rather than risk setting them off further."

King had represented the hope and promise of the civil rights movement and his death was a terrible, numbing blow for many people, but for African Americans serving in the armed forces, especially those stateside, there were very direct consequences. The pain, anger, hate, and frustration many people felt quickly became manifest in the form of riots that erupted in more than one hundred American cities. In Chicago, twenty blocks of the downtown business district became a battleground between police and rioters. Mayor Richard Daley ordered the police to shoot looters on sight, and Maryland Governor Spiro Agnew urged police in Baltimore to do the same, while blasting the city's black leaders for not doing more to contain the violence in their city. The police in most cities could not control the riots, thus authorities called in 23,000 regular army troops and 16,000 guardsmen to help quell the uprisings. Nearly 14,000 regulars and 1,850 National Guard were deployed to Washington, D.C., and thousands more to Chicago and Baltimore.

This was not the first time federal troops had been mobilized to support local law enforcement, but many black critics claimed that local, state, and federal authorities were far more likely to use troops during black disturbances than white ones. In reality, troops also preserved order at predominantly white antiwar protests. Still, blacks in the military feared riot duty because it meant confronting and possibly harming fellow African Americans in defense of a government that they perceived as unjust and racist.

Sympathy and concern for those back home meant that many black servicemen refused to do riot duty, fearful of harming other African Americans, whose frustrations and desires they understood all too well. Soldiers Richard Allen and John Chase both refused to go through the obligatory twenty-five hours of armed forces riot control training because they were convinced that they would have to fight against black militant groups like the Black Panthers or the Nation of Islam. One black officer, who wished to remain anonymous, told a reporter that he was leaving the military because he thought a war between blacks and whites was imminent, and he believed that black troops would have to kill black civilians. Some black soldiers refused to mobilize against civilians engaged in antiwar protests. In August 1968, forty-three African American soldiers—many of them Vietnam veterans—refused to move against antiwar protesters demonstrating outside the National Democratic Convention in Chicago. In 1969 and 1970, only 14 percent of black servicemen in Vietnam said that they would obey orders to perform riot duty without hesitation if ordered to do so back in the United States. However, not all blacks were sympathetic. Many denounced the rioters and rioting as the very antithesis of what the great civil rights leader stood for and what they believed they were fighting for in Vietnam. Others expressed concern that the violence threatened the stability and security of the United States and feared that it could lead to a communist takeover.

Although many whites were saddened by the assassination and alarmed by the riots, some were apathetic. Yet others openly celebrated King's death by parading with Confederate flags or wearing white Ku Klux Klan robes. These displays of racial hate and intolerance added fuel to a growing hostility between blacks and whites in the armed forces. It did not help the army's image when it became known after Dr. King's death that the army had been spying on King and other black activists. Many of those who had once believed in integration, and had praised the equal opportunity the armed forces seemed to promise, became disenchanted and pursued more aggressive methods of dealing with racism. The result was the rise of black militancy among black service personnel. Wallace Terry, an African American journalist covering the black experience in the war, noted this change in attitude during his frequent trips to Vietnam. In 1966, he found that few black soldiers identified with the extreme militants. By the spring of 1969, the situation had changed, and he saw many extremists and their sympathizers greeting each other with Black power salutes.

African Americans felt rejected by the armed forces. Blacks had once viewed the military as the most egalitarian and least bigoted institution in America. But the high death rate, discrimination in the draft, and personal and institutional racism in the military, in contrast to the strides civilian society had made in race relations, had steadily eroded the military's once favorable image. Many black soldiers now believed that the military, far from being a model for civilian society, was just as bad or worse when it came to race relations and discrimination. Many soldiers signaled their displeasure and disillusionment by leaving the military as soon as their enlistments were up. Moreover, the once high reenlistment rate of 66 percent in 1966 declined to less than 13 percent by 1970. How much of the decline was due to racism is hard to say, but it was obvious that African Americans no longer viewed the armed forces as a viable career or as a haven from racism.

Some of the black troops did not want to wait until their time was up and deserted. During the Vietnam War, African Americans accounted for about 20 percent of all army deserters, and many of them claimed that racism as well as general opposition to the war were their main reasons for doing so. In 1971, there were an estimated one hundred black deserters living on Saigon's "Soul Alley," many of them citing racism as the primary reason for desertion.

However, desertion was a drastic step that many men were not willing to take, and, disgruntled as they were, the vast majority stayed.

African Americans who remained in the armed forces often reacted to racism by seeking comfort and safety in racial solidarity and by establishing their own subculture within the military. They called each other "brother," "soul brother," or "bloods," and they were proud of being black. Two popular methods of greeting fellow black soldiers and demonstrating racial solidarity were the black power salute, a clenched fist in the air, and the "dap," which developed in Vietnam, probably among inmates at the notorious Long Binh Stockade. Dap is a corruption of the word "dep," Vietnamese slang for something beautiful. The dap, also known as "checking in," was an intricate ritualized handshake, involving numerous gestures and movements. There was no standard dap, but there were many common gestures. There were countless variations of the dap, and some of the more complex greetings could go on for five or more minutes. Each move had a specific meaning: Pounding the heart with a clenched fist, for example, symbolized brotherly love and solidarity; clenching fingers together and then touching the backside of the hand meant, "My brother, I'm with you." Most of the gestures signified solidarity, respect, and pride, but a few had darker meanings. A slicing movement across the throat symbolized cutting the throats of white MPs, never a favorite group with black radicals.

Many of the men also started carrying visible symbols of black power and racial pride, such as black power canes, made of ebony, an African wood. Others wore "slave bracelets," woven from their extremely long army bootlaces, and in off-duty hours they wore dashikis. Black power flags, displaying the colors black, green, and red, often flew over all-black barracks, or "hootches" in the field. Marcus Garvey had inspired the design, but black marines stationed at Danang modified the flag into a meaningful symbol for black warriors. It was red to symbolize the blood shed by African Americans in the war, with a black foreground representing black culture. In the middle of the flag were two crossed spears superimposed on a shield, surrounded by a wreath, signifying, "violence if necessary" but "peace if possible." Many of the flags carried slogans in Swahili, such as "I will stand by you my brother if you want my help" or a warning to one's enemies: "My fear is for you." The black power flag spread from Vietnam throughout the American military establishment, and variations of it flew at military installations from West Germany to South Korea.

Another aspect of this new black militancy was the tendency toward racial separation. Especially during off-duty hours, service personnel tended to socialize with other members of their racial or cultural group. Even black officers, who were generally more conservative than the young draftees, often preferred all-black social and recreational functions to integrated ones. Colin Powell recalled that his time at the Command and General Staff College at Fort Leavenworth was his first assignment where there were enough other blacks to form a critical mass. Training classes and formal gatherings were integrated, but during off-duty hours, black officers hung out together, put on parties, and had soul food nights.

For the militants, however, self-segregation went beyond mere convenience and commonality of interests. It was rooted in a proud and often aggressive philosophy that rejected a Eurocentric view of the world. Black power advocates were separatists by nature and had little desire to be part of a white world, civilian or military. The more militant among them believed that racial bonds were more powerful than those of patriotism or military loyalty and duty. Many African Americans rejected the military's attempts at unit cohesion and esprit de corps, in favor of racial solidarity. Their primary loyalty was to the race and not the armed service to which they belonged. Many young black recruits shared this attitude.

Racial separation was most noticeable in the off-duty hours and in the many nightclubs and eating establishments near military bases that catered to a racially exclusive clientele. In Saigon, for example, whites tended to go to Tu Do Street, where many of the bars featured country and western or rock music. Blacks, in general, did not feel comfortable there, preferring instead to party in the Khanh Hoi section of the city. Many bars and restaurants in this district were considered to be less expensive than Tu Do, but, more importantly, its businesses catered to black tastes. African Americans even dubbed Khanh Hoi "Soul Alley." At restaurants such as the L & M and the C. M. G. Guest House, for example, African Americans could get real soul food, prepared with turnips, barbequed ribs, and chitterlings. Many African Americans were also pleased to discover that there were black women in the district. In the 1950s, Khanh Hoi had been a popular destination for black Senegalese troops serving the French in the Franco-Vietminh War, and they left behind a racially mixed population. Many of the women working the bars and brothels there were either Cambodian or the daughters of a Vietnamese mother and Senegalese father.

Often, African Americans sought racially exclusive settings simply to avoid trouble and confrontation with hostile and bigoted whites. African Americans stationed in West Germany, for example, tended to stay away from the base clubs, because every time they brought German women there, drunken whites tried to pick a fight. White American military personnel also brought familiar patterns of racial segregation with them when stationed overseas. From Germany to Vietnam to South Korea, there were "whites-only" establishments. African Americans stationed in Saigon, Na Trang, Ua Nang, and some of the other large towns risked getting thrown out of entertainment establishments and bars simply for being black. Yet blacks often resisted desegregation because they had come to feel comfortable in black-only establishments. Air Force Sergeant Jack Smedley explained, "A man wants to relax, really relax, when he's off duty. . . . He doesn't want to listen with half an ear to hear if some drunken whites are going to call him a nigger."[8]

Housing was another contested area where the races sought separation and control of their living environment. Many commanders in Vietnam allowed their men to choose their "hootch" mates, a policy that often led to all-white or all-black hootches. After King's assassination, many of these hootches exhibited overt symbols of racial pride. Black hootches flew black power flags while white ones displayed the Confederate flag. What was a symbol of pride for one soldier, however, was a provocation for another. The use of the "Stars and Bars" was extremely irritating to African Americans in Vietnam, who complained that they were fighting for the United States of America, and not the Confederate States of America.

Most African Americans viewed their racial solidarity and separation as a defense mechanism against racism and an expression of black pride. Yet they also saw it as a way to gain power and control, two things whites were not likely to give to blacks. Most whites believed that black solidarity meant black favoritism and that African Americans would use whatever power and authority they might possess to aid a brother and discriminate against whites. Blacks admitted to and sometimes flaunted their newfound sense of power. For example, a white first sergeant placed a black cook on restriction because he had been dancing and listening to the radio instead of performing his "kitchen patrol" duties. The cook appealed to his black company commander on grounds of racial solidarity and the commander lifted the restriction and gave him a thirty-day pass to go on leave. Whites considered this racially based preferential treatment to be "reverse discrimination" and complained loudly about it. Many African Americans undoubtedly did extend favoritism to other brothers, but they were not alone in the practice of helping out a buddy. There were probably just as many complaints from black enlisted personnel that brother officers and NCOs showed them no favoritism and were tougher on them than they were on whites. Often it was a problem of perception, and some blacks believed that whites were overly sensitive to any expression of black pride and solidarity, viewing such expressions as threatening.

The stage was now set for major violent racial confrontations in the armed forces. By mid-1968, all of the elements necessary to spark widespread racial violence throughout the military establishment were in place. The rapid expansion of the armed forces in Vietnam had brought hundreds of thousands of draftees into the ranks who brought racist preconceptions with them. Black soldiers were less willing to tolerate racism and were more likely to protest or fight back. Conversely, many white Southerners believed African Americans had "forgotten their place" or were acting "uppity." Both sides found it difficult to coexist and cooperate with each other.

Notes

1. James E. Westheider, "Sgt. Allen Thomas, Jr.: A Black Soldier in Vietnam," in *Portraits of African American Life Since 1865*, ed. Nina Mjagkij (Wilmington, DE: Scholarly Resources, 2003), 229.

2. Wallace Terry, "Bringing the War Home," *Black Scholar*, November 1970, 8.

3. U.S. House, *Investigation of Attempts to Subvert the United States Armed Forces*, hearings before the Committee of Internal Security, 92nd Congress (Washington: U.S. Government Printing Office, 1972), 6568; and "The Fort Jackson Eight," *Black Panther*, May 4, 1969, 9.

4. CM Sgt. Milton White, "Malcolm X in the Military," *Black Scholar*, May 1970, 32–33.

5. "Hanoi Sends Condolences to Group Led by Dr. King," *New York Times*, April 9, 1968, 37. The Vietnam Youth Federation Central Committee also sent its condolences. See "On the Death of Dr. Martin Luther King," *Black Panther*, May 4, 1968, 3.

6. Hon. Ronald V. Dellums, "Institutional Racism in the Military," *Congressional Record*, March 2, 1972, 6740.

7. Westheider, "Sgt. Allen Thomas, Jr.," 230–31.

8. Sol Stern, "When the Black GI Comes Back from Vietnam," *New York Times Magazine*, March 24, 1968, 42; *New York Times*, April 29, 1969, 16; and Thomas Johnson, "Negro Expatriates Finding Wide Opportunity in Asia," *New York Times*, April 30, 1969, 18.

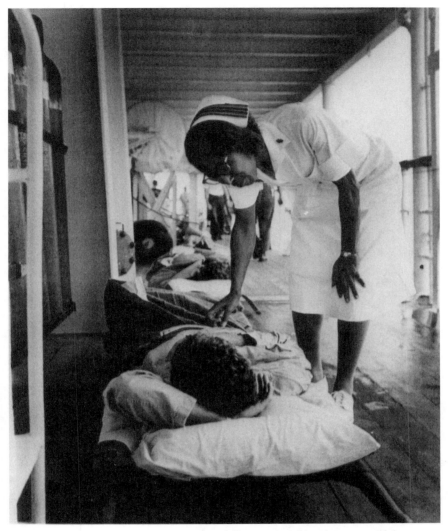

Black women served in Vietnam in many different specialties, but many of them were nurses. In this photo a black nurse tends to a patient on board the hospital ship, USS Repose, stationed off Vietnam in 1967. Photo courtesy of the United States Navy Historical Center.

Airman stands guard. Photo courtesy of the United States Air Force.

Alfonza Wright and Allen Thomas, August 2004. Photo courtesy Kimberley Henson, Broadway Photography, Cincinnati, Ohio.

African Americans were an integral part of the antiwar movement. In this photo Coretta Scott King leads an antiwar protest at the gates of the White House on May 17, 1967. Photo by Robert Knudsen, courtesy of the Lyndon Baines Johnson Presidential Library.

Black nationalists denounced the war in Vietnam and often expressed empathy with the other side. In this cartoon from the October 26, 1968, edition of the Black Panther newspaper a black solider daps with a Vietcong. Courtesy of the Huey Newton Foundation.
   Cartoon in the Black Panther Newspaper showing a black GI dapping hands with a Vietcong (Black Panther, October 26, 1968, p. 3).

During the later years of the Vietnam War, the U.S. Navy made a concerted effort to increase the number of African Americans in that service. These are three examples of navy recruiting posters aimed at African Americans. "You Can Be Black and Navy Too," issued in 1972, became one of the navy's main recruiting slogans in the early 1970s. Poster courtesy of the U.S. Navy Historical Center.

The 1971 "19 Weeks" poster was aimed at recruiting more African Americans to navy officer training. The poster reminded possible recruits that they could become an officer in only nineteen weeks. Poster courtesy of the U.S. Navy Historical Center.

"You Can Study Black History and You Can Make it," 1972 recruiting poster. Poster courtesy of the U.S. Navy Historical Center.

African Americans paid a high price for their reputation as good soldiers during the Vietnam War. In this photograph a wounded black soldier is being helped aboard a medivac helicopter. Photo courtesy of the United States Army.

President Johnson inspecting troops and shaking hands with a black soldier during a visit to Fort Campbell, Kentucky, in 1966. Photo courtesy of the Lyndon Baines Johnson Presidential Library.

During the Vietnam War, Samuel Gravely became the first black admiral in U.S. history. Photo courtesy of the U.S. Navy Historical Center.

In this photo a black sailor mans a .30-caliber machine gun on a utility boat during Operation Jackstay, in April 1966. Photo courtesy of the U.S. Navy Historical Center.

President Johnson met often with civil rights leaders, such as this meeting on January 18, 1964, with Dr. Martin Luther King Jr., Whitney Young, and James Farmer. Also present but not in the photo are Roy Wilkins and Lee White. In return for promoting civil rights issues, however, Johnson expected black support for the war in Vietnam. Photo by Yoichi R. Okamoto, courtesy of the Lyndon Baines Johnson Presidential Library.

Unlike most other civil rights leaders, Whitney Young of the Urban League remained a staunch supporter of Johnson and Vietnam till late in the war. In this photo President Johnson greets Young at the Oval Office on June 28, 1966. Photo by Yoichi R. Okamoto, courtesy of the Lyndon Baines Johnson Presidential Library.

THE NEW ACTION ARMY

You are offered a wide choice of duty stations and varied duties

1. SLAUGHTERING INNOCENT PEOPLE IN VIETNAM.

2. PUT DOWN THE FILTHY POOR OUT ON STRIKE.

3. BAYONET THE LONG HAIR HIPPIE SUBVERSIVES ON CAMPUSES THROUGHOUT THE STATES.

4. KILL BLACKS IN WATTS AND OTHER DIRTY GHETTOS.

5. CARRY MAIL WHILE MEN STARVE OUT ON STRIKE

6. FEATURING OUR NEW???? CAMBODIAN ACTION!!!!!

HELP FIGHT THE NEW ACTION ARMY! JOIN MDM!

MDM (Movement for a Democratic Military) is an organization which was begun by our Marine brothers at Camp Pendleton. MDM now is established at Marine camps, Army and Navy posts all over the West Coast and around the country. MDM IS COMMITTED TO FIGHTING THE REAL ENEMY: the pig that makes us fight our own brothers and sisters here in our own home, and makes us kill our brothers in other countries that are fighting for their freedom. The pig is US IMPERIALISM! MDM has a 12 point program which are demands for the GI brothers who want to fight the real enemy. The Armed Services is a system which lives on war. It's the government which makes war and not the people. DIG!

MDM STRESSES THAT ALL GI BROTHERS BEING OPPRESSED BY THE MILITARY SHOULD TAKE A FIRM STAND TO SMASH THE RACISM WHICH DIVIDES US AND CONTINUES OUR OPPRESSION IN THE ARMY. ALL GI BROTHERS MUST UNITE TO FIGHT THE REAL ENEMY - THE PIG!

ALL POWER TO THE PEOPLE

Support Our Brothers
ARMED FARCES DAY
MAY 16, 1970

Stop the war!!!

No More Kent States!

Black nationalist and radical organizations, such as the Movement for a Democratic Military, attempted to organize other military personnel against racism and the war in Vietnam. This is an MDM pamphlet announcing "Armed Farces Day" on May 16, 1970. Courtesy of the Division of Rare and Manuscript Collections, Cornell University Library.

Pamphlet announcing "Armed Farces Day" by Movement for a Democratic Military. U.S. House of Representatives, Investigation of Attempts to Subvert the United States Armed Forces, hearings before the Committee of Internal Security, 92nd Congress, (Washington: U.S. Government Printing Office, 1972), 6751.

Many African Americans in the armed forces used symbols and gestures denoting black pride and solidarity. Note the "black power" salute given by several black GIs in this photo with President Richard Nixon dated August 24, 1972. Photo courtesy of the White House Photo Office, National Archives and Records Administration.

Colin Powell would serve two tours of duty in Vietnam and become the first black chairman of the Joint Chiefs of Staff and the first African American secretary of state. Photo courtesy of the United States State Department.

African Americans served in every capacity in Vietnam. Commissaryman First Class Joshua Paige holds "sick call" for some children from Tam Toa village, near Danang, in November 1967. Photo courtesy of the U.S. Navy Historical Center.

Thousands of African Americans served with the "brown water" navy patrolling Vietnam's numerous rivers. Here, Seaman Lawrence W. Overton loads magazines for his M-16 rifle while standing watch on the LST Harnett County, on the Vam Co Dong River in May 1969. Photo courtesy of the U.S. Navy Historical Center.

Soldiers in combat units had to depend on one another and often developed a camaraderie that transcended race and ethnicity. In this photo a black trooper from the 101st Airborne stands guard over and comforts a fellow wounded white soldier. Photo courtesy of the U.S. Military History Institute.

Soldiers often chalked sayings on their helmets, often reflecting black power or racial pride in the case of African Americans. This one says, "We enjoy being black," surrounded by numerous names. Photo courtesy of the U.S. Military History Institute.

Black soldiers often wore symbols of racial pride, such as the "slave bracelet" worn by the soldier in the center of the photograph. Photo courtesy of the U.S. Military History Institute.

As they had in previous wars, Africans Americans proved courageous on the battlefield. Here, Sergeant Dwight Johnson receives the Medal of Honor from President Lyndon Johnson, in November 1968. Photo courtesy of the U.S. Military History Institute.

~

CHAPTER FIVE

Racial Violence in the Military and the Military Response

It was a widely held belief, among officers and Pentagon officials, that the rise of black solidarity and militancy in the armed forces was a product of civilian society, brought into the service by young recruits. General Westmoreland was typical in blaming civilian attitudes for black radicalism in the army, and many black officers shared this belief. But by 1968, many black soldiers believed that racial solidarity was simply self-defense against what they regarded as a racist institution. Racial tensions mounted throughout the military in the late 1960s and often turned to violence. While some of this violence was caused by minor slights or perceived insults, much of it grew from increasing frustration with the military's failed racial policies. Whatever the source of tension, it was clear that the military would have to make some changes.

One point of contention was the establishment of black "self-defense" organizations, modeled on the Black Panthers, in most of the military branches. These included the Blackstone Rangers, De Mau Mau in the army, and the Ju Ju in the Marine Corps. Most members of these organizations viewed them as protective in nature, claiming they defended African Americans in the military from white supremacist organizations, such as the Ku Klux Klan, which often operated rather openly among white soldiers. Members of these groups wore symbols of racial pride and defiance. The Ju Jus, for example, wore black shirts and black gloves into combat in Vietnam as symbols of their pride and frustration with racial conditions. Black service personnel in the United States also established self-defense groups. In late 1972, African Americans stationed in the San Diego area organized the Black Ser-

vicemen's Caucus to fight racism in the military and develop ties with the local black community. Whites, however, accused these self-defense organizations of being no more than violent gangs that roamed throughout the U.S.
military establishment provoking trouble and attacking innocent whites.
Compounding the problem was the fact that whites were also aggravated
over what they perceived to be, ironically, racial favoritism toward African
Americans at the expense of white enlisted personnel. Although the Pentagon was making every effort to suppress the black self-defense organizations
and drive their members out of the armed forces, most whites and blacks were
unaware of the military's internal war against perceived militants in the
ranks. Whites therefore believed that military authorities tolerated the existence of organizations such as De Mau Mau and the Ju Ju, which they saw as
black supremacist organizations.

Often, white perceptions of favoritism were the product of the Pentagon's
attempts to address some of the legitimate grievances of minority service personnel. Some whites, for example, considered a new Marine Corps directive
in the late 1960s, which required that at least one black or Puerto Rican be
appointed to boards in courts-martial involving a minority defendant, as
preferential treatment. Politicians also decried what they believed to be a
perceived double standard. Democratic Representative Dan Daniel of Virginia and several other members of the House Armed Services Subcommit-
tee on Recruiting and Retention denounced as reverse discrimination a Department of Defense policy that gave preference to minorities volunteering
for the reserves and National Guard. The Defense Department's investigation into military justice later in the war concluded that charges of reverse
discrimination were generally unfounded. However, many whites were convinced that they were victims of a racially based double standard and believed that African Americans got away with it because the chain of command was afraid of provoking black militants in the ranks. White resentment
of what they viewed to be official toleration of black militancy only added to
a growing racial polarity and hostility in the armed forces.

Racial antagonism increased alarmingly in the armed forces following
King's assassination. African Americans derisively called whites "Chucks,"
"whitey," "honkies," "Caucasians," "beasts," "dudes," "pigs," "foreigners," and
"rabbits"; and most whites believed that the "bloods" hated all whites. The
Department of Defense's Task Force on the Administration of Military Justice found that black self-segregation had increasingly hostile overtones. The
executive officer at the marine brig at Da Nang was convinced that most of
the black prisoners in maximum security were militants who thoroughly
hated whites.

There were plenty of white bigots and malcontents, and, like some of the black militants, they also reveled in abusing members of the other race. They had their own litany of racial profanities aimed at African Americans, calling them "spear chucker," "boy," "spook," and the always popular "nigger," all of which they used liberally in addressing black service personnel. In his first five months in Vietnam, African American Sergeant Willie E. Burney Jr. heard more whites refer to blacks as "niggers" than he had in a year while stationed at Biloxi, Mississippi. The word showed up as graffiti, such as "Niggers eat shit," and "I'd prefer a gook to a nigger," on the walls of bars and latrines in Vietnam and in suggestion boxes on military installations in the United States. The suggestion box at Camp Lejeune, North Carolina, often contained such racist rants as "Keep those niggers off the [dance] floor" and requests that the "Coons please go back to Africa." Black cadets at the Air Force Academy filed an official complaint about abusive language and asked that white cadets and instructors refrain from calling them "boy," "nigger," "snowflake," and "spook." Some whites enjoyed spreading malicious stories about African Americans, such as telling the Saigon bar girls that blacks were "animals" and "had tails." Others refused to extend common courtesies, like giving fellow enlisted men a ride in their jeep.

Militants and racists on both sides continued to provoke racial friction and violence, and one of their favorite ways of doing so was through symbols of racial "pride." In Tongduckon, South Korea, a drinking establishment catering to whites was damaged after a fistfight between a black and a white soldier escalated into a racial gang fight. What had triggered the confrontation was a black power flag flying over a predominantly black barracks. Dapping, especially in chow lines, was a never-ending source of friction between whites and blacks. Some daps were extremely elaborate, taking five to ten minutes to complete, and whites did not like waiting for their meals in line while blacks, who were ahead of them, went through a lengthy dap. Some whites appreciated the significance dapping had for African Americans but objected to the location and the time it took to complete. Most whites were less sympathetic. The dap was a reaffirmation of solidarity and brotherhood for African Americans, but many blacks did it simply to antagonize whites, and it worked. Some whites developed a "white power" salute of their own and harassed and insulted blacks engaged in dapping, which often led to confrontations and fights between the two groups.

In September 1969, the Marine Corps Commandant General Leonard F. Chapman issued a new policy on dapping designed to ease the tension between whites and blacks while respecting black cultural expressions. In essence, the directive banned dapping during working hours, as a salute to the flag or a commissioned officer, and in formation, but did not prohibit the practice entirely. Despite this new policy, dapping continued to spark interracial trouble. In 1971 in Japan, Marine Private Raymond Burns killed Marine Lance Corporal Thomas L. Bertler after Bertler ridiculed him for dapping.

Whites also used their own cultural expressions to antagonize and demean blacks. Black cadets at the Air Force Academy testified that they had been forced by white instructors to remain in push-up position for an hour for refusing to sing "Dixie." But it was white use of the Confederate flag, in particular, that infuriated blacks. Many whites argued sincerely that to them it embodied Southern pride and rebelliousness and was not intended as an insult to African Americans. But to most blacks, and a large percentage of whites, it was a symbol of racism and white supremacy. The "Stars and Bars" had been the banner of slavery, and white hate groups, such as the Ku Klux Klan, had adopted it. In the late fifties and early sixties, many Southern states added it to their flags in defiance of the civil rights movement and racial integration. To the vast majority of African Americans, it was a symbol as offensive as the Nazi swastika was to Jews. Blacks also noted a double standard that allowed whites to display their symbols of race and racial pride while military authorities suppressed corresponding black displays. One black marine in Vietnam told the *Pittsburgh Courier* he was angry and upset because whites could display Confederate flags, but he was forced to remove a "Black Is Beautiful" poster from the inside wall of his locker.

The symbol of the old Confederacy seemed to be everywhere, on the antennas of jeeps, in bars, and flying over all-white hootches, sometimes even on the base flagpole, directly under the American flag. It even made its way into a USO show, when six whites paraded with the Confederate flag in front of more than fifteen hundred troops gathered for a Bob Hope show on Christmas Day in 1965. The reaction of whites and blacks attending the event testified to the divisive nature of such symbols. After the show, white officers and NCOs proudly posed for pictures with the flag, a display that left one black soldier feeling like an outsider. Some African Americans tried to ban the use of Confederate flags. Two months after the incident at the USO show, the tristate director of the NAACP in Philadelphia, Phillip Savage, filed a formal complaint with Secretary of Defense Robert McNamara, requesting disciplinary action against military personnel who openly display rebel flags. Finally in 1969, the Pentagon agreed to ban the display of Confederate flags, but this announcement brought yet another hailstorm of protests, this time initiated by Southern politicians, who argued successfully that the "Stars and Bars" was part of many Southern states' flags and the armed forces could not legally prohibit the use of state flags by service personnel. A compromise of sorts was worked out prohibiting the public use of Confederate flags but still allowing state flags that contained the insignia.

The agreement to limit the use of Confederate insignia was seldom enforced, and rebel flags continued to fly openly and defiantly on many military installations throughout the Vietnam War. This practice disappointed but hardly surprised many African Americans in the armed forces, who were convinced that much of this activity indicated more than individual bigotry. As much as some whites claimed that military authorities tolerated black militant activities, African Americans were equally convinced that the armed forces were a haven for organized, hard-core white supremacists, especially members of the Ku Klux Klan. "Klaverns," or chapters of the terrorist organization, were known to operate openly on some military installations, and black soldiers reported finding Klan and other racist literature in places like the guardhouse, which was only accessible to commissioned officers and NCOs. Groups of whites, wearing real or impromptu Klan robes, were reported on numerous military bases in the United States and overseas. White racists in the armed forces also practiced cross burnings, another traditional Klan activity. In May 1969, two white sailors at Cam Ranh Bay burned a twelve-foot-high cross in front of a predominantly black barrack. In 1970, soldiers in Vietnam burned a cross outside the tent of Army Sergeant Clyde Brown, who had appeared on the cover of *Time* magazine in conjunction with an article entitled, "The Negro in Vietnam." Often these Klan-like activities seemed to occur with the tacit approval of those in command. Black air force cadets, for instance, were dismayed that Wing Staff had apparently allowed whites to fly a rebel flag and to burn a cross at a 1969 rally at the Air Force Academy.

In the wake of the assassination of Martin Luther King Jr., both the racist behavior of whites and the anger and frustration among African Americans touched off a wave of violence throughout the U.S. military establishment. Often the violence was simply a fistfight. At an army base in West Germany, a black soldier assaulted a white sergeant for referring to King's murder by saying, "Yeah, they finally got that son of a bitch." The black soldier avoided a court-martial, however, because the only witness to the attack was a white soldier who had been talking to him in the hallway and who refused to testify against his friend. Sometimes, however, the isolated fistfights escalated. For example, a racial gang fight erupted at the army's Manheim Stockade after a white prisoner made a racist comment shortly after King's death. There were certainly violent encounters between blacks and whites before the assassination, but the violence in the aftermath was a precursor of things to come. The feelings of anger and frustration did not fade in the weeks and months after the murder, but grew stronger instead.

Another element in the rising violence was the army's one-year rotation policy. Men went to Vietnam for a one-year tour of duty, replacing those who had died or returned to the United States. The constant shuffling of individuals in and out of units meant that many soldiers did not know each other very well. The physical nature of military bases did not help either. During the war, many defense installations were sprawling and overcrowded, with a large percentage of their population at any given time en route to or from an assignment. In these conditions, few long-term friendships developed to counteract negative racial stereotypes. Soldiers were more likely to socialize with members of their own ethnic group rather than across their unit.

The racial friction first erupted in the form of riots at two of the largest military prisons in South Vietnam. The first and smaller of the two disturbances occurred at the main naval brig at Da Nang on August 15, 1968. Black inmates fought with white prisoners and guards, and eventually gained control of the main compound. They held it for twenty hours before the military was able to restore order. Three days later prison officials authorized the use of tear gas to quell a second uprising of black prisoners. By the time the riots calmed down, the rioters had burned down a cellblock, and many of the most violent prisoners were placed in the sentry dogs' cages.

On August 29 a much larger racial uprising occurred at the army's Long Binh Stockade near Saigon. A fight between a small number of blacks and whites in the prison's medium-security area quickly escalated. The MPs, sent in to stop the fighting, were soon overwhelmed by black prisoners yelling, "Kill the chucks," and forced to retreat. The black prisoners then released other inmates from the maximum-security cells while others set fire to several buildings, including the administration building. About an hour after the riot began, reinforcements of military police arrived, and with the support of machine gunners in the guard towers ordered the prisoners to "cease and desist." Many of the prisoners obeyed the order, but about 250 inmates, the vast majority of whom were black, refused. MPs then fired tear gas at the rioters and entered the compound with bayonets, where inmates, armed with clubs, rocks, and metal rods, greeted them. When the battle ended, one white prisoner was dead and seventy black inmates and seventeen white MPs wounded.

Prison officials assumed they had quelled the riot. They divided the subdued prisoners into two groups: "cooperatives," those who had not been involved in the uprising or had surrendered; and "uncooperatives," the ones who continued to fight. Of the 220 uncooperatives, three were Puerto Ricans and the rest were black. The MPs herded this group into an enclosed section of the stockade, but the inmates once again seized control of the area. Many of them took off their military uniforms; some wore makeshift dashikis made of army blankets, while others wore bits of clothing as loincloths or remained naked. Uncertain how to react, military authorities decided to contain the uncooperatives in that small area and let the rebellion wear itself out. Guards tossed cases of food, known as C rations, over the fence into the compound each day to feed the prisoners. The army's show of patience worked, and the rebellion slowly fell apart. One by one the prisoners left the compound and surrendered, and after three weeks only thirteen hard-core resisters remained. In an attempt to find out what had sparked the riot, army psychologists and prison officials interviewed the inmates and questioned them about their grievances. Many inmates voiced complaints such as bad food and not enough mail, but several also claimed that cruel and racist guards and preferential treatment of white inmates had sparked the riot. Most of them just wanted to get out of the army, which they believed had mistreated them, and to go home.

Military officials were alarmed by the growing racial tension. The Marine Corps in particular was worried about racial conditions at Camp Lejeune, North Carolina, one of their key training centers in the United States. Like many other installations it was large and overcrowded; there were over forty thousand marines at the base in the summer of 1969. Moreover, it had a large transient population, as units constantly shipped in and out, causing authorities problems in monitoring and supervising personnel. The installation had already had its share of racial confrontations, usually during off-duty hours and in recreational facilities. Lejeune was the prototypical environment for producing racial violence in the armed forces. The Marine Corps began tracking racial assaults at the installation in August 1968 and recorded 160 of them before the end of the year. Conditions were so tense that a biracial committee of seven officers concluded that racism on the base and in the community contributed to an explosive situation. For the more militant and angry military personnel on both sides, the problems could not be fixed with race relations classes or more black products at the PX.

On the night of July 20, 1969, one of the worst racial gang fights erupted at Lejeune during a going-away party for a battalion that was departing the following day for duty in Spain. Around one hundred black marines and seventy-five white marines attended the festivities at the service club. There was friction between the two groups and a small fight occurred when a black marine cut in on a white sailor who was dancing with a black WAVE (member of the

Women's Naval Reserve). The shore patrol restored order and many marines left. Later that evening, however, a dazed and bloody white marine staggered into the club and announced that several black marines had attacked him. Within a half hour, fifteen additional injured white marines arrived. There was a gang fight raging in front of the dance hall between approximately thirty African Americans and Hispanics, and a small number of whites. By dawn, a twenty-year-old white marine lay dead as a result of fighting, and dozens more marines, both black and white, were hospitalized.

Ten days later, on the night of July 30, marines were involved in yet another racial fight at Millington Naval Air Station, outside Memphis, Tennessee. This time a gang of about fifteen whites armed with billy clubs ambushed African Americans, allegedly to prevent the black marines from attacking their barracks. The fight broke out when a group of blacks returned to the barracks from a night of drinking. For over fifteen minutes the combatants fought their way from the barracks to a nearby bar, but surprisingly there were no major injuries. Less than a month later a major fight broke out between white and black marines stationed at Kaneohe Marine Corps Air Station in Hawaii. Like much of the friction and violence, this fight was apparently triggered by a symbol of racial pride and resistance. Fifty black marines had made a clenched fist "black power" salute during the lowering of the colors, which ignited a four-hour-long brawl between approximately 250 combatants, roaming the installation armed with shovels, sticks, and pipes. Many of the soldiers involved were returning from tours of duty in Vietnam. This confrontation left sixteen white and black marines wounded and three hospitalized.

The racial violence that plagued the Marine Corps also erupted at other military institutions in the United States and overseas. Officials were especially concerned about problems on bases in West Germany in 1968 when Warsaw Pact forces invaded Czechoslovakia and the Cold War threatened to turn hot. In Bamberg, West Germany, there were serious confrontations, generally in the off-duty hours, and drug and racial problems plagued the barracks. The authorities, believing that troublemakers might try to seize weapons, took the unusual step of arming the sergeant in charge of the barracks at night with a .45 and giving him permission to use it. Taft Webster, a young African American stationed there, remembers manning a searchlight on a tank illuminating the parade ground so authorities could see and break up a racial gang fight one night.[1]

Racial violence continued to plague the armed forces for the next several years. Two hundred men were involved in a fight at Fort Bragg, North Carolina, in 1969. At Cam Ranh Bay there were regular gang wars between companies. In early 1971, a gunfight between a white and a black soldier at Camp Baxter, Da Nang, escalated into an armed standoff. Base authorities tried to disarm the soldiers, but a group of white soldiers seized machine guns and barricaded themselves in their barracks until military police restored order. In addition to riots, black and white soldiers ambushed each other. The attacks generally occurred at night in secluded areas of military installations. Often, victims were beaten and robbed. Much of the violence occurred during off-duty hours at or near recreational facilities, especially those where alcohol flowed and there was competition for women. Many of these establishments catered to large numbers of troops and had cramped conditions.

White officers were often the favorite targets of racial violence. At Chu Lai, for instance, angry blacks attacked and beat white officers for refusing to give them jeep rides. As morale in the United States armed forces began to sag and then collapse after the 1968 Tet Offensive, many enlisted personnel, regardless of race, took out their frustrations on their officers. Often this took the form of "fragging," the deliberate murder of an officer, or occasionally an enlisted person, by a fellow soldier. The term derived from the weapon of choice, fragmentation grenades. They were ubiquitous in Vietnam and had advantages; there was no reliable ballistics test for grenades as there was for guns, thus, they left little evidence. Soldiers who used this weapon did not have to be present for the attack; instead they attached the grenades or claymore mines to the door of the officers' latrine or barracks. By 1972, a total of 788 fraggings or attempted fraggings had occurred.

In May 1971, the *Pittsburgh Courier* reported that white officers in Vietnam had been "cowed" by the threat of being fragged by their own men. But not all of the fraggings were racially motivated; many were rebellions against authority, and even black officers felt the need to take some precautions. In 1969, Colin Powell moved his cot each night to avoid potential attacks from the Vietcong as well as members of his own battalion. As an authority figure, Powell was definitely in danger of being fragged. A lot had changed since Powell's first tour in Vietnam, and many enlisted men had no intention of dying in a war that they increasingly viewed as a lost cause.

It is difficult to assess how many fraggings were motivated by racial considerations, poor morale, drug-related problems, or any other reasons. One black Vietnam veteran recalled that the fragging of a white corporal in his unit was listed as race related, even though it was common knowledge in the company that the murder was over a drug deal gone bad. It is also difficult to assess the intensity of racial violence in the armed forces during the Vietnam War. Many confrontations between whites and blacks were not necessarily racially motivated, despite their outward appearances. Fights between whites and blacks in Captain Michael Colacicco's company at Bien Hoa in 1971 were more likely the result of personal animosity than racial antagonism. But many of the fights that started as personal misunderstandings developed into attacks on whites and the system in general. A 1972 riot at the Norfolk naval brig began with a fight between a white and a black inmate, but, as the fight expanded, African Americans armed with baseball bats beat several guards they considered racist.

Black frustration with racism in the military and their hatred and distrust of whites led to two of the worst racial incidents during the Vietnam War, the uprisings on the aircraft carriers *Constellation* and *Kitty Hawk* in 1972. The navy had its share of racial problems, but before 1972 it had a better record than either the army or the Marine Corps, partly because there was less strain on navy personnel and resources until the later stages of the conflict, and partly because there were fewer African Americans in that branch of the service earlier in the war. The navy's participation in the war had been extensive, including patrolling the Mekong Delta and the numerous rivers of South Vietnam, shelling suspected enemy locations from off shore, and conducting air operations against targets in both North and South Vietnam. But the navy had played a more limited role than the other service branches. It was also the most "lily white" of the services. In 1968, African Americans made up only 8 percent of the navy's enlisted personnel, a figure that decreased slightly to 5.5 percent in 1971. It was far worse in the officer corps, where the 540 black commissioned officers made up only 0.67 percent of the total. By comparison, there were over 77,000 white commissioned officers.

By the later stages of the war, however, black representation had substantially increased, due in large part to a recruitment effort initiated by Admiral Elmo Zumwalt. In 1971, the navy announced a five-year recruitment plan to increase the number of African Americans serving in that branch. The recruitment program tried to attract blacks to the predominantly white institution by using the slogan, "You can be Black, and Navy too." The navy also tried to increase the number of minority officers by establishing ROTC branches at historically black colleges, such as Savannah State in Georgia and Southern University in Louisiana. Though the new zeal for racial fairness angered and alienated many whites, it did have an impact. By 1972, the number of blacks in the navy had risen to 12 percent.

As in the other services, however, African Americans were still largely concentrated in the lowest and least rewarding military occupational specialties, and they constituted a tiny percentage of the commissioned officer corps. They made up a disproportionately high number of Captain's Masts and courts-martial, and there was increasing friction between white and black sailors. Compounding the problem was the fact that the navy was now taking on a larger part of the air war, as American ground and air forces in Vietnam were winding down operations. Ships were forced to remain longer "on station," meaning an extended time away from home and loved ones for the crews. Sailors, especially those on the carriers conducting air operations, worked eighteen-hour days, putting a strain on men, morale, and material in a war that virtually everyone now saw as a lost cause. The workday was long and arduous, but there was little or no threat of enemy attack. Thus, the camaraderie among crewmembers who faced a common threat did not develop. Much like the hootches in Vietnam and the barracks on military installations, racial separation was common on the ships. Blacks bunked with and hung out with other blacks. By mid-October 1972, all of these factors combined to produce some of the worst racial warfare the U.S. Navy had faced to that date.

The first ship affected was the aircraft carrier USS *Kitty Hawk*, under the command of Captain M. W. Townsend. Like many ships, the carrier had been forced to remain in the Pacific longer than originally planned. There was a history of friction between Townsend and the black sailors aboard the vessel, due to what blacks perceived as discriminatory use of nonjudicial punishment. There was also racial friction among the enlisted personnel. On October 10, 1972, while in port in the Philippines, a fight involving black and white members of the crew broke out at an enlisted men's club. The following day an officer from the ship attempted to question a black sailor regarding the on-shore incident, leading to another charge that white officers were only questioning and disciplining African Americans for the fight. Townsend did try to punish one African American sailor. In response, nine other black sailors decided to accompany him to his hearing with the investigating officer to air their grievances, but the meeting turned acrimonious, so the black sailor refused to cooperate with the investigation. Other African Americans, numbering somewhere between twenty and one hundred individuals, soon congregated in a mess area where they talked, dapped, and interfered with some white sailors waiting in the chow line. The two groups traded insults and racial epithets, and shortly thereafter a group of African Americans attacked and beat two white cooks. The captain dispatched a marine team to deal with the disturbances. An impasse soon developed when the black sailors refused to disperse and clear the passageway until a group of whites did the same. Soon afterward, a fight broke out between the marines and the black sailors. In all the confusion, rumors began to spread among the crew that Captain Townsend had either been killed or injured in the disturbances. Small groups of blacks, and possibly whites, roamed the ship waylaying sailors of the opposite race for the next few hours, until order was restored on the *Kitty Hawk* around 2:30 a.m. Many sources credit the ship's African American executive officer, Commander Ben Cloud, with defusing the situation.

The rioting on the aircraft carrier was just the beginning of a violent month and a half for the navy. A few days after the racial warfare on the *Kitty Hawk*, a similar incident erupted on the oiler *Hassayampa*, which ended with four white sailors in the hospital and eleven blacks in the brig. Likewise, the carrier *Constellation* experienced sporadic but often intense racial violence throughout the first two weeks of November. It began after a contentious meeting on October 12 between the ship's executive officer, Commander John Schaub, and representatives of the black sailors. After the meeting broke up, a white cook was attacked by a group of black sailors and suffered a broken jaw. Ship's officers singled out sixteen black sailors for their roles in the attack, and the following day Captain J. D. Ward initiated discharge procedures against six of the accused. This action sparked rumors that 250 of the *Constellation*'s black crewmen would be sent ashore and given undesirable discharges. This rumor set off a wave of racially motivated ambushes, counterattacks, and reprisals between black and white sailors, leading Ward to leave twenty African American crewmembers on shore when the ship sailed. Protesting the captain's actions, one hundred black sailors left the ship when it docked at San Diego on November 9, and they refused to go back on board. The navy charged, convicted, and fined all of them for being "absent without leave," but further trouble was avoided.

Though the incidents differed substantially, the underlying causes leading to racial violence on board the *Kitty Hawk* and the *Constellation* were similar. African Americans accounted for less than 10 percent of the crews on both vessels, and neither ship had many black officers. The *Kitty Hawk* was typical: Of 4,135 men and 348 officers assigned to the ship, only 297 enlisted men and five officers were black. Morale was poor, there was substantial antiwar sentiment and racial friction, and the men were tired from working long, stressful days. On both carriers, disciplinary action against black sailors, initiated by an overwhelmingly white chain of command, ignited the racial violence. The navy experienced similar violence on board various other vessels, including the aircraft carriers *Intrepid*, *Inchon*, and *Sumpter*. Naval shore installations were not exempt from the violence; indeed, one of the worst race riots occurred at the navy base on Midway Island on November 25.

The explosion of racial violence in the armed forces left military authorities searching for reasons why some units experienced racial violence and others did not. It also left them searching for answers to the racial problems threatening their ability to perform military missions with efficiency. Military authorities acknowledged that there were as many whites as blacks who were ready to engage in racial warfare. Most admitted that many of the complaints and grievances black service personnel voiced about personal and institutional racism in the armed forces were justified. This realization led to a wave of reforms to correct the problems. The Pentagon also initiated programs eliminating radicals from the ranks. Fortunately for the military, the racial violence did not seem to seriously affect the efficiency and fighting ability of the combat units.

In Vietnam, incidents of racial violence were confined largely to support and service units. Only a few active combat units reported significant incidents of racial friction or violence. In the combat units men had to depend on each other to survive, which forced them to develop cohesion. There was still a high degree of interracial cooperation, respect, and friendship, despite the racial polarization that was often prevalent outside the combat zone. Officers who had problems in support units found virtually none when they assumed command of units involved in active combat operations. Cecil F. Davis experienced his share of racially related problems in a noncombat support unit he had led, but in the infantry company he commanded in Vietnam, he had "absolutely nothing, we were all in there together."[2] Many elite combat units, such as the rangers, long-range reconnaissance, airborne, and special forces, had a higher degree of unit cohesion, pride, and esprit de corps, which further lessened the emergence of racial discord. Noncombat units that had a clearly defined mission and plenty of work to keep them busy also reported having few racial problems.

Leadership was an important factor determining whether or not a unit experienced racial problems or violence. Most Vietnam-era officers believed that poor or inexperienced leadership contributed significantly to the eruption of racial friction and violence. Black officers in general had fewer racial problems in their units, but there were too few of them. African Americans constituted only about 2 percent of the officer corps during the Vietnam War.

As early as July 1966, Whitney M. Young of the National Urban League and other civil rights leaders had urged President Johnson to increase the number of African American officers in the armed forces. After the outbreak of serious racial violence in the late 1960s and early 1970s, military officials were convinced that increasing the number of black officers could solve some of their problems. Black military personnel widely believed that they would be fairer to enlisted men and more likely enforce the Pentagon's equal opportunity policies and racial reforms.

Throughout the Vietnam War, the various branches of the armed forces made efforts to increase the number of black officers. One approach was to increase the number of black cadets at the service academies. From 1969 to 1972, however, there were only 105 African Americans graduates out of a total of nearly 19,000 graduates from West Point, Annapolis, and the Air Force Academy. The situation improved slightly by the end of the war. By 1971, there were 53 black cadets at West Point, and the following year Annapolis accepted 45 blacks, bringing the total number of black midshipmen at the academy to 150. The Air Force Academy admitted 25 black cadets to its first-year class in 1972. While a growing number of black officers were trained at the Officer Candidate Schools, the majority of African Americans commissioned during the war had been enrolled in the Reserve Officer Training Corps (ROTC) programs. Colin Powell, for example, was a product of the ROTC at City College of New York.

The army had a higher percentage of black officers than its sister services because of the presence of Army ROTC programs at historically black colleges, such as Howard University, Morgan State College, and Tuskegee University. Chappie James, for instance, was a cadet at Tuskegee when he enrolled at the school in 1937. The navy did not establish its first ROTC program at a predominantly black college until 1968. That year the navy initiated a program at Prairie View A & M in Texas, attracting twenty-four candidates. In 1971, the navy established additional programs at Savannah State University and Southern University, and in the following year, at Florida A & M University and North Carolina Central University. The army expanded its presence on black campuses during the Vietnam War, adding several new schools such as Norfolk State and Hampton to the list. By 1970, Army ROTC units were operating on fourteen historically black college and university campuses, and by 1972, on nineteen.

The marines were also concerned about raising the number of blacks in their officer corps. In May 1967, the Marine Corps appointed Lt. Colonel Kenneth H. Berthoud Jr., an African American, as the special advisor to the deputy chief of staff (manpower) for minority officer procurement, and charged him with the task of doubling the number of black officers in the corps. By 1972, there were 285 black officers in the Marine Corps, representing still only 1.5 percent of the total.

In general, black officers did have fewer racial problems in their units, but their ability to contain racial friction was often limited by their conservatism. African American military careerists were usually uncomfortable with and embarrassed by the more aggressive symbols of black solidarity such as the "dap." Like most white officers, black officers felt that it was a nuisance and supported efforts to suppress it. They viewed the black militants and their black power rhetoric as misguided, misinformed, and a threat to everything they had fought and worked hard to achieve. Colin Powell believed that the American dream was working for blacks in the military. Powell echoed the sentiments of most African Americans who hoped to make a career in military service, but his view was particularly indicative of the senior commissioned officers' disdain for black radicals in the ranks.

Noncommissioned officers who had chosen a military career also held the militants in contempt. Sergeant Alfonza Wright, a devout admirer of Dr. King, referred to black radical Eldridge Cleaver and his book *Soul on Ice* as despicable. He had no use for the Black Panthers or black power advocates such as Stokely Carmichael and H. Rap Brown. There were also serious divisions along gender lines. Though many black servicewomen supported the black power movement and participated in radical activities, many were turned off by the overt male chauvinism displayed by many of their allegedly enlightened revolutionary brothers.

Black military professionals may have seemed like patriotic "good soldiers" to much of the nation, but to black nationalists their loyalty and patriotism made them "Uncle Toms" who collaborated with the racist white power structure. In his final report to Congress as chief of staff, General Westmoreland admitted that many young black soldiers regarded black careerists with the same distrust they had for white officers and soldiers. The black draftees also criticized blacks involved in administering the armed forces' equal opportunity programs. Much of the scorn was aimed at the senior officers in particular. Sergeant Milton White, founder of the Malcolm X Society in the air force, derided General "Chappie" James as an "Uncle Tom" and the "only song and dance general in the history of the Armed Forces."[3]

Race relations and racial violence in the armed forces were complicated by numerous factors, but most whites in the armed forces were convinced that African Americans instigated much of the violence. Many of them believed that the racial violence was the result of a few but influential black militants. In December 1969, the House Armed Services Committee, for example, concluded that the riots at Camp Lejeune were generated in part by a few militant blacks who fanned the flames of racism. The House committee investigating racial warfare in the navy in 1972 fixed the blame on a few mentally deficient blacks.

Pentagon officials took steps to suppress both the racial violence in the armed forces and the militants they believed to be responsible for it. In many instances, African Americans suspected of fomenting trouble were taken care of informally at the company level. In Vietnam most African Americans believed that the white command structure routinely gave militants and troublemakers "shit" assignments and reassigned them to frontline units, where they were far more likely to come under hostile fire. Whites also resorted to violence and intimidation in their handling of outspoken black militants.

Military authorities suppressed black cultural expressions to eliminate friction between blacks and whites. In particular, they focused on dapping, which was often the catalyst for racial problems. During the Vietnam War, many base commanders banned the practice altogether. In 1972, Marine Private First Class Victor Lucky was court-martialed and sentenced to six weeks of solitary confinement for dapping in a mess hall. After the war both the navy and Marine Corps banned the practice on bases and on board ships during duty hours.

Many commanding officers also prohibited racially exclusive living quarters. It was standard procedure on many installations for military police or shore patrol to break up any large gathering of African Americans. Authorities also disciplined blacks involved in antiwar or black power protests. In 1971, African Americans attending a gathering organized by the Fort Hood United Front were first arrested by civil authorities and then charged with being AWOL by army officials. That same year Airmen Marty Dixon and Johny McRae were sentenced to eighteen months at hard labor and given bad-conduct discharges for their participation in a Malcolm X rally in South Korea and in the consequent riot that broke out.

Military authorities particularly targeted members of black organizations that they considered to be revolutionary or thought were contributing to racial friction or violence in the armed forces. The largest of these organizations operating in the armed forces was probably the American Servicemen's Union, founded in 1967. Most of the groups were relatively insignificant, had a small membership, and operated for a short period of time at only one installation. The People's Justice Committee, for example, existed only at Fort Hood, Texas. Simply being a member of a radical organization was not grounds for prosecution or discharge from the military, but there were procedures in place for identifying and eliminating personnel deemed hazardous to military discipline and security. Many of the so-called militant African Americans had powerful allies in the government, especially among the members of the Congressional Black Caucus. Nonetheless, most militants had no desire to fight the system and were willing to accept undesirable discharges to get out of the military. In December 1972, Admiral Zumwalt issued an order allowing sailors who had discipline problems to request a general discharge under honorable conditions. The program proved so successful that the navy extended it indefinitely.

In addition to eliminating alleged black troublemakers from the armed forces, authorities also realized that substantial reform was necessary to eradicate personal and institutional racism from the armed forces. In April 1969, Nixon's secretary of defense, Melvin R. Laird, formed the Domestic Action Council, which developed race relations programs for the armed forces. The various branches of the armed forces also established their own equal opportunity and race relations programs in response to racial problems. Beginning in 1970, officers had to include information on their handling of race relations in their efficiency reports, and success or failure in this area could affect their future assignments and chances of promotion. In November 1970, on recommendations from the Domestic Action Council, Westmoreland ordered the Continental Army Command to develop a mandatory race relations course for junior, warrant, and noncommissioned officers. Eventually this course became part of basic training for all enlisted personnel. Also that year he created a committee to evaluate and suggest improvements in all aspects of the army, ranging from official policies to products sold in the PXs. In the following year, the army sponsored a series of seminars at all major bases in the United States, aimed at finding possible solutions to the racial unrest and violence in the military. One result of these meetings was the establishment of the Department of the Army Race Relations and Equal Opportunity Committee in November 1971. The committee, which consisted of officers holding the rank of general, had a mandate to develop and oversee service-wide equal opportunity and affirmative action programs. By 1972, the army's new affirmative action plans included 138 separate initiatives and reforms designed to increase the number of African Americans in most military occupational specialties.

The Marine Corps, like the army, also began initiating a series of reforms in 1969. The marines set up an equal opportunity office, which established a Human Relations Training Program; an interracial Commandant's Advisory Committee on Minority Affairs, composed of uniformed personnel and prominent civilians; an Equal Opportunity Staff Section; and programs designed to recruit and retain more minority officers. Race relations and equal opportunity officers generally worked with and through existing race relations committees on the bases. Military authorities placed great hope in these programs, and commanders in Vietnam credited race relations committees for improving conditions in their units. By November 1969, marine commanding officers in I Corps, the northernmost section of South Vietnam, established almost 190 committees. It was the same in the United States. In July 1971, the Marine Corps established a Human Relations Institute at the Marine Corps Recruiting Depot at San Diego, California, with a mission similar to that of the Pentagon's Race Relations Institute. This program created mandatory race relations classes for all Marine Corps personnel, and by 1972 every marine, regardless of rank, had to complete a twenty-hour course.

The different service branches moved at their own pace, and reform in the navy and air force generally lagged behind that of the army and Marine Corps. In 1969, the air force began to assign at least one equal opportunity employment officer to each air force base and instituted a mandatory race relations class, but it was only a four-hour course. Not until 1971 did the air force expand the course to nine hours and make it part of both basic and officer candidate training. It also founded a Human Relations Institute at Lackland Air Force Base, nearly three years after similar measures had been implemented in the army and marines.

In the navy, serious racial reform dated from June 1970, when Admiral Elmo R. Zumwalt Jr. became chief of naval operations (CNO). As did Westmoreland in the army, and Chapman and Cushman in the marines, the feisty and resolute new chief of naval operations was determined to reform the most racist of all the military branches. By 1972, the navy had not only renewed its commitment to existing programs and policies but also started nearly two hundred new programs and initiatives designed to address both racial inequality and racial friction in that service. In addition to naming an African American, Lieutenant Commander William S. Norman, as his minority affairs assistant, Zumwalt oversaw the establishment of the navy's new Human Resource Project Office in June 1971. He intended the office to eradicate racism from the United States Navy, and like similar institutes in the other military branches, it trained race relations officers, known as race relations education specialists. These specialists conducted racial awareness and equal opportunity classes and seminars at most naval installations. But it was only in November 1972, after the incidents on board the *Constellation* and *Kitty Hawk*, that the navy launched Phase I of its new race relations program. Zumwalt's efforts to improve race relations were accompanied by a steady stream of "Z-Grams," as his operational directives were nicknamed. The Z-Grams emphasized the need for racial reform and prodded recalcitrant officers and enlisted personnel into implementing and supporting the new programs and initiatives.

In 1971, the Department of Defense created the Defense Race Relations Institute to train equal opportunity officers to conduct eighteen-hour courses on race relations, which were mandatory for officers and NCOs. Within a year, the institute had graduated over seven hundred instructors, who were assigned to installations throughout the military establishment. Once in place, they taught race relations classes, were responsible for monitoring compliance with the DOD's equal opportunity directives, investigated charges of racial prejudice and discrimination, and assisted in encouraging good relations between the races.

Despite good intentions, the military's programs to improve race relations were not without problems. Some critics claimed that a lack of experience was at fault; many officers never received any training during the war. Other times sincere attempts backfired. Officers were urged to hold race relations meetings in their units to allow the men to discuss their grievances, but instead of catharsis, these discussions often led to arguments and fights among the participants. Passions became so heated in some race relations classes that fist fights broke out.

Chief among the problems, however, was the fact that the very personnel charged with implementing the reforms, the commissioned and noncommissioned officers, were often apathetic about the equal opportunity and race relations programs and did little to implement the reforms. In many cases white officers were openly hostile and did their best to impede them. Proponents of racial reform believed that a lack of leadership was one of the major obstacles to successful racial reform in the armed forces. Some critics blamed senior officers and officials who talked about reform and demanded action from their subordinates without doing much to support them.

The ambivalence and hostility to racial reform permeated the chain of command. In 1969, the Marine Corps report on racial disturbances charged that most officers and NCOs were unenthusiastic about enforcing Marine Corps directives on racism and equal opportunity. Both Westmoreland and Zumwalt blamed recalcitrant officers for hindering racial reform in their respective services. Zumwalt's black advisors told him that white officers did not like his Z-Grams and openly resisted reform. In 1972, the chief of naval operations publicly blamed white senior officers for paying only lip service to his attempts at racial reform instead of trying to implement them. He issued several new Z-Grams ordering officers to enforce rigidly the new reforms, warning opponents of racial reform that "response which lacks commitment from the heart is obstructionist."[4]

Many commanders simply did not follow through on racial reforms. For instance, several equal opportunity directives had called for the creation of biracial command-community relations committees, but a 1972 study found that almost one-third of the commands surveyed had yet to do so. Of those that had formed committees, only sixty-one had local black civilian participation, as mandated by the directives. Many of those who did act on the directives were simply going through the motions. One marine commander in charge of an installation near Albany, Georgia, established a command-community relations committee, but when asked about the committee's achievements and activities, he replied "absolutely none." Having a talented and motivated equal opportunity officer was important if the reforms were to succeed, but commanding officers seldom assigned the task to their best and brightest subordinates. Officers did not view the job as having much prestige or as a route to advancement, so it was often given to relatively junior officers who were not viewed as particularly gifted or to officers already overburdened with other duties. A 1971 investigation found that of the equal opportunity officers on fifteen air bases, only three were qualified for and enthusiastic about their jobs. Even when individuals were motivated and capable, they seldom received much support from their superiors. It was little wonder that many African Americans considered the EO officers to be ineffective tools of the white establishment.

There were many reasons why base and senior commanders often failed to support racial reform. Some were immersed in other activities or programs and did not see racial reform as a priority. Many were overworked and did not want to assume new responsibilities. Others were racist and believed that minorities deserved inferior treatment and second-class status. Some did not want to admit the gravity of the situation or feared embarrassing and discrediting the armed forces. Many of them doubted the effectiveness of the programs even if they admitted that there were serious, racially motivated problems. A large number of officers believed that the racial violence was orchestrated by a handful of black militants and felt that the reforms would not solve the problem. Some critics claimed that the real issue was not lack of equal opportunity or white racism, but lack of discipline. Others argued that the reforms had made the situation worse by undercutting authority and giving the militants a forum from which to spread their message.[5]

As the Vietnam War wound down, military officials believed that they had won their internal struggle against black militants and racism. Racial violence did diminish in the ground forces as Americans withdrew from Vietnam, but in the case of the navy, the level of racial discord seems to have intensified. Westmoreland admitted later that although racial violence had declined by the end of the war, so had racial harmony in the army. In 1972, his counterpart in the navy, Admiral Zumwalt, admitted to reporters that the navy had not made acceptable progress on equal opportunity. The air force and Marine Corps also continued to experience racial problems, although to a lesser degree than the navy and army. Personnel of all races in all branches of the armed forces claimed that racial friction and racial violence remained endemic to the military after the war.

Often the impetus for reform came from outside the military establishment. The military also needed to reform its justice system, for example, which many critics charged was racist. Officials initially reacted to criticism of the military justice system by denying that racism was even a factor. Undoubtedly a few soldiers did use racism as an excuse for their own behavior, but a large number of complaints from black service personnel led to independent investigations, by the NAACP and the Congressional Black Caucus, of charges of racism in nonjudicial punishment and the discharge system. In general, military authorities cooperated with the investigations in an effort to help resolve the problems. But many military officials were reluctant to admit that there was a problem. They believed that the inquiries were misguided and unfair to the armed forces, given the military's record and initiative on many race-related issues. The list of apologists included most senior black officers. One of the most vocal defenders of the military was General "Chappie" James, who openly deplored black criticism of the armed forces. Some white officers and political leaders reacted to the inquiries with less-than-veiled hostility. Military officials often treated the Congressional Black Caucus in particular with disdain and defiance. For example, the House Armed Services Committee denied a request from the black caucus to allow one of its members to sit in on hearings into the *Kitty Hawk* and *Constellation* uprisings. In November 1971, members of the Congressional Black Caucus visited numerous military installations around the country, gathering evidence and testimony in an effort to document the scope of the abuses. They often found base commanders and other officers to be ambivalent and uncooperative.

All of the investigations, whether they focused on a single topic, such as military justice, or the entire system, reached essentially the same conclusion: that racism, both personal and institutional, did create a double standard and conditions prejudicial to African Americans. The DOD study found that racism was particularly evident in the administration of military justice. All urged immediate action, and most suggested some possible remedies. One group recommended that the Pentagon immediately adopt reforms in the use of nonjudicial punishment, in particular.

In the early 1970s and in the wake of the investigations, the Department of Defense did initiate reforms, which focused on eliminating the worst abuses of nonjudicial punishment. Beginning in 1972, it required publication of all Article 15s—nonjudicial punishments—given to personnel in the lowest four pay grades. Much like police officers, who had to read civilians their "Miranda" rights, military officers had to inform personnel facing nonjudicial punishment of their rights, including the right to appeal a decision and demand a court-martial in lieu of an Article 15 or Captain's Mast. Finally, the Defense Department placed limits on the use of pretrial confinement. The Department of Defense was convinced, and with some reason, that some of the racial problems that plagued the armed forces during the Vietnam War stemmed in part from the conditions in the stockades and brigs; thus, overhauling the military prison system became a priority. Overcrowding, one of the key factors that contributed to racial friction in prisons, was reduced at many facilities. Between 1968 and 1971, for example, the prison population at the Camp Pendleton, California, brig was reduced from more than one thousand to less than five hundred. Similar reductions occurred at other stockades in the United States and Vietnam, although the reductions in Vietnam had more to do with troop withdrawals than reform. The Department of Defense also emphasized the need for modern and professional training of prison officials. Many prison wardens were professionals, and in most prisons the guards received better training and the abusive ones faced elimination.

Although the system of courts-martial received less attention, the military did make a few important reforms in this area. One of the most important came early in the war. Under the Military Justice Act of 1968, the military had to provide legal counsel at the accused's request. The army now provided for special courts-martial to handle bad-conduct discharges, and the office of the Judge Advocate General tried to recruit minority lawyers. The Department of Defense did show a genuine commitment to reforming the military justice system, and many of the changes reflected the concerns of black service personnel. The reforms came rather late to have much impact on the vast majority of men who served during the Vietnam War—conditions would improve, however, for future generations of African Americans in the military establishment.

The Department of Defense also became sensitive to black cultural expressions and demands for black products. PXs began stocking dashikis and popular hair care products, such as Afro-Sheen. Books on black history and culture were now available at most post libraries. The military featured more black music on its radio stations and in the service clubs, and it made a concerted effort to entice more black entertainers to tour Vietnam. By 1973, the armed forces even permitted a modified Afro haircut for servicemen, and post barbers were trained to cut black hair to conform to the newer style. The military also made an effort to honor its black heroes. In January 1970, the Marine Corps named a barracks at Quantico in honor of the first black marine recipient of the Medal of Honor, Private First Class James Anderson Jr., and in April 1974 the corps activated Camp Gilbert H. Johnson, named after one of the first African Americans to serve in the marines.

The armed forces entered the Vietnam War with a reputation for racial fairness and equal opportunity. But as the war progressed, African Americans in the military increasingly voiced their displeasure with racism. This in turn contributed to an unprecedented rise in racial violence. Military authorities responded by suppressing the dissidents but also by instituting reform throughout the system, most notably in the areas of military justice, testing, and promotion. The Pentagon recognized African American military heroes and honored them by naming buildings and barracks after them. As American involvement in the war in Vietnam declined, conditions in the armed forces were still far from perfect, and there would be sporadic racial violence into the 1970s, but due to both outside pressure and internal reform, the military had made major strides in eliminating not only the vestiges of institutional racism but also most outward manifestations of personal racism. However, most black Vietnam-era veterans did not remain in the armed forces and consequently did not enjoy the benefits of reform. Instead, they returned to a civilian world as changed individuals and with new challenges facing them.

Notes

1. William H. McMichael, "A War on Two Fronts," *Newport News-Hampton, Virginia Daily Press*, Williamsburg Edition, July 27, 1998, 1, A4–A6.

2. Major Cecil F. Davis Interview, Senior Officer Oral History Project, 1982, 4.

3. Milton White, "Self-Determination for Black Soldiers," *Black Scholar*, November 1970, 42.

4. "The Navy's New Racial Crisis," *Newsweek*, November 20, 1972, 36; and Jack D. Foner, *Blacks and the Military in American History* (New York: Praeger, 1973), 222.

5. Foner, *Blacks and the Military*, 248–53; and "Fleet Racism Whitewash," *Camp News*, February 15, 1973, 7.

CHAPTER SIX

~

Vietnamization and Going Home

In 1968, Richard Nixon had won a close and bitterly contested presidential election against Democratic rival Vice President Hubert Humphrey and "Dixiecrat" George Wallace by running on a "law-and-order" platform and promising to end the war in Vietnam. In the summer of 1969, he announced his Vietnamization program that called for the removal of U.S. troops from the war and promised to achieve peace with honor. At the same time, he initiated peace talks in Paris with Hanoi. In effect, Nixon planned to reduce the number of American combat troops in Vietnam while training the South Vietnamese army to be able to stand on its own against its Vietcong and North Vietnamese opponents. At the end of 1968, at the height of American involvement, there were over 543,000 American troops in Vietnam. In June 1969, Nixon announced the withdrawal of 25,000 of them. The number of American military personnel in South Vietnam steadily fell to 475,000 by the end of 1969, to 335,000 in 1970, and to 157,000 by the end of 1971.

On January 23, 1973, Secretary of State Henry Kissinger and Le Duc Tho, the chief North Vietnamese negotiator, signed the Paris Peace Accords, which officially ended American participation in the Vietnam War. The agreement, which went into effect on the evening of January 27, stipulated that the United States remove all of its military forces from South Vietnam and that the North Vietnamese and Vietcong release all American POWs in their custody. For the Vietnamese people, the fighting finally ended on April 30, 1975, when North Vietnamese armed forces took Saigon, ending the decades-long war that had savaged their country and reuniting their nation.

In Vietnam, morale among American military personnel began to plummet, contributing to a host of problems that plagued U.S. forces until the end of American involvement. Signs of poor morale and motivation among U.S. troops were visible throughout Vietnam. After 1968, there were numerous incidents of "combat refusals," in which individual soldiers, or sometimes entire units, refused a direct order to move forward or to attack the enemy. In 1969, a company of the 196th Light Infantry Brigade refused orders and sat down despite their commander's pleas. The event was televised on the CBS evening news. Later that year, a company from the First Air Cavalry Division flatly refused to advance down a dangerous road. Units on patrol or on search-and-destroy missions purposely advertised their presence or wore red bandanas, which signaled to the Vietcong that they would fight only if attacked. Search and destroy had become search and evade. Many men simply avoided going out in the field or slowed their work pace. Almost all counted down the weeks and days they had left in Vietnam before they could go home.

Unlike the two world wars, in which military personnel served for the duration of the conflict, army personnel assigned to Vietnam had a fixed one-year tour of duty. Thus, most soldiers knew the exact date they could leave the war and return to the "world." A soldier with only a few months left on his tour was a "short timer." He had to worry about "short-timer's disease," which meant losing one's concentration out in the field and getting hurt or killed because one was daydreaming about going home. Going home meant the realization and the reality that no one was likely to be trying to kill you on a regular basis anymore, and there were loving relatives and the creature comforts of home to look forward to, but the actual transition from war zone to civilian society could be an abrupt one. Some men received their orders home while they were still out at a remote firebase or just coming in from a patrol. In less than seventy-two hours a man could go from an environment of kill or be killed, where he was heavily armed, dirty, and sweaty, to sitting in the lobby of an airport in Tacoma or Los Angeles in a pressed and starched dress uniform.

Approximately fifty thousand African Americans returned from Vietnam each year at the height of the war in the late 1960s, and for them, as for all returning veterans, the joy of coming home was tempered by a host of new issues and challenges confronting them upon their return to the world. Some had to deal with the physical scars of war, including the loss of a limb or limbs, reoccurring and debilitating diseases such as tropical malaria, severe burns and wounds that refused to heal, or the insidious effects of Agent Orange, a powerful chemical defoliant used by the United

States that killed its handlers with cancers and other maladies as efficiently as it wiped out tropical jungles.

A large percentage of returnees had injuries that were neither physical nor readily visible, but wounds nonetheless. By the time Sergeant Dwight Johnson received his Medal of Honor from President Lyndon Johnson at a White House ceremony in November 1968, the physical wounds he had received in combat had all but healed, but the psychological trauma from his ordeal had not. After earning his nation's highest honor, Dwight Johnson was admitted to a military hospital in Valley Forge, Pennsylvania, for psychological treatment. In May 1971, believing he was not a threat to himself or to others, Johnson's physicians gave him a five-day pass to go home and see his wife, but he never made it home. The owner of a "party" store in Detroit that he purportedly attempted to rob shot him to death. Johnson and numerous others suffered from a variety of psychological disorders. The most prevalent was post-traumatic stress disorder (PTSD), which causes patients to experience physical symptoms and psychological problems in response to catastrophic events. Symptoms include nervousness, anxiety, nightmares, flashbacks, depression, and anger. The one-year rotation policy for tours of duty in Vietnam was supposed to help remedy the problem and reduce the rate of incidence, but apparently it did not. It could strike anyone but was more likely to affect men who had served in combat, especially heavy fighting. Given the concentration of African Americans in the combat arms, it is not surprising that they suffered a higher incidence of PTSD than whites. A Veterans Administration study found that 40 percent of black veterans suffered from the disorder compared to 20 percent of white veterans.

For African Americans the problems of transition from the military to civilian society were compounded by racism and lack of job opportunities. Many were apprehensive about the rioting and racial violence in the United States, and some felt they were safer in Vietnam than in their own communities. Some hoped to go home to a nice quiet life with their family. Others worried about confronting civilian racism. Many African Americans returning from Southeast Asia did not wear their uniforms off-base if they were stationed in the South, not because of any animosity generated by the war but because of the racist reaction it often prompted from many whites. For some returning veterans, the indignities continued even after they had given their lives for their country and were brought home for burial. At least two black soldiers, Army Privates Jimmy Williams and Bill Terry, were denied burial in all-white cemeteries after being killed in the war. In June 1966, Williams was buried with full military honors at the National Military Cemetery in Andersonville, Georgia. It was one hundred miles from his hometown of Wetumpka, but it was the closest available integrated graveyard. After a lengthy court battle Terry was finally laid to rest as he wished at the previously all-white Elmwood cemetery near Birmingham, Alabama, in January 1970.

Black veterans came home to communities where the jobless rate for blacks was often three times the national average. Unemployment was an issue for all veterans, but the situation was worse for blacks. By 1973, the unemployment rate for returning white veterans between the ages of twenty and twenty-four hovered around 5.7 percent, but for comparable black veterans it was nearly 33 percent. A Detroit-area study that same year reported that 25 percent of black veterans were still jobless six months after leaving the services. In desperation, Casper Smith moved to Washington, D.C., because there were no employment opportunities for blacks in his small hometown in South Carolina, but even in the nation's capital, the best he could do was get a part-time job selling insurance. The jobs that were available were often menial and low-paying positions. Otilio Mighty directed an Urban League program to find employment for returning veterans, and while it was generally successful, most of the positions he could find only paid wages comparable to what a white worker without a high school diploma could expect to receive. For many veterans the frustration of not being able to find a decent job or career continued for years after they left the armed forces. In 1977, the unemployment rate for black veterans was still much higher than for African Americans overall or for the nation at large. It was especially bad for those between the ages of twenty and twenty-four. Nearly 31 percent of them were unemployed compared to 21 percent for African Americans who had not served in the armed forces.

Some programs and agencies did help Vietnam veterans make the transition to civilian life. Beginning in 1967, minority and economically disadvantaged service personnel could sign up for job counseling and training under a new Pentagon program called "Project Transition." Even more important was the new GI Bill passed that year. Veterans interested in starting a small business or buying a home could apply for low-interest loans. Moreover, the bill provided tuition and a living stipend to veterans wishing to attend college or a trade school. The stipends were modest; single veterans received $130 per month, while married ones got $160 per month. Nonetheless, the money often enabled African Americans to obtain an education that had previously been out of reach.

In addition to federal programs, many states, municipalities, and private organizations provided counseling, educational opportunities, and job placement. Among the private organizations, the Urban League in particular took the lead. In 1967, it established a Veteran's Affairs Program (VAP) to aid the returning black veterans, particularly with job placement. The pilot program was so successful that the League eventually opened VAP offices in nine major American cities. The League boasted of an 80 percent success rate in its job placement, with many of its clients finding career-oriented opportunities. Within days of his discharge from the military, Bill Robinson was working as an account executive with a Manhattan dry-cleaning firm. Twenty-one-year-old Raul Ferran found employment as an apprentice mechanic in New York City with the Clarke Equipment Company. Veterans also formed self-help groups, often with the aid of an established organization. With support from both the American Association of Junior Colleges and the American Legion, Alfonza Wright, Kenneth Jackson, and other black veterans at the Community College of Baltimore founded a "veteran's club," aimed at facilitating and coordinating job training and placement. Eventually they found work for many of their fellow vets in the construction and steel industries.

Vietnam veterans paradoxically got little help or empathy from the members of most established veterans' organizations, which considered them losers. Vietnam veterans in general, but black veterans in particular, were not welcome in many veterans' organizations, which were dominated by World War II–era white veterans who had served in a segregated military and wanted to keep their posts and chapters racially exclusive. Until the mid-1960s, some groups had official restrictions in their charters prohibiting integration, and many maintained segregation unofficially for decades afterward. An all-white American Legion post close to his neighborhood in Covington, Kentucky, originally rejected Allen Thomas for membership. Vietnam veteran Bill O'Neill told a reporter that as late as 1986, he and a group of Vietnam veterans were asked to leave an American Legion Post in Newport News, Virginia, because of the "loser" stigma and because of race. In the mid-1980s, Vietnam veterans were relegated to the basement by the Veterans of Foreign Wars chapter in Norfolk, Virginia. Initially they met without incident, until a World War II veteran found out that many of the Vietnam vets were black, precipitating a confrontation between the two groups.

State, local, and federal governments, as well as private organizations, all helped, but it was not nearly enough. The private organizations had limited resources. As successful as the Urban League's Veteran's Affairs Program might have been, it operated in only a few cities and left veterans living in rural areas with little or no organized assistance. Many minority veterans did not even know that they were entitled to government benefits or that federal programs such as Project Transition existed to help them. Some critics claimed that the GI Bill was underfunded and failed to provide adequate benefits to those who needed them most. The net result was that black veterans often found themselves back where they had started and worse off for their experiences. The failure of the federal government to help black veterans kick drug addictions, which they had acquired while in the military, rankled many African Americans in particular.

The war in Vietnam may have been over, but the following years were some of the toughest for the armed forces. Morale was at an all-time low, the volunteers entering the armed forces lacked the college educations many draftees had possessed, and enlistees of all races were from some of the poorest and toughest neighborhoods in America. The result was that drug use and violence continued to be problems for the military. Moreover, charges of institutional and personal racism persisted. In August 1974, a racially mixed group of fifty-five sailors refused to board the aircraft carrier *Midway* in Japan, claiming racism on board the ship. As late as June 1979, the ACLU and two California congressmen, Don Edwards and Ron Dellums, a long-time critic of the Pentagon, charged that there was widespread discrimination in the navy due to bias in its entrance exams. Racial violence continued to flare up. Between 1976 and 1978, racial gang fights in barracks, attacks on individuals, and other forms of racial violence reminiscent of the Vietnam War occurred throughout the military establishment.

The postwar years also saw a resurgence of white supremacy in the ranks. In December 1976, the Marine Corps admitted to a Klan presence at Camp Pendleton, California, and in June 1979, the Pentagon warned of a dramatic increase in Ku Klux Klan activity among off-duty service personnel. That summer three white sailors wearing sheets and hoods sparked a "black power" demonstration on the *Independence* in the Mediterranean Sea. There appear to have been active Klan members on at least two other ships in the Atlantic Fleet. In 1980, the army relieved five military policemen from duty at Fort Monroe, Virginia, when they admitted that they were members of the KKK.

By 1980, however, the racial climate in the military had improved. "Things got better for some of us after Vietnam," recalled Allen Thomas Jr. "The military had the ability, the power. . . . [I]t cannot control your thinking, but it can control the way you act. It was a lot better because some things were just no longer permitted."[1] One reason for the improvement in race relations was the higher recruiting standards for the all-volunteer army that emphasized education and provided bonuses for enlistment, which attracted higher-caliber recruits instead of "troublemakers." African American military personnel who had pressed military officials for reform and equal opportunity were instrumental in the change, as were reformers like Admiral Zumwalt. "In my opinion, Admiral Zumwalt was the greatest individual, one of the bravest men I ever met in my life," stated African American retired Master

Chief Petty Officer Ron Carter. "To stand for what he felt and implement it. . . . [H]e's a hero in my book."[2]

Perhaps most importantly, there were now more black officers in the armed forces, and they were making a difference in race relations by their sheer presence. The numbers of black officers increased, due both to Vietnam War–era recruitment efforts to expand the presence of the armed forces at all-black schools, and to the decline in popularity of ROTC programs at predominantly white schools as a result of an antiwar backlash. In addition, the war had contributed to double-digit inflation and a lack of job opportunities in the civilian sector, making a career in the armed forces more attractive to talented and ambitious minorities.

By the mid-1980s, the armed forces had again become an attractive career path for many minorities, and the number of African Americans in the military remained high. High reenlistment rates and not necessarily new enlistments, however, were largely responsible for the high percentage of African Americans in the armed forces. As early as 1972, 20 percent of all African American first-term enlistees in the army decided to re-up. By 1981 two-thirds of black first-term enlistees decided to stay for another tour, and a staggering 80 percent of all blacks in the armed forces eligible to reenlist did so, compared to only 20 percent of whites.

The large number of minorities in the armed forces led to concerns that nonwhites would suffer disproportionate casualties in any future war. In 1990 and 1991, when the United States entered the First Gulf War, its military forces were heavily black. A quarter of the five hundred thousand American troops that went to the Middle East were African Americans. Sixty-three African Americans were among the 375 American fatalities during operations Desert Shield and Desert Storm, accounting for 16.8 percent of American deaths. Considering that black soldiers made up 25 percent of the armed forces that fought in these wars, this casualty rate was low.

Many African Americans made a career in the military. In 1976, for example, Samuel Gravely was promoted to vice admiral and assumed command of the Third Fleet, thus becoming the first African American to command an American naval fleet. Clifford L. Stanley, who joined the Marine Corps as a second lieutenant in 1969 after graduating from college, served thirty-three years in several prestigious assignments. He retired in 2002 as a major general. Taft Webster, a young African American stationed at Bamberg, Germany, also remained in the army and as of 1998 was the command sergeant major at Fort Monroe, Virginia. Arguably the most illustrious black Vietnam veteran is Colin Powell. In 1989, he became the first African American chairman of the Joint Chiefs of Staff, the highest uniformed position in the military hierarchy, and from 1990 to 1991 he directed the successful international coalition forces in the First Gulf War. Under President George H. W. Bush, Powell became the first African American to serve as national security advisor, and in 2001 he was appointed secretary of state under President George W. Bush, retiring from that position in 2005.

Most African Americans did their stint in the armed forces and returned to civilian life. Some POWs came home to a hero's welcome. On February 12, 1973, the North Vietnamese released POW Norman McDaniel after six and a half years of captivity. When McDaniel finally returned home, the chamber of commerce of Greensboro, North Carolina, held a community banquet in his honor. Others, such as James Daly, returned from Vietnam only to be accused of collaborating with the enemy. In July 1974, the army and navy dropped all charges against Daly and the other POWs.

Many of the deserters returned as well. In an attempt to help heal the wounds of war, President Gerald Ford announced on September 16, 1974, that Vietnam-era draft evaders or deserters could apply for clemency. His successor Jimmy Carter expanded this policy into a more inclusive amnesty program. Terry Whitmore remained in Sweden in the years immediately following the war and tried to build a life and a career. He got married and briefly tried his hand at an acting career. He also published a memoir of his Vietnam years and his sojourn to Sweden as a deserter. Whitmore worked a variety of jobs before settling down as a bus driver and then as a buyer for a large company. In 1977, he took advantage of Carter's amnesty program and returned to the United States for the first time since his desertion in 1967 to see his daughter Tonya, who was being raised by Whitmore's mother. Like many Vietnam War–era deserters or draft resisters, Whitmore believed that he was a patriotic American who took a principled stand against an immoral war, and he did not regret his actions.

Neither did the most famous draft resister of the Vietnam War, Muhammad Ali. Even before his conviction for draft evasion was overturned in 1971, Ali resumed his career in the ring. In 1974, he finally reclaimed the world championship title that he had lost because of his opposition to the war and his refusal to serve in the armed forces. Ali retired from boxing in 1981. In 1996, Ali was honored when he served as the main torchbearer at the opening ceremonies for the Olympic Games in Atlanta.

In 1966, war critic John Lewis stepped down after three years as the chairman of the Student Nonviolent Coordinating Committee to become director of the federally funded Voter Education Project, started by Robert F. Kennedy in 1961 to register black voters in the South. Under his guidance the VEP enrolled nearly four million minority voters. In 1977, President

Jimmy Carter appointed him director of ACTION, the agency in charge of coordinating all federal volunteer agencies, such as the Peace Corps and Job Corps, and in charge of 250,000 volunteers nationwide. Four years later he entered politics and was successful in his bid for a seat on the Atlanta City Council. In 1986, Lewis was elected to the United States Congress where he continues to serve as the representative for Georgia's Fifth Congressional District. In 1969, Stokely Carmichael moved to Guinea, West Africa, and changed his name to Kwame Ture. Carmichael died of prostate cancer at age fifty-seven in November 1998. Fellow SNCC activist and draft resister Cleveland Sellers returned to college and earned an Ed.D. in history from the University of North Carolina, Greensboro, in 1987.

Decades after the fall of Saigon, the military establishment is still dealing with the legacy of Vietnam and the bitter racial divisions that plagued the armed forces during that war. The swift and overwhelmingly decisive triumph of the American-led coalition against Iraq in the First Gulf War and its subsequent action in Bosnia and then again in Iraq helped the armed forces eradicate the ghost of Vietnam and restored the image of the U.S. armed forces as a potent and victorious military. In the years since the Vietnam War ended it has also restored its reputation for racial fairness and equal opportunity. According to sociologist Charles Moskos, arguably the best authority, not a single racial incident significant enough to warrant military police occurred in the First Gulf War, Bosnia, or Somalia. As reporter Mark St. John Erickson observed in the late 1990s, "Since . . . President Harry S. Truman signed an executive order calling for equality of treatment in the armed forces, few parts of American culture have had so much impact on how everyone else gets along."[3] The Vietnam War and black unrest in that era forced the military to reexamine its racial programs and priorities, and commit itself again to racial fairness and equal opportunity. Despite its faults and shortcomings, the military in the early twenty-first century is still a model of integration and race relations when compared to any other major institution or segment of American society.

Notes

1. James E. Westheider, *Fighting on Two Fronts: African Americans and the Vietnam War* (New York: New York University Press, 1997), 173.

2. William H. McMichael, "In Fight against Bias, Victory Is Never Secure," *Newport News-Hampton, Virginia Daily Press*, July 28, 1998, A1, A4.

3. Mark St. John Erickson, "Military Has Become Model for Race Reform, Experts Say," *Newport News-Hampton, Virginia Daily Press*, July 28, 1998, A1.

APPENDIX A

~

Commissioned Officer Ranks during the Vietnam War Era

Rank in Descending Order

General—Air Force, Army, Marines
Admiral—Navy, Coast Guard

Lieutenant General—Air Force, Army, Marines
Vice Admiral—Navy, Coast Guard

Brigadier General—Air Force, Army, Marines
Rear Admiral—Navy, Coast Guard

Colonel—Air Force, Army, Marines
Captain—Navy, Coast Guard

Lieutenant Colonel—Air Force, Army, Marines
Commander—Navy

Major—Air Force, Army, Marines
Lieutenant Commander—Navy

Captain—Air Force, Army, Marines
Lieutenant—Navy

First Lieutenant—Air Force, Army, Marines
Lieutenant, Junior Grade—Navy

Second Lieutenant—Air Force, Army, Marines
Ensign—Navy

Warrant Officer—Air Force, Army

APPENDIX B

~

Enlisted Ranks during the Vietnam War Era

Rank in Descending Order

Sergeant Major of the Army / E-9—Army
Sergeant Major of the Marines / E-9—Marines
Chief Master Sergeant of the Air Force—Air Force
Master Chief Petty Officer of the Navy / E-10—Navy

Command Sergeant Major / E-9—Army
Sergeant Major/Master Gunnery Sergeant / E-9—Marines
Chief Master Sergeant—Air Force
Master Chief Petty Officer / E-9—Navy

Staff Sergeant Major / E-9—Army
First Sergeant / E-8—Marines
First Sergeant / E-8—Air Force
Senior Chief Petty Officer / E-8—Navy

Master Sergeant / E-8 or Sp-8—Army
Master Sergeant / E-8—Marines

Sergeant First Class / E-7 or Sp-7—Army
Gunnery Sergeant / E-7—Marines
Senior Master Sergeant—Air Force
Chief Petty Officer / E-7—Navy

Staff Sergeant / E-6 or Sp-6—Army
Staff Sergeant / E-6—Marines
Staff Sergeant / Technical Sergeant—Air Force
Petty Officer First Class / E-6—Navy

Sergeant / E-5 or Sp-5—Army
Sergeant / E-5—Marines
Sergeant / Senior Airman—Air Force
Petty Officer Second Class / E-5—Navy

Corporal / E-4 or Sp-4—Army
Corporal/Sergeant / E-4—Marines
Petty Officer Third Class / E-4—Navy

Private First Class / E-3 or Sp-3—Army
Lance Corporal / E-3—Marines
Airman First Class—Air Force
Seaman / E-3—Navy

Private / E-2 or Sp-2—Army
Private First Class / E-2—Marines
Airman—Air Force
Seaman apprentice / E-2—Navy

Private / E-1 or Sp-1—Army
Private / E-1—Marines
Airman—Air Force
Seaman recruit / E-1—Navy

APPENDIX C

~

Service Statistics

Table C.1. Service Population (Officer and Enlisted) by Race (June 30, 1972)

		White		Black		Other		Total
		#	%	#	%	#	%	#
Army	Officer	121,290	95.7	4,788	3.9	497	0.4	126,575
	Enlisted	557,061	81.8	116,825	17.1	7,524	1.1	681,410
Navy	Officer	72,154	98.7	660	0.9	128	0.4	72,942
	Enlisted	382,426	87.4	31,825	7.3	23,476	5.3	437,727
Air Force	Officer	118,671	97.8	2,124	1.7	673	0.5	121,468
	Enlisted	519,559	86.6	75,628	12.6	4,793	0.8	599,980
Marine	Officer	19,164	98.1	285	1.5	93	0.4	19,542
Corps	Enlisted	151,543	85	24,439	13.7	2,403	1.3	178,385
All	Officer	331,279	97.2	7,857	2.3	1,391	0.4	340,527
Services	Enlisted	1,610,589	84.9	248,717	13.1	38,196	2	1,897,502

Table C.2. African Americans as Percentage of U.S. Army Forces in Vietnam

Year	% African American
1964	8.7
1965	12
1966	15
1967	10
1968–1972	9.5–10

Table C.3. Discharges Issued under Other-than-Honorable Conditions, 1970

	Army							
	Total		Undesirable		Bad Conduct		Dishonorable	
Race	#	%	#	%	#	%	#	%
White	15825	80.8	14246	80.7	1400	83.6	179	73
Black	3607	18.4	3283	18.6	260	15.5	64	24
Other	149	.8	133	.7	14	.8	2	
Total	19581	100	17662	100	1674	100	245	100

	Marine Corps							
	Total		Undesirable		Bad Conduct		Dishonorable	
Race	#	%	#	%	#	%	#	%
White	8226	80.3	6987	80.5	1192	79.5	47	71.2
Black	1924	18.8	1617	18.6	288	19.2	19	28.8
Other	92	.9	72	.9	20	1.3	0	0.0
Total	10242	100	8676	100	1500	100	66	100

	Navy							
	Total		Undesirable		Bad Conduct		Dishonorable	
Race	#	%	#	%	#	%	#	%
White	2656	90.6	1836	92.0	810	87.9	10	83.3
Black	237	8.1	146	7.3	89	9.7	2	16.7
Other	36	1.3	14	.7	22	2.4	0	0.0
Total	2929	100	1996	100	921	100	12	100

	Air Force	
Race	Undesirable Discharges and Discharges for the Convenience of the Government under Other-than-Honorable Conditions	
	#	%
White	361	69.5
Black	158	28.9
Other and Unknown	8	1.6
Total	527	100

~

Documents

President Truman's Executive Order 9981, July 26, 1948

In 1948, President Harry Truman issued Executive Order 9981 ending segregation in the armed forces and calling for equal opportunity. Hampered by a conservative coalition in Congress, Truman could not get support for any significant civil rights legislation. Nonetheless, as head of the executive branch and commander-in-chief, he did have authority to make changes in these branches and so used executive orders as a way to bypass Congress. He made the Fair Employment Practices Committee permanent and extended its reach to government subcontractors, and he established a committee to investigate race relations in the United States, among other measures. Truman's desegregation of the military was perhaps the most far reaching of these changes, however, as it not only affected the soldiers, but the civilians who worked on the military bases, most of which were in the South. Desegregation was not complete until 1953, and desegregation did not bring an end to discrimination, but it did mean that the government had committed itself to equal treatment within the armed forces, and many blacks began to see the military as a good career opportunity. Many Southern whites who fought in desegregated units in the Korean War began to change their views of the abilities of African American soldiers.

Executive Order 9981
Harry S. Truman
July 26, 1948

Establishing the President's Committee on Equality of Treatment and Opportunity in the Armed Forces.

WHEREAS it is essential that there be maintained in the armed services of the United States the highest standards of democracy, with equality of treatment and opportunity for all those who serve in our country's defense:

NOW THEREFORE, by the virtue of the authority vested in me as President of the United States, by the Constitution and the statutes of the United States, and as Commander in Chief of the armed services, it is hereby ordered as follows:

1. It is hereby declared to be the policy of the President that there shall be equality of treatment and opportunity for all persons in the armed services without regard to race, color, religion or national origin. This policy shall be put into effect as rapidly as possible, having due regard

to the time required to effectuate any necessary changes without impairing efficiency or morale.

2. There shall be created in the National Military Establishment an advisory committee to be known as the President's Committee on Equality of Treatment and Opportunity in the Armed Services, which shall be composed of seven members to be designated by the President.

3. The Committee is authorized on behalf of the President to examine into the rules, procedures and practices of the Armed Services in order to determine in what respect such rules, procedures and practices may be altered or improved with a view to carrying out the policy of this order. The Committee shall confer and advise the Secretary of Defense, the Secretary of the Army, the Secretary of the Navy, and the Secretary of the Air Force, and shall make such recommendations to the President and to said Secretaries as in the judgment of the Committee will effectuate the policy hereof.

4. All executive departments and agencies of the Federal Government are authorized and directed to cooperate with the Committee in its work, and to furnish the Committee such information or the services of such persons as the Committee may require in the performance of its duties.

5. When requested by the Committee to do so, persons in the armed services or in any of the executive departments and agencies of the Federal Government shall testify before the Committee and shall make available for use of the Committee such documents and other information as the Committee may require.

6. The Committee shall continue to exist until such time as the President shall terminate its existence by Executive order.

Harry Truman
The White House
July 26, 1948

Courtesy of the Truman Library.

Letters Authorizing the Establishment of JFK's Committee on Equal Opportunity—The Gesell Committee, 1962

To further racial equality in the armed forces President John F. Kennedy empowered the Committee on Equal Opportunity, chaired by Gerhard A. Gesell, to study and make recommendations. Members of the committee included Joseph O'Meara, Nathaniel Colley, Abe Fortas, Benjamin Muse, John Sengstacke, and the National Urban League's Whitney Young. In 1963, the Gesell Committee reported on conditions on and surrounding bases as well as attitudes of officers in the armed forces. They discovered what black soldiers already knew firsthand—racial discrimination existed both on and off military bases. In response to their report, Secretary of Defense Robert McNamara issued new departmentwide guidelines to combat the worst problems and created the post of Assistant Secretary of Defense for Civil Rights to monitor compliance.

President John F. Kennedy to Gerhard A. Gesell, June 22, 1962
Dear Mr. Gesell:

The Department of Defense has made great progress since the end of World War II in promoting equality of treatment and opportunity for all persons in the Armed Forces. The military services can take justifiable pride in their outstanding accomplishments in this area over the past ten years.

It is appropriate now, however, to make a thorough review of the current situation both within the services and in the communities where military installations are located to determine what further measures may be required to assure equality of treatment for all persons serving in the Armed Forces.

There is considerable evidence that in some civilian communities in which military installations are located, discrimination on the basis of race, color, creed, or national origin is a serious source of hardship and embarrassment for the Armed Forces personnel and their dependents.

In order that I may have the benefit of advice from an independent body of distinguished citizens on the most effective action that can be taken to cope with the problem I am establishing a Committee on Equality of Opportunity in the Armed Forces, and I ask that you serve as Chairman of the Committee.

The Committee will include in its consideration of the general problem the following specific questions:

1. What measures should be taken to improve the effectiveness of current policies and procedures in the Armed Forces with regard to equality of treatment and opportunity for persons in the Armed Forces?
2. What measures should be employed to improve equality of opportunity for members of the Armed Forces and their dependents in the civilian community, particularly with respect to housing, education, transportation, recreational facilities, community events, programs and activities?

The Secretary of Defense will make all necessary facilities of the Department of Defense available to the Committee for carrying out this important assignment.

Sincerely,
Gerhard A. Gesell, Esquire   /s/ John F. Kennedy
Union Trust Building
Washington 5, D. C.

Assistant Secretary of Defense Norman S. Paul Memorandum on Gesell Committee to Under Secretaries of the Army, Navy, and Air Force, August 13, 1962
ASSISTANT SECRETARY OF DEFENSE
WASHINGTON 2[8], D.C.
MANPOWER   AUG 13 1962

MEMORANDUM FOR THE UNDER SECRETARY OF THE ARMY
                         THE UNDER SECRETARY OF THE NAVY
                         THE UNDER SECRETARY OF THE AIR FORCE

SUBJECT: President's Committee on Equal Opportunity in the Armed Forces
    The President recently established the Committee on Equal Opportunity in the Armed Forces. . . . The Chairman, Mr. Gerhard A. Gesell, has scheduled the first meeting of this Committee during the first week of September. In connection with this meeting he asked for the following material relating to policies and practices affecting members of the active and reserve forces:

1. Regulations and/or directives setting forth policies of the military departments on equality of treatment and opportunity (including instructions issued to implement policies and instructions issued by the Office of the Secretary of Defense).
2. Any studies or reports in the area of equality of treatment and opportunity for members of the armed forces.
3. Departmental regulations regarding community relations, particularly as they pertain to problems of equality of treatment and civil rights. Also, provide specific examples of community problems affecting minority groups which were handled through community relations.
4. A listing of major problems regarding equality of treatment and opportunity, either on or off-base, such as the non-availability of community housing or recreational facilities for minority group members, with an indication as to the scope and approximate frequency of such problems.
5. Any experience with racial problems affecting minority groups other than Negro, e.g., Mexicans, Puerto Ricans, etc.
6. A list of major military bases in the Continental United States, to include military population, dependent population and the population of the nearest community or communities to the base.

It also is requested that the Under Secretary of the Army, in cooperation with the Under Secretary of the Air Force, develop a statement concerning the status of integration in the Army and Air National Guard. Included in this statement, as a minimum, should be the following information, along with any other narrative or statistical information which will be of assistance in apprising the Committee of the nature and scope of problems relating to discriminatory practices in the Army and Air National Guard:

1. A listing of specific state laws or other regulations which preclude integration in the National Guard or require separate Negro and white units.
2. A listing of states which by practice segregate personnel and units of the National Guard, along with a narrative statement as to the situation in each such state.
3. A statement of the actions taken by the Departments of the Army and Air Force, through consultation or other means, to encourage states having discriminatory practices to discontinue them and of any progress being made.

In connection with the above, an appropriate representative should be available to brief the Committee at the first meeting. Further details as to time and place will be provided in advance of the meeting.

It is requested that the above material be furnished by August 27, 1962 in ten copies each so that they may be made available to members of the Committee.

Norman S. Paul

Medal of Honor Citations

African Americans demonstrated tremendous skill and bravery in Vietnam, once again defying stereotypes about black abilities. Yet proof of ability often combined with prejudice to keep black soldiers in more dangerous assignments for longer. Black infantrymen often served on point—a sign of their skill but also, many believed, because white officers thought them expendable. Many civil rights groups cited the disproportionately high casualty rates among black soldiers as signs of discrimination. The soldiers also had to face discrimination at home. After he left the military, Dwight Johnson suffered from psychological problems, common among many Vietnam veterans. On a pass from a psychiatric hospital, he was shot by a storeowner in Detroit who claimed Johnson was trying to rob him. Nonetheless black soldiers served with distinction and earned numerous medals, proving again that the military did recognize ability regardless of race. The following citations are for two of the twenty-one Medals of Honor awarded to African Americans during the Vietnam War.

Charles Rogers's Medal of Honor Citation

ROGERS, CHARLES CALVIN

Rank and organization: Lieutenant Colonel, U.S. Army, 1st Battalion, 5th Artillery, 1st Infantry Division.

Place and date: Fishhook, near Cambodian border, Republic of Vietnam, 1 November 1968.

Entered Service at: Institute, W Va.

Born: 6 September 1929, Clarement, W Va.

Citation:

For conspicuous gallantry and intrepidity in action at the risk of his life above and beyond the call of duty. Lt. Col. Rogers, Field Artillery, distinguished himself in action while serving as commanding officer, 1st Battalion, during the defense of a forward fire support base. In the early morning hours, the fire support base was subjected to a concentrated bombardment of heavy mortar, rocket and rocket propelled grenade fire. Simultaneously the position was struck by human wave ground assault, led by sappers who breached the defensive barriers with bangalore torpedoes and penetrated the defensive perimeter. Lt. Col. Rogers with complete disregard for his safety moved through the hail of fragments from bursting enemy rounds to the embattled area. He aggressively rallied the dazed artillery crewmen to man their howitzers and he directed their fire on the assaulting enemy. Although knocked to the ground and wounded by an exploding round, Lt. Col. Rogers sprang to his feet and led a small counterattack force against an enemy element that had penetrated the howitzer positions. Although painfully wounded a second time during the assault, Lt. Col. Rogers pressed the attack killing several of the enemy and driving the remainder from the positions. Refusing medical treatment, Lt. Col. Rogers reestablished and reinforced the defensive positions. As a second human wave attack was launched against another sector of the perimeter, Lt. Col. Rogers directed artillery fire on the assaulting enemy and led a second counterattack against the charging forces. His valorous example rallied the beleaguered defenders to repulse and defeat the enemy onslaught. Lt. Col. Rogers moved from position to position through the heavy enemy fire, giving encouragement and direction to his men. At dawn the determined enemy launched a third assault against the fire base in an attempt to overrun the position. Lt. Col. Rogers moved to the threatened area and directed lethal fire on the enemy forces. Seeing a howitzer inoperative due to casualties, Lt. Col. Rogers joined the surviving members of the crew to return the howitzer to action. While directing the position defense, Lt. Col. Rogers was seriously wounded by fragments from a heavy mortar round which exploded on the parapet of the gun position. Although too severely wounded to physically lead the defenders, Lt. Col. Rogers continued to give encouragement and direction to his men in the defeating and repelling of the enemy attack. Lt. Col. Rogers' dauntless courage and heroism inspired the defenders of the fire support base to the heights of valor to defeat a determined and numerically superior enemy force. His relentless spirit of aggressiveness in action are in the highest traditions of the military service and reflects great credit upon himself, his unit, and the U.S. Army.

Dwight Johnson's Medal of Honor Citation
JOHNSON, DWIGHT H.
Rank and organization: Specialist Fifth Class, U.S. Army, Company B, 1st Battalion, 69th Armor, 4th Infantry Division
Place and date: Near Dak To, Kontum Province, Republic of Vietnam, 15 January 1968
Entered service at: Detroit, Michigan
Born: 7 May 1947, Detroit, Michigan

Citation:
For conspicuous gallantry and intrepidity at the risk of his life above and beyond the call of duty. Sp5c. Johnson, a tank driver with Company B, was a member of a reaction force moving to aid other elements of his platoon, which was in heavy contact with a battalion size North Vietnamese force.

Sp5c. Johnson's tank, upon reaching the point of contact, threw a track and became immobilized. Realizing that he could do no more as a driver, he climbed out of the vehicle, armed with only a .45 caliber pistol. Despite intense hostile fire, Sp5c. Johnson killed several enemy soldiers before he had expended his ammunition. Returning to his tank through a heavy volume of antitank rocket, small arms and automatic weapons fire, he obtained a submachine gun with which to continue his fight against the advancing enemy. Armed with this weapon, Sp5c. Johnson again braved deadly enemy fire to return to the center of the ambush site where he courageously eliminated more of the determined foe. Engaged in extremely close combat when the last of his ammunition was expended, he killed an enemy soldier with the stock end of his submachine gun. Now weaponless, Sp5c. Johnson ignored the enemy fire around him, climbed into his platoon sergeant's tank, extricated a wounded crewmember and carried him to an armored personnel carrier. He then returned to the same tank and assisted in firing the main gun until it jammed. In a magnificent display of courage, Sp5c. Johnson exited the tank and again armed only with a .45 caliber pistol, engaged several North Vietnamese troops in close proximity to the vehicle. Fighting his way through devastating fire and remounting his own immobilized tank, he remained fully exposed to the enemy as he bravely and skillfully engaged them with the tank's externally-mounted .50 caliber machine gun; where he remained until the situation was brought under control. Sp5c. Johnson's profound concern for his fellow soldiers, at the risk of his life above and beyond the call of duty are in keeping with the highest traditions of the military service and reflect great credit upon himself and the U.S. Army.

Courtesy of the US Army Center for Military History.

Interview with Sergeant Allen Thomas Jr.

Allen Thomas was one of nearly three hundred thousand African Americans to serve in Vietnam. Sergeant Thomas served three tours, and his experiences are representative of what many African Americans experienced in Vietnam. Drafted on his eighteenth birthday in 1957, Thomas served in the army in the Signal Corps and in security until 1978. He served three tours of duty in Vietnam in 1965–1966, 1967–1968, and 1970–1971. Despite encountering racism on both a personal and institutional level, Allen stayed in the military for twenty-one years and found it a good career.

Westheider: Where were you stationed?

Thomas: I was an advisor to a Thai unit my first tour, and spent time in both Vietnam and Thailand. In my second and third tours I was with the Fourth Infantry Division at Kontum and Dak To.

Westheider: How old were you when you went to Vietnam and what was your rank?

Thomas: I was 25-26 my first tour and E-5 going over, but an E-6 coming home.

Westheider: How did you feel about the war when you went to Vietnam the first time?

Thomas: First tour? I was brainwashed. I was career military, and war was what the military did, and I was anticommunist, so I pretty much supported the war.

Westheider: How did you feel about the war after serving in Vietnam?

Thomas: When I went back in 1967–1968 the whole tone had changed. My first tour we were mostly professionals but by my second tour it was a lot of draftees. I changed real quick; watching people do things they were not supposed to do, atrocities, and people murdered. There was more disobedience by the troops in the second tour. Third tour was just survival, everybody just wanted to stay alive.

Westheider: What was your opinion of whites before serving in Vietnam?

Thomas: I grew up in a segregated society, and my opinion of whites was formed early. There was some name-calling, but no violence. I watched my father, uncle, etc., they knew what to do. I never got angry and there was no fear, just confident in the belief that if you did your best you could do you could get ahead. We were looking for opportunity not revenge. We were trying to get along but the whites were not.

Westheider: What was your opinion of whites after serving in Vietnam?

Thomas: Vietnam and age changed my opinion. I was very good at what I did. Got lots of rewards, recognition, free vacations to Munich and Stuttgart. We imported racism into Germany. Frankfort, Ansbach, Wurtzburg, had segregated bars, restaurants, clubs, just like being in Georgia. It happened anywhere there was a U.S. presence, Germany, Thailand, the Philippines. Things did change though from 1958 to 1970.

Westheider: Did you feel that the military was generally fair to African Americans? How did it compare to civilian society?

Thomas: Things were better in the military. Hard given the conditions everyone is under not to treat someone as a person. Attitudes change. Things got better for some of us after Vietnam. The military had the ability, had the power to change things. They cannot control your thinking, but they can control the way you act. It was a lot better because some things were just not permitted.

Westheider: What was your opinion of white commissioned officers?

Thomas: Generally good. Both black and white officers tended to be pretty good.

Westheider: Do you believe that such things as promotion, assignments, and the military justice system were fair to African Americans? In particular, what about the use of nonjudicial punishment?

Thomas: I got good assignments, good duty, but racism was rampant. There was a six-month rotation policy between the front and rear areas for my MOS. Eighteen of the twenty-five E-5s in my platoon were black, but the blacks stayed at the front as the whites got rotated back. It also had a lot to do with lack of promotion. I was at the front and was not notified about a pending promotion board until 11:00 the night before. I had to ride in a truck all night long just to try and get there on time. No promotion. It was much easier for whites.

Military justice was racist, especially the use of Article 15s, or nonjudicial punishment. The officers had too many discretionary powers, and could write someone up for anything. There was a double standard. If you were black and spoke up you were a troublemaker, instigator, whatever. If you were white, you were an innovator. "Conduct unbecoming" was often used. A lot of black NCOs did the same thing, had a double standard. They had bought into the system and didn't even realize they were doing it. It was so ingrained. They thought they were good officers and NCOs and they were harder on blacks. We had to give 110 percent, live up to expectations. Elite units were different. The command structure in many was entirely black. I thought of myself as a teacher, a trainer, I had a different idea on how things should be done.

Westheider: Was racial tension a problem in your unit? Were there any major incidents?

Thomas: It was there but we never had any outbreaks. Everybody got along, intermingled together. There were a few all-white hootches, and some predominantly black ones, but it was divided up more into juicers and hard-core drug users. The NCOs were mixed up. We had to get along with each other black and white. There were the typical day-to-day problems, but I would not classify them as racial incidents. I had one young trooper tell me that he "would not take orders from a nigger," but the guy turned out to be a real good kid, just young, from rural Louisiana. We got along great after he spent thirty days in the stockade.

Westheider: What about incidents or racial problems in other units?

Thomas: I heard about some in other units.

Westheider: What about after the assassination of Dr. King?

Thomas: The young guys wanted to hurt somebody. We sat down in the field, a couple of hundred troops, didn't do anything for several days. Many of them just drank, smoked pot. We (the black NCOs) went to the officers, asked them to back off. The last thing you wanted to do was set them off, seasoned veterans with guns. Let them get over their anger and hurt. We had good officers, and were in stand down at the time. There were some fistfights between black and white but nothing serious, no one hurt or killed. No weapons, lots of talking. We were a more elite unit and had better educated people than most others.

Westheider: What black leaders influenced you the most? Who did you admire?

Thomas: I latched on to a few. Randolph, Dr. King, I read all their stuff. I was in the civil rights movement. Malcolm at the time scared the hell out of me. I was searching for respectable equality. I was too young and didn't appreciate what he was all about. My heroes were the people in my neighborhood, the local pastor, the Pullman porter. . . .

Allen Thomas Jr. Interview with the Author, March 22, 1995.

The Black Panthers Express Condolences
on the Death of Ho Chi Minh, 1969

As some African American activists adopted more militant attitudes in the late 1960s, many came to equate the plight of African Americans with that of the North Vietnamese, who they saw as fellow victims of racial oppression from white people. The North Vietnamese and Vietcong consciously courted black soldiers with propaganda and actions. Ho Chi Minh had toured the United States in the 1920s and had seen racial segregation firsthand. He also visited Harlem and sympathized with the plight of African Americans. When the Vietminh captured black soldiers, they often treated them more leniently in order to win their support. The majority of black soldiers did not sympathize with the communists, however many problems they faced in their own country. But many recognized the hypocrisy of a military fighting for the rights of a foreign nation while denying rights to citizens at home. The Black Panthers, attracted by a Marxist interpretation of racial problems, often expressed understanding and solidarity with the Vietcong and North Vietnamese.

To the Courageous Vietnamese People, Commemorating the Death of Ho Chi Minh, *Black Panther*, September 13, 1969

To die for the fascist imperialistic warmongers of the U.S. and others in the world; to die for the oppressive ruling circles of the bourgeoisie exploiters; to die for the capitalistic, aggressive, inhumane, atrocious, genocidal regimes is a death lighter than a feather which a destructive windstorm can blow about at random will.

But to die for the people; to die for the correct socialistic development of mankind; to die in the midst of socialistic revolutionary change for human survival; to die for your nation and peoples' right to self-determination in their land, home and community; to die for the freedom of all from oppression that the Black Panther Party has witnessed in the proletarian internationalism practiced by the Vietnamese peoples' revolutionary representatives that we have met; to die after all the great heroic and dedicated years of sacrifice to bring to the world and its people an end to the murderous, stormy winds of capitalism's fascist, aggressive imperialism; to die because he loved the people of his nation and humans of the world (and Brother Ho Chi Minh had practiced this all the days of his life); to die for all of this is a death heavier than the highest mountain in the world of which no, not any destructive fascist imperialistic storm can blow away at will.

Who can find the feather or feathers that were blown away by the destructive windstorm? I can't find any. Who can see the mountains since the windstorm is gone? I can see many, they still stand. There! That mountain will always stand and Ho Chi Minh is that mountain—a death heavier than Mt. Thai.

Courtesy of the Huey P. Newton Foundation.

Letters from Disgruntled Black GIs in Vietnam

African Americans disillusioned with the war or the armed forces often vented their discontent in the "GI Letters" section of the Black Panther *newspaper. These letters reflect a growing frustration with racism in the military. One inmate describes deplorable conditions for military prisoners, a large number of whom were African American or other ethnic minorities. Others show that the movement toward black nationalism affected black servicemen as much as black civilians. Soldiers in Vietnam often used black power symbols on their helmets and flew black power flags from their hootches. They developed elaborate handshakes, known as "daps," to show racial solidarity, and they wore "slave bracelets" woven from bootlaces. The following letters describe some of the conditions the soldiers faced and demonstrate their increasing impatience with the military's ability to deal with the problems.*

"GI Letters," *Black Panther*, September 27, 1969
STOCKADE SADIST
Dear Friend:

The story I tell you in this letter is 100% fact, I may be court-martialed like many others and it is so important that my story pierce the ears of the people in the world outside the stockade. Chances are that when you read this I will be taken to court, but that is beside the point as long as you discover and can see what the army is really like.

In this testimony I will talk mostly about the Military Police Company working in the stockade. Th[o]se most involved are the 532nd and the 759th, but the 532nd are, in my opinion, the worst. I think that these M.P.s, with a few exceptions, must be psychopathic. Certainly their anti-social and immoral conduct would indicate something like that for they are sadists.

If you think that torture is no longer used you are wrong. The army has devised these leather belts which they call straps. Straps are put on your wrists with your wrists twisted behind your back as far as they can go and tied to your ankles and you lie with all your weight on your stomach on the wooden bunk because in that position your chest can't even touch the ground.

With this in mind let me give you a few cases. I'll start with Jimmy Friend (of course that is not his real name because I don't have permission to use it). I was in Mental Hygiene when I looked out the window and saw this prisoner being taken into segregation. He was being hit on top of the head when all of a sudden he let one go and landed on Sgt. Branhover's face. (Sgt. Branhover is a lifer). Then they really put it to him. The word from Major Casey was, "Drop him." As I went then to my cell I saw big bruisers go in his cell and they followed Major Casey's orders with enthusiasm. He was in the straps about five or six hours. He was laid on a bunch of boards about eight inches off the ground and every thirty minutes or so he was picked up and let fall hitting his head and abdomen, each time from higher up. As a result the man was unable to use his legs without support, his face was bashed up and he couldn't use his arms. He was in extreme pain in every muscle, bone and pore of his body. How long he endured this completely useless and unbearable pain I don't really know. He was in cell 12 and I was in 14. The next day he was processed out of the pound. . . .

[Serviceman Carlos Rodriguez, writing to the Workers Defense League from the stockade at Fort Dix, New Jersey]

GI LETTERS
NAVY
Dear Brothers:

Just a few lines to explain a few things about myself and the Naval service. I'm in the service and I have been for 7 months. I would like to tell all the brothers and sisters to stay away from the White pigs' war. I've done all I can to get out but there is no hope. I want to be a Black Panther and hold a position as one who will tell you how phony the swine is. I've written over 14 people with Congressional power and all I've gotten from them was, "No." I want to be right here in the service and still help my Black people. I need your help, and you the Black people on the outside need mine.

I promise to keep you informed on what's happening. I live in Brooklyn, New York, 39 Moffat Street, but I want you to write me in the service. I want the whole world to know how this place is. I want you to know how to get out, and how to stay in, if you want to be the White man's flunky. Please send me your Code of Ethics, and some Black literature, and buttons. Please, I need your help and you need mine.

Sincerely from a Brother,
Paul Isaac Murray
P.S. Write me back. Please, I have a lot to tell you!

ARMY
Dear Sir,

Hello there, my name is Lionel Anderson, and I am from New Orleans.

I was just released from the United States Army, which was the sorriest thing that ever happened to me in my life. The way they used me and my fellow brothers to wage war on oppressed people in Vietnam. Knowing that we are oppressed here in the States, discriminated against as individuals. I was released under a bad conduct discharge for failure to comply with the ruling class rules.

As of now I am an organizer, working here at the Oleo Strut Coffee House. My job is to talk and organize Black men from Fort Hood Post.

I have been keeping up with your literature and politics. And would like to know a little more about your projects. I would appreciate a reply from you as soon as possible. I am interested in getting involved with your organization. Thank you very much for letting me take up some of your time.

Yours Truly
Lionel Anderson
Kil[l]een, Texas

NAVY
Dear fighting Black brothers:

I'm sending my money to help in the struggle. I would like you to send me the Black Panther News as soon as you can.

I am in the White man's Navy, but my heart is in the street fighting by the sides of Black men for the rights of Black people.

I was born in West Oakland and will soon be back in Oakland, as my time will soon be up. I made the mistake of coming in the service, thinking that maybe it's better being in the Navy. But the man got me in a box along with a lot of other Black men. But when we get out, "the sky is the limit," and I will put to good use the training that the White man has taught me. I need some written support from YOU to help me teach my Black brothers on the ship.

Most of the brothers are from the South and are scared to speak out. I have been telling them about the ways of the White man, but I want them to read it for themselves.

My birth name is Thomas Walker, but the name Thomas don't get it. Could you tell me a name for a Black warrior?

Thomas F. Walker BM-3
Deck Div.
U.S.S. AGEKHOLM DD826
c/o FPO San Fransisco, Ca. 96601

p.s. The ship is in Viet Nam, so please send as soon as you can.
Power to the People
Right On!

Courtesy of the Huey P. Newton Foundation.

Organized Protest: The Fort Hood United Front and the People's Justice Committee

Black nationalist and black power organizations sprang up on many military bases in the late 1960s and early 1970s. At Fort Hood, Texas, the People's Justice Committee began after a series of hearings on racism. Black soldiers at Fort Hood, Texas, met with Representative Louis Stokes, a member of the Congressional Black Caucus, and complained about the absence of black officers and racism in the military justice system, the promotion of military personnel, and duty assignments as well as discrimination suffered by members of the Nation of Islam. The discussion inspired the soldiers to take action. This pamphlet describes the visit and consequent formation of the all-black People's Justice Committee to protest racism on the base. Such organizations often became targets for military officials, and members faced harassment and even "undesirable" discharges. The Fort Hood United Front was a predominantly white organization that opposed the war in Vietnam and supported soldiers' rights in general.

"Black Organization Grows from Hearing on Racism,"
November 15, 1971

Fort Hood United Front
PO Box 1265
Killeen, TX 76541
(817) 634-9405
November 15, 1971
BLACK ORGANIZATION GROWS FROM HEARING ON RACISM

Ft. Hood, Texas

What may well develop into a post-wide black organization to combat racism on Ft. Hood was sparked November 15 by the visit of Rep. Louis Stokes, a member of the Congressional Black Caucus. Stokes came to Ft. Hood to begin hearings on racism in the military. The hearings, conducted by the Black Caucus, will continue Nov. 16 to 18 in Washington, D.C.

The organization, called the Peoples' Justice Committee (PJC), was formed when it became obvious in the course of the hearing that simply talking with Rep. Stokes would not solve the problems of racism in the military. The Brothers decided that what was needed was a strong, independent organization of Black enlisted men that could defend and support itself.

In a press release issued by the Black Caucus before the hearing, "military justice" was cited as one of the things the Caucus would be seriously investigating. "For instance, Black GI's represent 30.6% of the population of the

Army's world wide confinement facilities and in the Air Force they represent the incredible figure of 53.4% of the inmates of this service's confinement facilities. Similarly the Navy and Marine Corps have in their stockades a [disproportionate] number of Black GI's, these figures being 16.2% and 21.0% respectively. Additional reason for concern in this area is the too frequent occa[s]ion of 'lily-white justice.' Blacks constitute less than 1% of the military lawyers and little is being done to correct this situation." To say the least, those words were proven true at today's hearing.

The stage was set by the Brass's blatant refusal to provide decent facilities for the hearing. In a letter to General George Seneff (commander of Ft. Hood), Rep. Ronald Dellums of the Black Caucus asked "That Rep. Stokes be provided with a theater or meeting room capable of seating a least 200 persons." Yet when GI's began arriving at the appointed place for the hearing in the morning they were handed numbers and told they would be talking with Rep. Stokes "one at a time." But the 100–150 people who gathered decided they would rather talk in a group, and Stokes agreed. So the hearing was moved to a condemned barracks that was no longer in daily use.

Most of those in attendance had been informed of the hearing by members of the Ft. Hood United Front, who had worked with Stokes to coordinate the activities. The Army, although it had received advanced word of the hearing and its nature, put out little if any publicity. Some companies were told at morning formation that Stokes would be on fort, and anyone who wanted to go could talk with him. But no mention was made of the fact that he had come to investigate racism.

Before the hearing began, the press was asked to leave by the brothers who had come to testify. Most had seen how the press had handled the question of racism in the past, and all were aware of the rep[e]rcussions that would come as a result of them appearing in local media. The reporter for the *Fatigue Press*, Ft. Hood's GI newspaper, was allowed to stay.

When the press was gone, the hearing got underway. Testimony was given regarding racism in promotions, Military Occupational Specialties, duty assignments, MP activities, and the military justice system.

A Black MP from 518 MP's testified about the racist police policies on Ft. Hood. "Blacks are in trouble as far as police are concerned." He gave the example of a "riot" that took place in 42nd Signal [Battalion] about four months ago. When he arrived, there were eight blacks on the ground with 40 shotgun-carrying MP's around them. Since there wasn't really a "riot," the MP's stormed the barracks, dragged people out of bed, and arrested them. Nineteen blacks and one white were arrested. "If the Blacks on this post get [any] shit together, they'd better have full field gear and a couple of tanks, 'cause them police are gonna have all their equipment—there's gonna be a lot of dead Black people here." He said that in his entire [battalion] there isn't one Black officer.

A Black Muslim from 36th Medical Battalion testified to consistent harassment from Captain Markum and other lifers in his company. That includes weekly Article 15's (nonjudicial punishment—[meted] out at the Captain's discretion). He signed (accepted) the last one because a military lawyer told him he couldn't be acquitted in a court-martial with his beliefs. The Muslim diet prevents him from eating messhall food, but no provisions are made for separate rations. In fact the Muslim religion is not recognized by the Army, which denies Muslims religious freedom, not to mention political freedom.

One Brother testified that he and a white enlisted man had both been charged with the same incident of "AWOL from KP." No action was taken against the white, but the Black was given an Article 15.

Another man testified that the Army hadn't paid him in 4 months. He said that everytime he went to the finance office they told him to come back later. "My parents are both dead, I got two little sisters back in DC, and a brother in the hospital with a piece of glass in his spine—I'm all they got for support, to eat, you know—the most basic thing in life. And those motherfuckers keep telling me to come back later."

Brother after Brother testified about the racism that is part of everyday life on Ft. Hood. The fact that Blacks are given infantry and artillery jobs; the fact that Blacks are prosecuted for 5 minutes AWOL; the fact that Blacks are thrown into the stockade arbitrarily and with little reason. Anger was high during the hearing, showing the extent and depth of racism on Ft. Hood, the military, and American society as a whole.

A number of times Stokes was asked just what he was going to do with the information gathered. "Since racism is necessary to the military, what are you planning on doing to combat it?" one Brother asked. "Are you just here to bullshit for a while, to pacify us and go back and tell your boss what's happening?" Stokes answered "I do not represent the U.S. Government. My constituency is in Cleveland—they elected me to represent them. I'm not here for votes or anything other than to investigate racism." "That's your rap, but is it reality? If you don't have a boss, why don't you just go out there and tell these people you're gonna do this thing and then do it?"

Stokes's answer was that General Seneff's "Volar plan" included a "Human Relations Unit" to deal with racial questions, led by a Black Command S[e]rgeant Major. The Unit has not yet been established.

After Stokes had left for lunch, a meeting of about 50 Brothers took place. It broke up for lunch and regrouped later with over 150 present. One Brother explained the purpose for the meeting: "There are all these people who came here with individual problems for the Congressman—but there's a Brother over here with a problem, and there's another over there with the same dam[n]ed problem. We ain't got no personal problems—we're oppressed people! Blacks are just flunkies around here. We can't solve our problems individually, but as a group."

For the first time in over a year, a Black organization was formed on Ft. Hood. Another meeting was held that night at the Oleo Strut Coffeehouse to formulate a structure. The name "People's Justice Committee" was chosen.

In the past, Black organizations have been dealt with viciously by the Ft. Hood Brass—such as the case of the Ft. Hood 43 (43 Black GI's who helped formulate demands against racism in response to the order to got to Chicago in the summer of '68. They were court-martialed as a result of the meeting to formulate the demands). As such, the Brothers of the PJC expect serious harrassment and repression. The group is young and building, along with the Ft. Hood United Front, a predomina[nt]ly white organization. Spirit and energy are high, and the Brothers understand along with Bobby Seale that "If we worry about what's going to happen to us, we'll never get anything done. Justice is gonna come when the masses rise up and see justice done."

Courtesy of the Division of Rare and Manuscript Collections, Cornell University Library.

Free the Camp Allen Brothers, Pamphlet

This pamphlet, drafted by the Defense Committee at Camp Allen, Virginia, called attention to the plight of sixteen black sailors accused of participating in a riot on post. In the late 1960s, the stockades were the setting for a series of riots involving black inmates who made up a disproportionate percentage of the inmates due to racism in the military judicial system. In 1968, racial violence erupted at the main naval brig at Da Nang and the army's Long Binh Stockade near Saigon. This violence spread throughout the armed forces. In 1969, there were racially motivated "gang" fights at the Marine Corps' Camp Lejeune in North Carolina, Millington Naval Air Station in Tennessee, and Kaneohe Marine Corps Air Station in Hawaii, among other locations. By the early 1970s, there were fights on ships and aircraft carriers like the USS Kitty Hawk. The Defense Committee urged concerned African Americans to petition the Congressional Black Caucus to investigate the incident.

FREE THE CAMP ALLEN BROTHERS

The trials grind on in the case of the Camp Allen Brothers, sixteen Norfolk sailors accused of participating in a so-called brig "riot" last Nov. 26. All of them are enlisted men, all of them are Black. Since Nov. they have been threatened, harassed, isolated, racially insulted and beaten. The brothers are under a tremendous strain, and the brig today is just as explosive as it was at the time of the so-called "riot." Instead of stopping this racist harassment of the prisoners, the brig and base commanders seem to encourage it as if trying to provoke a confrontation.

To get to the bottom of what led up to the rebellion of the 26th, the Defense Committee, the GI project organizing the defense, started a petition campaign to get a Congressional investigation of the situation. Rep. Shirley Chisholm, (D-NY), responded and agreed to send two aides to the brig. When they attempted to see the Brothers, the Navy responded with red tape and bureaucratic excuses, fearing what they might find. Ms. Chisholm expressed her "total disgust with the Dept. of Navy," and pledged to "pursue the matter to the fullest extent possible." The brass clearly can't have the conditions in their prisons being made too public.

As the Defense Committee noted, the whole question is not "who did what," but "what" was the situation in the brig last Nov. and "why" did the prisoners feel that the base and brig commands were unable or unwilling to change it? The point is, "these men wouldn't be on trial now if they weren't enlisted and Black. . . . Officers don't go to the brig, because the brig isn't meant for them. The brig is really just a POW camp for enlisted men. Just like in all other POW camps, enlisted men in brigs fight back."

The need for support of the Camp Allen Brothers has become critical. Of the seven who have already been tried, all but one received brig time, (1–4 months), and all received Bad Conduct Discharges. Of the six remaining, at least 3 or 4 will receive General Courts-martial where they could be put away for many years, if convicted.

WHAT YOU CAN DO:

—Write or wire the Black Caucus to encourage a Congressional Investigation: The Congressional Black Caucus, c/o Hon. Louis Stokes, 315 Cannon Bldg., Wash, DC 20515.

—Send a letter of support to the Camp Allen Brothers.

—Send a contribution to help publicize the trials.

—And for more information write:

THE DEFENSE COMMITTEE
BOX 1492, Norfolk, VA. 23501

Courtesy of the Division of Rare and Manuscript Collections, Cornell University Library.

"Z-Grams": Admiral Elmo Zumwalt
Promotes Equal Opportunity, 1970

Chief of Naval Operations Admiral Elmo Zumwalt worked tirelessly to reform the Navy and make it racially egalitarian. He sought to ensure equal access to housing and ordered stores on military installations to carry products for black personnel. A similar order mandated that all navy libraries and other reading areas carry books, magazines, and records by and about African Americans. Furthermore, he suspended all so-called Mickey Mouse rules that regulated the physical appearance of navy personnel, including haircuts and dress codes, which often affected African Americans who sometimes wore distinctive haircuts or facial hair as expressions of cultural pride. Racist officers would use these distinctions as excuses to punish black sailors they thought were "troublemakers."

Z-gram #57: 10 November 1970
ELIMINATION OF DEMEANING OR ABRASIVE REGULATIONS

1. THOSE DEMEANING OR ABRASIVE REGULATIONS GENERALLY REFERRED TO IN THE FLEET AS "MICKEY MOUSE" OR "CHICKEN" REGS HAVE, IN MY JUDGMENT DONE ALMOST AS MUCH TO CAUSE DISSATISFACTION AMONG OUR PERSONNEL AS HAVE EXTENDED FAMILY SEPARATION AND LOW PAY SCALES. FOR THIS REASON, SHORTLY AFTER TAKING COMMAND I REQUESTED A COMPREHENSIVE REVIEW OF CURRENT NAVAL POLICIES AND REGULATIONS. I DESIRE TO ELIMINATE MANY OF THE MOST ABRASIVE POLICIES, STANDARDIZE OTHERS WHICH ARE INCONSISTENTLY ENFORCED, AND PROVIDE SOME GENERAL GUIDANCE WHICH REFLECTS MY CONVICTION THAT IF WE ARE TO PLACE THE IMPORTANCE AND RESPONSIBILITY OF "THE PERSON" IN PROPER PERSPECTIVE IN THE MORE EFFICIENT NAVY WE ARE SEEKING, THE WORTH AND PERSONAL DIGNITY OF THE INDIVIDUAL MUST BE FORCEFULLY REAFFIRMED. THE POLICY CHANGES BELOW ARE EFFECTIVE IMMEDIATELY AND WILL BE AMPLIFIED BY MORE DETAILED IMPLEMENTING DIRECTIVES TO BE ISSUED SEPARATELY.

A. IT APPEARS THAT MY PREDECESSOR'S GUIDANCE IN MAY ON THE SUBJECT OF HAIRCUTS, BEARDS AND SIDEBURNS IS INSUFFICIENTLY UNDERSTOOD AND, FOR THIS REASON, I WANT TO RESTATE WHAT I BELIEVED TO BE EXPLICIT: IN THE CASE OF

HAIRCUTS, SIDEBURNS, AND CONTEMPORARY CLOTHING STYLES, MY VIEW IS THAT WE MUST LEARN TO ADAPT TO CHANGING FASHIONS. I WILL NOT COUNTENANCE THE RIGHTS OR PRIVILEGES OF ANY OFFICERS OR ENLISTED MEN BEING ABROGATED IN ANY WAY BECAUSE THEY CHOOSE TO GROW SIDEBURNS OR NEATLY TRIMMED BEARDS OR MOUSTACHES OR BECAUSE PREFERENCES IN NEAT CLOTHING STYLES ARE AT VARIANCE WITH THE TASTE OF THEIR SENIORS NOR WILL I COUNTENANCE ANY PERSONNEL BEING IN ANY WAY PENALIZED DURING THE TIME THEY ARE GROWING BEARDS, MOUSTACHES, OR SIDEBURNS.

B. I VIEW THE PROHIBITION AGAINST THE WEARING OF CLEAN, NEAT WORKING UNIFORMS OR DUNGAREES TO AND FROM WORK AS UNWARRANTED AND I NOW DIRECT THAT IT BE SUSPENDED FOR THE CONVENIENCE OF ALL CONCERNED.

C. TO STANDARDIZE CURRENT PRACTICES, WORKING UNIFORMS, DUNGAREES, AND FLIGHT SUITS ARE AUTHORIZED IN ALL NAVAL COMMISSARIES. EXCHANGES, SNACK BARS, DISPENSARIES, DISBURSING OFFICES, AND OTHER SERVICE TYPE FACILITIES, AND NO ONE WILL BE DENIED ENTRANCE FOR BEING IN THE "IMPROPER" UNIFORM, ASSUMING THOSE WORN ARE CLEAN, NEAT, AND IN GOOD CONDITION. BASE COMMANDERS WILL REVIEW SIMILAR RESTRICTIONS APPLICABLE TO DEPENDENTS AND ADOPT REGULATIONS CONSISTENT WITH CURRENT FASHIONS.

D. THE REQUIREMENT FOR OFFICERS AND MEN TO SHIFT INTO THE UNIFORM OF THE DAY FOR THE EVENING MEAL WILL BE DISCONTINUED, EXCEPT FOR CEREMONIAL OR OTHER SPECIAL OCCASIONS OR BY DECISION OF THE GROUP OF PERSONNEL INVOLVED.

E. AT LEAST ONE ROOM OF EVERY NAVAL OFFICER, CPO, AND ENLISTED CLUB SHALL PERMIT THE WEARING OF INFORMAL AND CASUAL CLOTHES (SPORT SHIRT) AND NAS CLUBS SHALL SIMILARLY PERMIT FLIGHT SUITS IN AT LEAST ONE ROOM OF EACH CLUB.

F. WHERE OPTIONAL UNIFORMS ARE SPECIFIED BY THE AREA COMMANDER, THIS WILL MEAN OPTIONAL TO THE INDIVIDUAL AND NOT TO THE LOCAL COMMANDS, EXCEPT FOR SPECIAL OCCASIONS, SUCH AS INSPECTIONS, WHERE UNIFORMITY IS REQUIRED. . . .

H. THE REQUIREMENTS TO CERTIFY THE POSSESSION OF SUFFICIENT FUNDS OR TO ACKNOWLEDGE GEOGRAPHICAL LIMITATIONS FOR LEAVE (EXCEPT FROM VIETNAM WHERE SPECIAL REGULATIONS APPLY) OR LIBERTY PURPOSES, TO PRODUCE PERSONAL PROPERTY PASSES, OR TO SHOW CERTIFIED PERMISSION TO BE AWAY FROM DUTY STATION (WALKING CHITS) PRESUPPOSES A GENERALIZED IRRESPONSIBILTY WHICH I DO NOT ACCEPT, AND THESE REQUIREMENTS WILL BE ELIMINATED. . . .

J. OVERNIGHT LIBERTY WILL NOT BE TREATED AS A PRIVILEGE FOR WHICH A SPECIAL REQUEST CHIT MUST BE SUBMITTED, BUT RATHER AS THE NORMAL FORM OF LIBERTY FOR OUR RESPOSIBLE SAILORS. EXCEPTIONS TO THIS POLICY WOULD BE MADE ONLY FOR EXTRAORDINARY CIRCUMSTANCES SUCH AS GOVERNMENT IMPOSED CURFEW OR EXTREMELY UNSATISFACTORY ENVIRONMENT, AND THEN ONLY UPON DETERMINATION OF THE SENIOR OFFICER PRESENT.

K. THE REQUIREMENT FOR LINE HANDLERS, REFUELING PARTIES, TOPSIDE WATCH STANDERS IN INCLEMENT WEATHER, BOAT CREWS IN HEAVY WEATHER, AND OTHERS WHO ARE ENGAGED IN WORK WHICH WOULD UNDULY SOIL OR DAMAGE SUCH UNIFORMS, TO PERFORM THE JOBS IN WHITES OR BLUES IS UNREASONABLE AND IS TO BE DISCONTINUED, EXCEPT FOR MOST UNUSUAL CEREMONIAL OCCASIONS.

L. THE OCCASIONAL PRACTICE OF REFUSING TO FORWARD A REQUEST FROM AN INDIVIDUAL TO HIGHER AUTHORITY WILL BE DISCONTINUED. IF PERSONNEL IN THE CHAIN HAVE GOOD REASON FOR NOT RECOMMENDING APPROVAL OF A REQUEST, THEY SHOULD, OF COURSE, SO STATE, BUT THEY MUST FORWARD IT EXPEDITIOUSLY ONE WAY OR ANOTHER.

M. I AM NOT SUGGESTING THAT A MORE LENIENT ATTITUDE TOWARD IRRESPONSIBLE BEHAVIOR BE ADOPTED, BUT I DO BELIEVE THAT WE CANNOT PERMIT GENERAL POLICIES TO BE DICTATED BY THE NEED, WHICH I SUPPORT, TO CONSTRAIN THOSE FEW INDIVIDUALS WHO DO NOT RESPOND TO THE TRUST AND CONFIDENCE EXPRESSED IN MORE FLEXIBLE AND LESS RESTRICTIVE REGULATIONS.

E. R. ZUMWALT, JR., ADMIRAL, U.S NAVY,
CHIEF OF NAVAL OPERATIONS.

Z-gram #66: 17 December 1970
EQUAL OPPORTUNITY IN THE NAVY . . .

1. THE PURPOSE OF THIS NAVOP IS TO EXPRESS MY WHOLE-HEARTED SUPPORT OF THE POLICIES ON EQUAL OPPORTUNITY STRONGLY REAFFIRMED BY THE SECRETARY OF THE NAVY IN ALNAV 51, TO EXPRESS MY GENERAL GUIDANCE FOR IMPLEMENTATION OF THESE POLICIES, AND TO DIRECT IMPLEMENTATION OF A FEW OF THE ACTIONS WE CAN TAKE IMMEDIATELY.

2. LAST MONTH, SECRETARY CHAFEE AND I, ALONG WITH OTHER SENIOR OFFICIALS OF THE NAVY DEPARTMENT, MET ON ONE OCCASION WITH REPRESENTATIVE BLACK NAVY OFFICERS AND THEIR WIVES AND LATER WITH A REPRESENTATIVE GROUP OF BLACK ENLISTED MEN AND THEIR WIVES. PRIOR TO THESE MEETINGS, I WAS CONVINCED THAT, COMPARED WITH THE CIVILIAN COMMUNITY, WE HAD RELATIVELY FEW RACIAL PROBLEMS IN THE NAVY. HOWEVER, AFTER EXPLORING THE MATTER IN SOME DEPTH WITH THESE TWO GROUPS, I HAVE DISCOVERED THAT I WAS WRONG—WE DO HAVE PROBLEMS, AND IT IS MY INTENTION AND THAT OF SECRETARY CHAFEE TO TAKE PROMPT STEPS TOWARD THEIR SOLUTION.

3. WHAT STRUCK ME MORE THAN ANYTHING ELSE WAS THE DEPTH OF FEELING OF OUR BLACK PERSONNEL THAT THERE IS SIGNIFICANT DISCRIMINATION IN THE NAVY. PRIOR TO THESE MEETINGS, I SINCERELY BELIEVED THAT I WAS PHILOSOPHICALLY PREPARED TO UNDERSTAND THE PROBLEMS OF OUR BLACK NAVYMEN AND THEIR FAMILIES, AND UNTIL WE DIS-

CUSSED THEM AT LENGTH, I DID NOT REALIZE THE EXTENT AND DEEP SIGNIFICANCE OF MANY OF THESE MATTERS.

4. THERE ARE TWO KEYS TO THE PROBLEM. FIRST, WE MUST OPEN UP NEW AVENUES OF COMMUNICATION WITH NOT ONLY OUR BLACK PERSONNEL, BUT ALSO WITH ALL MINORITY GROUPS IN THE NAVY SO THAT WE MAY LEARN WHAT AND WHERE THE AREAS OF FRICTION ARE. SECOND, ALL OF US IN THE NAVY MUST DEVELOP A FAR GREATER SENSITIVITY TO THE PROBLEMS OF ALL OUR MINORITY GROUPS SO THAT WE MAY MORE EFFECTIVELY GO ABOUT SOLVING THEM. OUR MEETINGS HERE IN WASHINGTON WERE A BEGINNING, BUT NO MORE THAN THAT. MUCH REMAINS TO BE DONE.

5. FOR EXAMPLE, I AM PARTICULARLY DISTRESSED BY THE NU-MEROUS EXAMPLES OF DISCRIMINATION BLACK NAVY FAMI-LIES STILL EXPERIENCE IN ATTEMPTING TO LOCATE HOUSING FOR THEIR FAMILIES. THIS SITUATION AND OTHERS LIKE IT ARE INDICATIVE IN SOME CASES OF LESS THAN FULL TEAM-WORK BEING BROUGHT TO BEAR BY THE WHOLE NAVY TEAM ON BEHALF OF SOME OF OUR MEMBERS AND FAILURE TO USE EXISTING AUTHORITY AND DIRECTIVES TO ENFORCE THEIR RIGHTS (SECNAV INST 5350.12). IN SOME PLACES HOUSING PER-SONNEL ARE TACITLY CONTRIBUTING TO DISCRIMINATION IN HOUSING.

6. SECRETARY CHAFEE AND I HAVE ASKED OUR STAFFS TO BE-GIN WORK WITH OTHER MEMBERS OF THE NAVY DEPARTMENT TO MAKE AN IN-DEPTH INVESTIGATION OF THIS PROBLEM AND PRESENT TO US WITHIN 60 DAYS PROPOSALS WHICH WILL HELP ALLEVIATE THE MOST ACUTE HOUSING PROBLEMS. MEAN-WHILE, THERE ARE MANY THINGS THAT CAN BE ACTED UPON IMMEDIATELY. THEREFORE, BY 15 JANUARY 1971 I EXPECT AC-TION TO BE TAKEN AS FOLLOWS:

A. EVERY BASE, STATION AND AIRCRAFT SQUADRON COM-MANDER AND SHIP COMMANDING OFFICER SHALL APPOINT AN AWARE MINORITY GROUP OFFICER OR SENIOR PETTY OFFI-CER AS HIS SPECIAL ASSISTANT FOR MINORITY AFFAIRS. THIS OFFICER OR PETTY OFFICER SHOULD HAVE DIRECT ACCESS TO

THE COMMANDER/COMMANDING OFFICER AND WILL BE CON-
SULTED ON ALL MATTERS INVOLVING MINORITY PERSONNEL.
EXCEPTING THOSE COMMANDS ALREADY HAVING MINORITY-
AFFAIRS OFFICER BILLETS, THE INITIAL ASSIGNMENT WILL BE
ON A CONCURRENT DUTY BASIS. (I CAREFULLY WEIGHED THIS
ITEM WITH MY DESIRE, . . .TO REDUCE COLLATERAL DUTY AS-
SIGNMENTS. HOWEVER, AFTER DISCUSSING THIS WITH SEV-
ERAL BLACK OFFICERS I BECAME CONVINCED THAT THEY
WOULD IN FACT, CHERISH THIS AS A COLLATERAL DUTY.)

B. ALL SHORE BASED COMMANDERS SHALL ENSURE THAT A MI-
NORITY GROUP WIFE IS INCLUDED IN THE NAVY WIVES OM-
BUDSMAN CONCEPT SET FORTH IN REF B.

C. THE PROGRAMS ALREADY BEGUN BY COMNAVSUPSYSCOM
TO ENSURE THAT THE SPECIAL NEEDS OF MINORITY GROUPS
ARE RECOGNIZED AND PROVIDED FOR SHALL BE EXPEDITED,
NAMELY:

(1) SUITABLE COSMETICS AND OTHER PRODUCTS FOR BLACK
PERSONNEL AND THEIR DEPENDENTS WILL BE STOCKED IN
NAVY EXCHANGES.

(2) SHIP'S STORES WILL STOCK BLACK GROOMING AIDS.

(3) EVERY BASE AND STATION, WILL EMPLOY, AS SOON AS POS-
SIBLE, AT LEAST ONE QUALIFIED BLACK BARBER/BEAUTICIAN IN
MAJOR BARBER AND BEAUTY SHOPS, AND WILL WORK TOWARD
THE GOAL OF HAVING SUFFICIENT BARBERS/BEAUTICIANS
QUALIFIED IN HAIR CARE FOR BLACK PERSONNEL TO PROVIDE
SERVICE FOR ALL BLACK PATRONS.

(4) ALL MAJOR COMMISSARIES SHALL STOCK FOODS AND PRO-
DUCE FREQUENTLY REQUESTED BY MINORITY GROUPS. AS A
MINIMUM, SPECIFIC RECOMMENDATIONS SHOULD BE SO-
LICITED FROM MINORITY PERSONNEL AND THEIR FAMILIES
AND ACTED UPON BY LOCAL COMMISSARY MANAGERS.

D. SPECIAL SERVICES OFFICERS WHICH DEAL IN DISCOUNT
TICKETS FOR VARIOUS ENTERTAINMENT PROGRAMS WILL

ALSO OBTAIN DISCOUNT TICKETS TO EVENTS OF SPECIAL IN-
TEREST TO MINORITY GROUPS WHENEVER SUCH TICKETS ARE
AVAILABLE.

E. A REPRESENTATIVE SELECTION OF BOOKS, MAGAZINES AND
RECORDS BY AND ABOUT BLACK AMERICANS WILL BE MADE
AVAILABLE IN NAVY LIBRARIES, WARDROOMS, CLUBS AND
OTHER READING AREAS.

ANY OF THE ABOVE WHICH CAN'T BE ACCOMPLISHED WITHIN
THE TIME SPECIFIED ABOVE WILL BE REPORTED VIA CHAIN OF
COMMAND TOGETHER WITH A SUMMARY OF CIRCUM-
STANCES PREVENTING TIMELY IMPLEMENTATION.

7. IN ORDER THAT I MAY REACH A MORE COMPLETE UNDER-
STANDING OF THE PROBLEMS EXPERIENCED BY OUR MINORITY
PERSONNEL, IN ADDITION TO SECNAV/OPNAV/BUPERS TEAM
VISITS I AM DIRECTING MY SPECIAL ASSISTANT FOR MINORITY
AFFAIRS, LCDR NORMAN, TO VISIT MAJOR NAVAL ACTIVITIES
WITHIN CONUS TO MEET WITH INDIVIDUAL COMMANDING
OFFICERS AND WITH MINORITY MILITARY PERSONNEL AND
THEIR DEPENDENTS. BY LEARNING IN DEPTH WHAT OUR PROB-
LEMS ARE, I BELIEVE WE WILL BE IN A BETTER POSITION TO
WORK TOWARD GUARANTEEING EQUAL OPPORTUNITY AND
TREATMENT FOR ALL OF OUR NAVY PEOPLE.

8. THIS IS THE FIRST OF MY REPORTS TO YOU ON MINORITY AF-
FAIRS. SECRETARY CHAFEE AND I WILL BE LOOKING INTO ALL
AREAS OF MINORITY AFFAIRS AND WILL BE ISSUING FURTHER
REPORTS AS OUR PROBLEMS BECOME MORE CLEAR AND THEIR
SOLUTIONS BECOME MORE APPARENT. IT IS EVIDENT THAT WE
NEED TO MAXIMIZE OUR EFFORTS TO IMPROVE THE LOT OF
OUR MINORITY NAVYMEN. I AM CONVINCED THAT THERE IS
NO PLACE IN OUR NAVY FOR INSENSITIVITY. WE ARE DETER-
MINED THAT WE SHALL DO BETTER. MEANWHILE, WE ARE
COUNTING ON YOUR SUPPORT TO HELP SEEK OUT AND ELIMI-
NATE THOSE DEMEANING AREAS OF DISCRIMINATION THAT
PLAGUE OUR MINORITY SHIPMATES. OURS MUST BE A NAVY
FAMILY THAT RECOGNIZES NO ARTIFICIAL BARRIERS OF RACE,

COLOR OR RELIGION. THERE IS NO BLACK NAVY, NO WHITE NAVY—JUST ONE NAVY—THE UNITED STATES NAVY.

E. R. ZUMWALT, JR., ADMIRAL, U.S. NAVY,
CHIEF OF NAVAL OPERATIONS

Courtesy of the U.S. Navy.

"Racism in the Military":
The Congressional Black Caucus Report, 1972

In response to numerous requests by black service personnel, the Congressional Black Caucus initiated hearings to investigate racism in the armed forces. Many groups charged that African American military personnel suffered unfair punishments and unfavorable discharges due to racism. A particular target was the prejudicial use of nonjudicial punishment. Known as Article 15 hearings in the army and Captain's Masts in the navy and marines, nonjudicial punishment procedures allowed officers to decide punishments for minor infractions. Unlike in formal hearings, defendants had no rights to representation, and racist NCOs often wrote up black soldiers and sailors for punishment when they did not report white soldiers for similar violations. Blacks often received the maximum punishment in these hearings. African Americans were also more likely to receive unfavorable discharges than whites in the military. Many African Americans believed that the military used less-than-honorable discharges to rid the armed forces of black militants. Military officials generally cooperated with investigations but were reluctant to admit problems of institutional racism. They were particularly scornful of the Congressional Black Caucus, which they saw as a group of troublemakers. Nonetheless, following this report and others like it, the Department of Defense began instituting reforms to make the judicial system within the military more fair.

"Racism in the Military," October 13, 1972
HON. LOUIS STOKES OF OHIO IN THE HOUSE OF REPRESENTATIVES
Friday, October 13, 1972

Mr. STOKES. Mr. Speaker, almost 1 year ago, the Congressional Black Caucus began its investigation of racism in the military. We began with onsite visits to 10 military installations in this country followed by 3 days of open hearings in Washington. Our findings and recommendations, as set forth in the following "Congressional Black Caucus Report on Racism in the Military," have been forwarded to the Department of Defense and the House Armed Services Committee. . . .

II. COMMITMENT AND COMPLIANCE
A. Job assignment

The Black serviceman usually receives his first dose of military racism on the day that he is inducted. Upon entering the service, each enlisted man is given a series of tests to determine his suitability for placement in one of the many military occupational specialties. The racial and cultural biases in these tests combine with the often low educational training and experience of the minority inductee to insure that he is assigned primarily and permanently to those low-skilled, dead-end jobs which the military terms "soft core." . . .

B. Promotion

When the time for promotion occurs, the Black serviceman finds once more that he is at the complete mercy of a system stacked against him. And it is here that the racism of individual officers and NCO's makes its appearance. Testimony by Black servicemen as well as the military's own data give ample evidence of the systematic exclusion of Blacks from promotion lists. Locked into a promotion system dominated by White NCO's and officers, Black servicemen stand by, sometimes [quietly], while his White barracksmate easily advances to higher grades. In 1971 while Blacks made up 12.1% of enlisted strength, they were concentrated most heavily in the second lowest pay grade (15.7% at E-2 level) and they were represented in the smallest proportion at the top enlisted grade (4.2% at the E-9 level). . . .

C. Command

One particular tactic often mentioned by Black officers is the practice of refusing to give them command level positions so necessary to advancement in the officer ranks. . . .

As a consequence Blacks not only receive fewer promotions, receive less pay while in the service, and of course, receive smaller benefits upon retirement. Faced with discrimination in the promotion system, it is not surprising that both morale and reenlistment rates have reached new lows for the Black soldier. According to figures supplied on the Army for 1970, 87.2% of those eligible to reenlist refused to do so, while in 1969, 84.7% chose not to reenlist.

It is interesting to note that in 1972 for the first time a Black general has been placed in command of a division. (General Fred Davison, U.S. Army, Europe.)

D. Equal opportunity

Adding to the problem of inequities in the job assignments and promotion areas is the realization that the only appeal the Black serviceman can make regarding discriminatory practices is into the system from which the discrimination originated. . . .

E. Housing and medical problems

Racism and discrimination as it affects housing and medical problems in the military are magnifications, rather than reflections, of the same problems which affect Black civilians. Because of the location of most military bases, away from the major urban centers, the Black serviceman in the United States finds that the level of discrimination and open hostility which block him in his attempt to find suitable housing near his duty station is even greater than that which he faces as a civilian.

Congressman Charles Rangel, during his one day visit to Fort Bragg was greeted with a big sign which said, "Welcome to Fayetteville, Home of the Ku Klux Klan. Fight Communism and Integration." Such a welcome from the local branch of the KKK, which for many years has greeted Black and White servicemen arriving at Fort Bragg, is an accurate indication of the problems which will face the Black serviceman once he goes outside the base in search of housing for himself and his family. . . .

III. MILITARY JUSTICE
A. Article 15

No military procedure has brought forth a greater number of complaints and evidences of racial discrimination than has administration of non-judicial punishment (Article 15). Article 15 punishments, administered at the discretion of individual commanders for "minor" offense, has without doubt, resulted in irreparable damage to the service careers of Blacks vastly out of proportion to Black enrollment in the military. . . .

B. Pretrial confinement

Another judicial area in which the discretionary powers of commanders exerts itself to the detriment of Black servicemen is through the use of pretrial confinement. Although Black enlistment in the Air Force was only 10.6% in 1971, Department of Defense figures show that more than 50% of the airmen being held in pretrial confinement were Black. While pretrial confinement is designed to detain offenders whom the authorities believe might otherwise escape to avoid prosecution for a serious offense, testimony and military records amply substantiate the charges that, for Blacks, pretrial confinement is more often used as punishment for trivial offenses and is even used where there has been no offense. . . .

D. Discharges

Given the effect of discharges on both the military and civilian survival of GI's, generally, the disproportionate number of less than honorable discharges given to Black GI's is of major concern to the Caucus. There can be little doubt as to the impact of the arbitrary standards used in the dispensing of military discharges. In 1970 Black servicemen made up 11.7% of the total

Air Force strength. In the same year, they received 28.9% of the Air Force's discharges issued under other than honorable conditions. For the combined Armed Forces, Black servicemen are many times more likely to receive a less than honorable discharge than are Whites. For example, recent Department of Defense figures show that of the total of all discharges given Blacks in 1970, 5% were given under conditions other than honorable, as compared to only 3% given to Whites under the same condition. . . .

IV. RECOMMENDATIONS . . .

The recommendations of the Congressional Black Caucus are based on the belief that racism in the military must be eliminated not only because of its debilitating effect on racial minorities, but also because racism in the military poses a serious threat to our National Security. . . . It is therefore obvious that drastic and far reaching changes must be immediately initiated to insure that discrimination in the military is eliminated.

The Congressional Black Caucus therefore recommends that the following action be taken.

1. We recommend that definite goals be established and adhered to, in order to assure that minority servicemen and women are equally represented with[in] all the military occupational specialties. To accomplish this task, special efforts will have to be made to recruit minorities for the specialized fields of medicine, law, and those technical fields which require previous educational experience. . . .

2. We recommend that promotion boards be restructured to include a certain percentage of blacks, other minorities, and women. This percentage could be based on the percentage of these groups in the Service as a whole.

3. We recommend that officer fitness reports also include an evaluation in the area of race relations by the officer's own men. Since an evaluation of equal opportunity effectors are now included on the officer fitness reports, we believe that the best group available to comment on his fairness in this area is his own men. . . .

4. We recommend that definite goals be established to place all minority groups in ranks and in command positions by a definite date. As the Caucus report states very clearly, minorities make up over 11% of the service personnel while they comprise only 2.2% of the officers. If minorities are to be recruited and retained in the Armed Forces, they need to be assured through example, that they can also progress at the same rate as their White counterparts. . . .

5. We recommend the creation of an assistant secretary of defense for civil rights, who would have direct access to the Secretary of Defense as well as the Secretaries of each branch of service. The hearings pointed out repeat-

edly, the failure of the Equal Opportunity Programs both in the Pentagon and on the bases to deal effectively with the problems of discrimination. . . .

6. We recommend that off base housing problems and policies be handled by the Assistant Secretary of Defense for Civil Rights.

7. We recommend that article 15's be removed entirely from any discharge action in the future. Testimony was received throughout the hearings that the Article 15 punishments were administered at the discretion of the commanding officer and used as a basis for undesirable discharges. It is proposed that they be removed entirely from any discharge action. To insure this is done, the Article 15 will be removed from both the base and Department of Defense personnel files exactly one year after the article was given.

8. We recommend that the military code be amended to allow the accused adequate time to confer with counsel before accepting or rejecting an article 15. The administration of justice differs from the problems of discrimination in housing, in restaurants, and in bars, in that the dispensation of justice is totally within the control of the American military officials. We propose that since they have been issued with such arbitrary authority that strong controls be placed on their use.

9. We recommend that more explicit pretrial confinement conditions be established, allowing the accused to be released upon his request or that of his legal counsel unless substantial and convincing evidence was presented to the appropriate JAG official as outlined in Department of Defense directives. . . .

10. We recommend a complete revision of the Uniform Code of Military Justice which would remove from its jurisdiction any offense which is already covered by existing civilian law. This would mean that such charges as rape, assault, murder, theft, etc. would be tried in civilian federal courts instead of by the military. The military courts would have jurisdiction only over those offenses considered peculiar to the military such as AWOL, Desertion, disrespect, missing movement. . . .

11. We recommend that the Uniform Code of Military Justice be amended so that discrimination be an offense considered punishable by court martial just as any other form of misconduct. At the same time the court martial conviction would be removed from the code as a federal offense, but would remain as a form of military punishment.

12. We recommend that the court martial boards be organized to insure representation by all minorities, by women and by rank to be drawn from the total population of the base.

13. We recommend that the Department of Defense contract with civil rights organizations such as the National Association for the Advancement

of Colored People, Legal Defense and Educational Fund, Inc., The National Association for the Advancement of Colored People, and The National Conference of Black Lawyers to provide counsel for Black servicemen until the proportion of Black attorneys in the military begin to equal the percentage of Blacks in the military. . . .

14. We recommend that legislation be introduced to eliminate all punitive discharges and to establish in their place a certificate of service. This certificate would be applicable to the diploma issued upon completion of high school. However, the certificate of military service would indicate the length of service, any special awards or decorations received and a notification as to whether it was issued for medical reasons. Each person upon completion of 181 days of service, would be eligible for any veteran' s benefits provided for under current law. The military would continue to have the authority to discharge a soldier and to punish him for violations of their law; however, they will not be able to mark him for life. Therefore, if the service decides to discharge an individual after this given period of time they will not be able to strip him of his benefits. The ability to function well in the Army bears little relationship to being able to function in civilian society.

15. We recommend that the military justice task force be given the power to evaluate current regulations of the military which are felt to be discriminatory against minority servicemen (e.g. handshake, hair length, beards, arm bands).

16. We recommend the elimination of foreign aid and the removal of all military bases from host countries failing to insure fair treatment of minority servicemen. Without such action there exists a kind of tacit approval of such practices. (e.g. Korea)

17. We recommend that the Department of Defense set timetables for the implementation of these recommendations at the earliest date practicable. The Caucus should be informed as soon as possible of these timetables.

Extensions of Remarks, **Congressional Record, 92nd Congress, 2nd Session, October 14, 1972 (Washington, DC: U.S. Government Printing Office, 1972), 36582–85.**

~

Bibliographic Essay

Probably the best general history of African Americans in the armed forces and one of the first to examine the black experience in Vietnam is Jack D. Foner, *Blacks and the Military in American History* (New York: Praeger Publishers, 1974). More recent studies include Bernard C. Nalty, *Strength for the Fight: A History of Black Americans in the Military* (New York: Free Press, 1986); Michael Lee Lanning, *The African-American Soldier: From Crispus Attucks to Colin Powell* (Secaucus, NJ: Carol Publishing, 1997); Gerald Astor, *The Right to Fight: A History of African Americans in the Military* (Novato, CA: Presidio, 1998); Gail L. Buckley, *American Patriots: The Story of Blacks in the Military from the Revolution to Desert Storm* (New York: Random House, 2001); and Robert B. Edgerton, *Hidden Heroism: Black Soldiers in America's Wars* (Boulder, CO: Westview Press, 2001).

Benjamin Quarles, *The Negro in the American Revolution* (Chapel Hill, NC: Institute of Early American History and Culture, 1961), is still one of the best sources on the war for independence. On black participation in the Civil War, see Dudley T. Cornish, *The Sable Arm: Black Troops in the Union Army, 1861–1865* (Lawrence: University Press of Kansas, 1987); and James M. McPherson, *The Negro's Civil War: How American Blacks Felt and Acted during the War for the Union* (New York: Pantheon Books, 1965). A good primary account is Thomas Wentworth Higginson, *Army Life in a Black Regiment* (East Lansing: Michigan State University Press, 1960). Arthur E. Barbeau and Florette Henri have written one of the few histories of African Americans in World War I, *The Unknown Soldiers: Black American Troops in*

World War I (Philadelphia: Temple University Press, 1974). Emmett J. Scott, *Official History of the American Negro in the World War* (New York: Arno Press, 1969); and Kelly Miller, *History of the World War for Human Rights* (New York: Negro Universities Press, 1969), both published shortly after the end of the war, are dated but still useful. See also Charles H. Williams, *Negro Soldiers in World War I: The Human Side* (New York: AMS Press, 1970).

Much has been written about the black experience in World War II. Lou Potter, William Miles, and Nina Rosenblum, *Liberators: Fighting on Two Fronts in World War II* (New York: Harcourt Brace Jovanovich, 1992), is a good introductory history into the black experience, as is A. Russell Buchanan, *Black Americans in World War II* (Santa Barbara, CA: Clio Books, 1977). For a biography of Benjamin O. Davis Sr., the only black general in World War II, see Marvin E. Fletcher, *America's First Black General: Benjamin O. Davis, Sr., 1880–1970* (Lawrence: University Press of Kansas, 1989). A fine work highlighting the famed Tuskegee Airmen is Lynn M. Homan and Thomas Reilly, *Black Knights: The Story of the Tuskegee Airmen* (Gretna, LA: Pelican Publishing, 2001). Brenda L. Moore, *To Serve My Country, To Serve My Race: The Story of the Only African American WACS Stationed Overseas during World War II* (New York: New York University Press, 1996), ably chronicles the story of the 6888th Central Postal Directory Battalion. For the Korean War, see Lyle Rishell, *With a Black Platoon in Combat: A Year in Korea* (College Station: Texas A & M University Press, 1993); William T. Bowers, *Black Soldier, White Army: The 24th Infantry Regiment in Korea* (Washington, DC: Center of Military History, U. S. Army, 1996); and Charles M. Bussey, *Firefight at Yechon: Courage and Racism in the Korean War* (Washington, DC: Brassey's, 1991).

For a comprehensive study of African Americans and the Vietnam War, see James E. Westheider, *Fighting on Two Fronts: African Americans and the Vietnam War* (New York: New York University Press, 1997). Robert Mullen, *Blacks in America's Wars: The Shift in Attitudes from the Revolutionary War to Vietnam* (New York: Pathfinder Press, 1973), does a good job detailing the range of arguments and opinions concerning the war in the black community. Herman Graham III, *The Brothers' Vietnam War: Black Power, Manhood, and the Military Experience* (Gainesville: University Press of Florida, 2003), looks at the impact Vietnam had on black masculinity, arguing that several new models emerged from the war. For the impact of black nationalism on African Americans in the armed forces see Alvin J. Schexnider, "The Development of Nationalism: Political Socialization among Blacks in the U.S. Armed Forces" (Ph.D. dissertation, political science, Northwestern University, 1973). Martin Binkin and Mark J. Eitelberg examine the role of blacks in the armed forces from a sociological perspective in *Blacks and the Military* (Washington, D.C.: Brookings Institution Studies in Defense Policy Series, 1982). Maurice Zeitlin, Kenneth G. Lutterman, and James W. Russell, "Death in Vietnam: Class, Poverty, and the Risks of War," in *American Society Inc.: Studies of the Social Structure and Political Economy of the United States*, ed. Maurice Zeitlin (Chicago: Markham Publishing, 1970), looks at the impact of social class on African Americans.

Several excellent firsthand accounts can be found in Wallace Terry, *Bloods: An Oral History of the Vietnam War* (New York: Random House, 1984); and Stanley Goff and Robert Sanders, *Brothers: Black Soldiers in the Nam* (New York: Berkeley Books, 1985). Colin L. Powell's memoirs, coauthored with Joseph E. Persico, *My American Journey* (New York: Random House, 1995), discuss Powell's two tours in Vietnam at length, and it is one of the few accounts by a black officer who served in the war. David Parks, *GI Diary*, reprint edition (Washington, DC: Howard University, 1982), looks at the war in the early years of direct American involvement through the eyes of an upper-middle-class African American. Clyde Taylor, *Vietnam and Black America: An Anthology of Protest and Resistance* (Garden City, NY: Anchor Press, 1973), was one of the first accounts of black antiwar activity and resistance. James A. Daly and Lee Bergman, *A Hero's Welcome: The Conscience of Sergeant James Daly versus the United States Army* (Indianapolis, IN: Bobbs-Merrill, 1975), is Daly's account of his time as a POW and attempts by the U.S. government to brand him a collaborator. For a black deserter's perspective see Terry Whitmore, *Memphis, Nam, Sweden: The Autobiography of a Black American Exile* (Garden City, NY: Doubleday, 1971). For accounts of black women in Vietnam, see Kathryn Marshall, *In the Combat Zone: An Oral History of American Women in Vietnam, 1966–1975* (Boston: Little, Brown, 1987); and Keith Walker, *A Piece of My Heart: The Stories of 26 Women Who Served in Vietnam* (Novato, CA: Presidio Press, 1985). For biographies of black generals during the war, see J. Alfred Phelps, *Chappie: The Life and Times of Daniel James, Jr.* (Novato, CA: Presidio Press, 1991); and Benjamin O. Davis Jr., *Benjamin O. Davis, Jr., American: An Autobiography* (Washington, DC: Smithsonian Institution Press, 1991).

The armed forces have produced several useful studies on the black military experience. For a general study of the black military experience, see Office of the Deputy Assistant Secretary of Defense for Equal Opportunity, *Black Americans in Defense of Our Nation* (Washington, DC: U.S. Government Printing Office, 1981). A good source for primary documents relating to the black experience in the military since the Civil War is Bernard C. Nalty and Morris MacGregor, eds., *Blacks in the Military: Essential Documents*

(Wilmington, DE: Scholarly Resources, 1981). The integration of the armed forces is thoroughly documented in Morris J. MacGregor, *Integration of the Armed Forces, 1940–1965* (Washington, DC: Center of Military History, U.S. Army, 1981). A comprehensive study of equal opportunity in the early years of the war can be found in Morris J. MacGregor and Bernard C. Nalty, *Blacks in the United States Armed Forces*, vol. 11, Fahy Committee Report (Wilmington, DE: Scholarly Resources, 1977). For black officers in the Marine Corps, see Alphonse G. Davis, *Pride, Progress, and Prospects; The Marine Corp's Efforts to Increase the Presence of African-American Officers (1970–1995)* (Washington, DC: History and Museums Division, Headquarters, U.S. Marine Corps, 2000). The Pentagon's findings on racism in the armed forces can be found in Task Force on the Administration of Military Justice in the Armed Forces, *Report of the Task Force on the Administration of Military Justice in the Armed Forces* (Washington, DC: U.S. Government Printing Office, 1972).

Many scholars have examined the civil rights and black power movements in relation to the Vietnam War. Two good general articles to start with are Herbert Shapiro, "The Vietnam War and the American Civil Rights Movement," *Journal of Ethnic Studies* 16 (1989): 117–41; and Adam Fairclough, "Martin Luther King, Jr. and the War in Vietnam," *Phylon* 45 (1984): 19–39. For the best treatment of SNCC, see Clayborne Carson, *In Struggle: SNCC and the Black Awakening of the 1960s* (Cambridge: Harvard University Press, 1981). Philip S. Foner, ed. (editor), *The Black Panthers Speak* (Philadelphia: J. B. Lippincott Co., 1970), offers some insightful documents and excerpts from the Black Panther newspaper, but there is not much analysis or discussion of the material.

Several anthologies contain chapters on either African Americans or racial violence during the Vietnam War. See Paul L. Savage and Richard A. Gabriel, "Cohesion and Disintegration in the American Army, an Alternative Perspective," *Armed Forces and Society* 2 (May 1976): 340–76; James E. Westheider, "African Americans and the Vietnam War," in *A Companion to the Vietnam War*, ed. Marilyn B. Young and Robert Buzzanco (Oxford:Blackwell, 2002), 333–47; and James E. Westheider, "Sgt. Allen Thomas, Jr.: A Black Soldier in Vietnam," in *Portraits of African American Life Since 1865*, ed. Nina Mjagkij (Wilmington, DE: Scholarly Resources, 2003), 219–36.

Probably the best single book written on the Vietnam-era draft is Lawrence M. Baskir and William A. Strauss, *Chance and Circumstance: The Draft, the War, and the Vietnam Generation* (New York: Knopf, 1978). Also worth consulting is Michael S. Foley, *Confronting the War Machine: Draft Resistance during the Vietnam War* (Chapel Hill: University of North Carolina

Press, 2003); and Roger W. Little, *Selective Service and American Society* (New York: Russell Sage Foundation, 1969).

For issues concerning African Americans and the post-Vietnam all-volunteer armed forces see Herbert R. Northrup, *Black and Other Minority Participation in the All-Volunteer Navy and Marine Corps* (Philadelphia: Wharton School, University of Pennsylvania, 1979); Martin Binkin, *Who Will Fight the Next War: The Changing Face of the American Military* (Washington, DC: Brookings Institution, 1993); and William Bowman, Roger Little, and G. Thomas Sicilia, *The All-Volunteer Force after a Decade: Retrospect and Prospect* (Washington, DC: Pergamon-Brassey's, 1986). The government's assessment of the all-volunteer armed forces can be found in Thomas Gates, *A Summary of the Gates Commission Report: The Report of the President's Commission on an All-Volunteer Armed Force* (Washington, DC: U.S. Government Printing Office, 1970).

There are numerous general studies on the Vietnam War. George C. Herring, *America's Longest War: The United States and Vietnam, 1950–1975* (New York: McGraw Hill, 1996), is a good one to start with. Also recommended are Stanley Karnow, *Vietnam: A History* (New York: Viking Press, 1983); and George Moss, *Vietnam: An American Ordeal* (Upper Saddle River, NJ: Prentice Hall, 1998).

Index

absent without leave (AWOL), 57
ACB. *See* Army Classification Battery
ACTION, 113
Adams, Maurice L., 50
AFQT. *See* Armed Forces Qualification Test
African Americans in military, xvii–xxi, 113; chronology of, xi–xvi; and civil rights movement, 68–69; disillusionment with Vietnam War, 63–79, 137–40; history of, 1–15; officers, 2, 6–7, 93–95, 111; record of, 51–52; return from war, 106–13; subculture of, 76; in Vietnam, 39–62, 119. *See also* black
Agent Orange, 106–7
Agnew, Spiro, 74
Air Force, U.S.: history of African Americans in, 7; population by race, 119; race reform in, 98
Air Force Academy, Colorado Springs, CO, 94
Ali, Muhammad, xiii, xv, 30–32, 112
Allen, Doris "Lucki," 50
Allen, Richard, 74

all-volunteer army, and race relations, 110–11
American Civil Liberties Union, 28, 110
American Legion, 109
American Revolution, 1, 21
American Servicemen's Union, 96
Anderson, James, Jr., xv, 52, 102
Anderson, Lionel, 139
Annapolis Naval Academy. *See* West Point
antiwar movement, 63–79; African American soldiers on, 68–69; after war, 112–13; race relations in, 65–66
Armed Forces Qualification Test (AFQT), 42–44
Armed Forces Reserve, 34–36, 82
Army, U.S.: and desegregation, 8; population by race, 119; race reform in, 97; after Vietnam, 110
Army Classification Battery (ACB), 44
Article Fifteen, 55, 157. *See also* nonjudicial punishment
assignments, racism and, 42–46, 49–50, 95–96, 155–56
attrition strategy, 73

bad conduct discharge, 60–61
bad-paper discharge, 61
Baez, Joan, 33
Baker, Newton D., 3
basic training, 41–42
Belieu, Kenneth E., 69
Bell, David, 36
Berthoud, Kenneth H., Jr., 94
Bertler, Thomas L., 84
Bevel, James, 64
black(s). *See* African Americans
black militants, 24–25; black officers
    and, 94–95; discharge of, 96;
    influence of, 69–70, 72, 75; military
    response to, 95–96; terminology of,
    82
black nationalists, 24–25; and Vietnam
    War, 64–65
black officers: character of, 94–95; early
    history of, 2; increase in number of,
    93–94; and race reforms, 111; in
    World War II, 6–7
Black Panther Party for Self-Defense,
    xiii, 24; and death of Ho Chi Minh,
    70, 135–36; and Vietnam War, 63–65
black power canes, 76
black power flags, xx, 76, 78, 83
black power salute, 76, 88
Black Servicemen's Caucus, 82
Blackstone Rangers, 81
Bond, Julian, 29, 31, 66
boot camp, 41–42
Bosworth, Crispus, 39–40
Branch, Frederick C., xii
Breedlove, John "Jackie," 40
Brown, Beauregard, 50
Brown, Clyde, 85
Brown, James, 52
Brownsville Riot, xi–xii, 3
Brown v. Board of Education, 8, 11
Buffalo Soldiers, xi, 2
Burden, Tommy, 69
burial, racism and, 107–8

Burney, Willie E., Jr., 9, 83
Burns, Raymond, 84
Bush, George W., 35

Camp Allen Brothers, 145–46
Camp Gilbert H. Johnson, 102
Camp Lejeune, NC, racial violence at,
    xiv, xx, 87–88
canes, black power, 76
Captain's Mast, 55. *See also* nonjudicial
    punishment
Carmichael, Stokely, 25, 113; on
    casualty rates, 48; and draft, 31, 33;
    and Vietnam War, 64–66, 70
Carter, Jimmy, 112–13
Carter, Ron, 40, 44–46, 110–11
casualty rates, xx, 21; in Civil War, 2;
    race and, 47–50
Chafee, John, 150–51, 153
Chapman, Leonard F., 83
Chase, John, 74
checking in. *See* dapping
Chisholm, Shirley, 66, 145
Civil Air Transport, 19
Civil Rights Act, xii, 11, 14, 63; and
    housing discrimination, 10
civil rights movement, 24–25; division
    in, 66–67; and draft, 32–33
Civil War, 1–2, 21
Clark, Frank, 31
Clark, Ramsey, 32
Clay, Cassius. *See* Ali, Muhammad
Clay, Lucius, 66
Clay, Sonji, 31
Cleaver, Eldridge, 25, 70, 95
clothes: dashikis, 53, 76, 87, 102;
    reform and, 148–49
CO. *See* conscientious objector status
Colacicco, Michael F., 39, 90
Colley, Nathaniel, 124
Collins, Walter, 25, 36
Colored Officers' Training Camp, xii,
    xviii, 3

combat units; assignment to, 44; and casualty rates, 49; and racial violence, 93; refusal of orders by, 106; in World War I, 4

command, African Americans and, 3; racism and, 156

commissioned officer ranks, 115–16

Committee on Equal Opportunity in the Armed Forces: establishment of, 124–25; memorandum on, 126–27

Confederate flags, 78, 84–85

Congressional Black Caucus: investigation by, 141–44; and military justice system, 101; report of, 155–60; and Vietnam War, 66

Congress of Racial Equality (CORE), xiii, 25, 31, 68

conscientious objector (CO) status, 27, 29–31

conscription, 21–36

Constellation, racial violence on, xv, 90, 92

containment, 19

Conyers, John, 26

CORE. *See* Congress of Racial Equality

courts-martial, 54–55, 57–58; minority representation on boards, 82; reform of, 102

Crawford, Jeanette, 32

Crawford, Warren, 36

cross burnings, 85

cultural expression. *See* racial emblems

Cummings, Tom, 40

Daley, Richard, 74

Daly, James, 29, 40, 71, 112

Da Nang Brig, 59, 82, 86

Daniel, Dan, 82

Daniels, George, 59

dapping, xx, 83; ban on, 83–84, 96; black officers and, 94–95; term, 76

dashikis, 53, 76, 87, 102

Davis, Benjamin O., Jr., xii, xv, 5

Davis, Benjamin O., Sr., xii, 2, 5

Davis, Cecil F., 93

Davis, Hubert, 32

Davison, Frederic E., xiii, 50–51, 156

death penalty, 59

Defense Race Relations Institute, 98

deferments, 22, 26–27

Dellums, Ron, 66, 110, 142

De Mau Mau, 81

Deputy Assistant Secretary of Defense for Civil Rights, xii

desegregation of military, xix, 7–8

desertion, 75–76; and return, 112

Dewey, Thomas, 7

DI. *See* drill instructor

Diggs, Charles, 26

discharge system, 60–61; and black militants, 96; Congressional Black Caucus on, 157–58; other-than-honorable, by race, *120*

dishonorable discharge, 60–61

Dixon, Marty, 96

Domestic Action Council, xiv, 97

domino theory, 19

Double V program, xviii

Douglass, Frederick, xvii

draft, 21–36

draft boards, 27–28; minority representation on, 28–29

drill instructor (DI), 41–42

drug abuse, in military, 110

Drummond, Roscoe, 15

DuBois, W. E. B., 3

Ebony, 54

economic issues: and draft, 26, 34; and enlistment, 9; and return from war, 108

education: *Brown v. Board of Education*, 8, 11; and courts-martial, 58; GI Bill and, 108; of military dependents, 11–12; and test performance, 43

educational deferments, 22, 26–27

Edwards, Don, 110
Edwards, Reginald, 9
enlisted ranks, 117–18
enlistment, rationale for, 9–10
entertainment: racism and, 52–53;
    reform and, 152–53; voluntary
    segregation and, 77
Erickson, Mark St. John, 113
Evers, Charles, 28
Executive Order no. 8802, xviii, 5
Executive Order no. 9981, xii, xix, 7,
    122–23

Fair Employment Practices Commission
    (FEPC), xviii, 5
Ferran, Raul, 109
First Gulf War, 111–12
Fitt, Alfred, 13
flags, black power. See black power flags
Flipper, Henry O., xi
Florida A & M University, 94
FO. See forward observer
Ford, Gerald, 112
Forman, James, 63
Forrestal, James, 7
Fortas, Abe, 124
Fort Des Moines, xii, xviii, 3
Fort Hood United Front, 56–57, 141–44
forward observer (FO), 46
fragging, 89–90; term, 89

Garland, Stanley L., 32
Garvey, Marcus, 76
general discharge, 60
Gesell, Gerhard A., 124
Gesell Committee: establishment of,
    124–25; memorandum on, 126–27
GI Bill, 108–9
GIs United Against the War, xiv, 69
Glenn, Rinell R., 53
Gravely, Samuel L., Jr., xv, 41, 111
Great Depression, 5
Gulf of Tonkin Resolution, xiii, 20

hair-care products, 54, 102; reform and,
    152
hairstyles: and nonjudicial punishment,
    56; reform and, 102, 147–48, 152
Hall, Joseph H., 72
hardship deferments, 27, 29
Hare, Nathan, 66
Harlem Hellfighters, 4
Harper, Richard W., 50
Harvey, William, Jr., 59
Hassayampa, 92
Hauser, Pinkie, 50
Hershey, Lewis, 32
historically black colleges and
    universities: and antiwar movement,
    65–66; and ROTC, 94
Ho Chi Minh, xii, 17–19, 71; death of,
    70, 135–36
Holloman, Lawrence, 46, 68
honorable discharge, 60
Hope, Bob, 52–53, 84
housing: Congressional Black Caucus
    on, 156–57; desegregation of, 10; off-
    base, discrimination in, 10, 12–15;
    reform and, 151; voluntary
    segregation and, 78, 96
Houston Riot, xii, 4
Howard University, 66
Humphrey, Hubert, 105

Inchon, 92
institutional racism: versus legal racism,
    40; in military, 40–47; whites and,
    46–47
Intrepid, 92
Islam, 29–32, 57, 143

Jack, Alex, 33
Jackson, Kenneth, 109
Jackson State College, 66
James, Daniel "Chappie," xv, 51, 94–95,
    101
James, Robert, 32, 36

Japan, 17–19
Jenkins, William K., 8
Jet, 54
Johnson, Dwight H., 107, 129–30
Johnson, Gilbert H., 102
Johnson, Lyndon B.; and antiwar movement, 66–67, 72; and civil rights movement, xii, xiii, 63; and housing guidelines, 10; and James, 51; and Vietnam War, 20–21
Johnson, Thomas, 48
Jones, Allen E., 42
Jones, Nathaniel, xv
Jones, Robert E., 68
Jordan, Mayanard III, xv, 69
Judge Advocate General's Office, racial composition of, 58–59
Ju Ju, 81

Kaneohe Marine Corps Air Station, HI, racial violence at, xiv, 88
Karenga, Maulana, 64
Kelley, Roger T., 41
Kennedy, John F., 10–11, 20, 124–25
Kennedy, Robert, 11, 112
Kent State University, 66
King, Coretta Scott, 67
King, Martin Luther, Jr., 25, 31; assassination of, xiv, 71–75, 82, 85, 133–34; and split in civil rights movement, 66–68; and Vietnam War, xiii, xix–xx, 63
Kissinger, Henry, xv, 105
Kitty Hawk, racial violence on, xv, 90–92
Knox, Frank, 7
Korean War, xii, 8
Kraft Foods, 54
Ku Klux Klan, 5, 75, 81, 84, 157; and draft boards, 29; in military, 85
Kushner, Floyd, 40

Laird, Melvin R., xiv, 97
Lawson, Phillip, 70

leadership: and race reforms, 99–100; and racial violence, 93–94
Le Duc Tho, xv, 105
legal racism, versus institutional, 40
Lester, Julius, 70
Lewis, John, 32–33, 112–13
liberty, reform and, 149
Liston, Sonny, 30
Long Binh Stockade, xiv, 59, 86–87
lottery system, for draft, 26–27
Louis, Joe, 30
Lucky, Victor, 96
Lynch, Lincoln, 64

MAAG. *See* Military Assistance and Advisory Group
MacArthur, Douglas, 8
magazines, black, 53–54; reform and, 153
Malcolm X Society, xv, 69
Manheim Stockade, 85
manhood, and enlistment, 9–10
manpower channeling, 22
Marine Corps, U.S.: and black officers, 94; and desegregation, 8; history of African Americans in, 5; population by race, *119*; race reform in, 97–98; and racial violence, 88
Marshall, George C., 6
Marshall, Thurgood, 8
Maxwell, Hurdle L., 45
McCloy, John, xviii–xix
McDaniel, Norman A., 72, 112
McNamara, Robert, xii, xiii; and antiwar movement, 72–73; on casualty rates, 48; and housing guidelines, 10, 12–13; and National Guard, 35; and racial emblems, 84
McRae, Johny, 96
Medal of Honor: citations for, 128–30; recipients of, 2, 52, 107
medical deferments, 27
mentors, 45–46

Mickey Mouse regulations, 56
Midway, race relations on, xvi, 110
Mighty, Otilio, 108
Miles, Joseph, xiv, 69
Military Academy, West Point, NY, 2,
  5, 94
Military Assistance and Advisory
  Group (MAAG), 19
military bases, physical nature of, and
  racial violence, 86
Military Justice Act, 102
military justice system: Congressional
  Black Caucus on, 157–58; racism
  and, 54–61; reform of, 100–2; Stokes
  and, 141–43; Thomas on, 133
Military Occupational Specialty
  (MOS), 4, 43–45
Militia Act of 1792, xi, 1
Miller, William, 10
Millington Naval Air Station, TN,
  racial violence at, xiv, 88
Mississippi Freedom Democratic Party,
  25
MOS. *See* Military Occupational
  Specialty
Mosby, Priscilla, 53
Moses, Robert, 63–64
Moskos, Charles, 113
Moton, Robert R., 3
Motown Records, 54
Movement for a Democratic Military,
  xiv
Muhammad, Elijah, 30–32, 64
Murray, Paul Isaac, 138
Muse, Benjamin, 124
music, 54; racism and, 52; voluntary
  segregation and, 77
Muslims, treatment of, 29–32, 57, 143

Nash-Bevel, Diane, 70
National Association for the
  Advancement of Colored People
  (NAACP): and draft, 28–29; and
  military justice system, 101; and
  racial emblems, 84; and Vietnam
  War, 66–68; and World War I, 3
National Black Anti-War Anti-Draft
  Union, 64
National Guard, 34–36, 82
National Liberation Front, 20
National Urban League, 66–68; on
  African American performance in
  military, 51; and returning veterans,
  108–9
Nation of Islam, 24, 29–31, 64
Naval Academy, Annapolis, MD, 94
Navy, U.S.: history of African
  Americans in, 4–5, 7; population by
  race, *119*; race reform in, 98, 100,
  110–11, 147–54; and racial violence,
  90–92; recruitment, 90–91
New Mobilization Committee to End
  the War in Vietnam, 70
Newton, Huey, xiii, 24, 70
Ngo Dinh Diem, 20
Nguyen Ai Quoc. *See* Ho Chi Minh
Ninety-second Division, 4
Ninety-third Division, 4
Ninth Cavalry Regiment, xi, 2
Nixon, Richard M., 72, 105
noncommissioned officers, 95
nonjudicial punishment, 54–57;
  Congressional Black Caucus on, 157;
  reform of, 101–2; Stokes and, 143;
  Thomas on, 132–33
Norman, William S., 98
North Carolina Central University, 94

occupational deferments, 22
off-base housing, 20; Congressional
  Black Caucus on, 156–57;
  discrimination in, 10, 12–15; reform
  and, 151; voluntary segregation and,
  78, 96
off-base recreation, voluntary
  segregation and, 77–78
Office of Strategic Services, xviii
Officer Candidate Schools, 6, 94

officers: black, 2, 6–7, 93–95, 111;
noncommissioned, 95; Thomas on,
132; white, 3, 89, 99–100
Olive, Milton Lee III, 52
O'Meara, Joseph, 124
O'Neill, Bill, 109
one-year rotation policy, 106; and draft,
23; and post-traumatic stress
disorder, 107; and racial violence, 86
over-strength program, 35–36

Paris Peace Accords, xv, 105
Parker, Henry L., 49
Parks, David, 46
Patterson, Floyd, 31
Patti, Archimedes, 19
Paul, Norman S., 126–27
Peace Committee, 71
penalties, in military justice system,
racism and, 59–61
People's Justice Committee, 96, 141–44
Peoples Liberation Armed Forces
(PLAF), 20
Pershing, John J., 4–5
personal racism, in military, 39–40
Petersen, Frank E., Jr., xiii, 8, 51
Pham Van Dong, 17
Poole, Cecil, 34
post exchanges: racism and, 53–54;
reform and, 102, 152
post-traumatic stress disorder (PTSD),
23, 107
Powell, Adam Clayton, Jr., 26
Powell, Colin; on assignments, 50; and
black militants, 95; career of, 9,
111–12; and civil rights movement,
68; and fragging, 89; on housing, 12;
and mentoring, 45; military record
of, 51; and ROTC, 94; on voluntary
segregation, 77
POWs. See prisoners of war
Prairie View A& M, xiv, 94
President's National Advisory Council
on Civil Disorders, 34–36

pretrial confinement, 57–58, 157
Price, George B., 45
pride, and enlistment, 9–10
prison: draft evasion and, 36; military,
59, 102
prisoners of war (POWs), 105, 112;
African American, treatment of,
71–72
Project 100,000, xiii
Project Transition, 108
promotion process: racism and, 40,
45–46, 156; Thomas on, 132–33
PTSD. See post-traumatic stress disorder
Pulley, Andrew, 69

race reforms in military, xx–xxi,
90–103; barriers to, 99–100;
Congressional Black Caucus on,
158–60; negotiation of, 61–62, 74;
Zumwalt and, 147–54
racial emblems, xx, 76, 83–85; and
housing, 78; and nonjudicial
punishment, 56; reform and, 102;
suppression of, 96
racial stereotypes: and draft boards, 29;
in military, 40
racial violence, xi–xii, 3–4, 23–24, 35,
74, 110; in military, xx, 81–103, 113;
military response to, 81, 87, 92–103;
music and, 52; Thomas on, 133
racism in military, xx, 83–85, 110; in
basic training, 42; Congressional
Black Caucus report on, 155–60; and
draft boards, 29; institutional, 40–47;
personal, 39–40; Stokes and, 141–44;
terminology of, 83; Thomas on,
132–33; in World War II, 6
Randolph, Asa Philip, xviii, 7, 68, 134
Rangel, Charles, 157
Ray, James Earl, xiv
recreation, off-base, voluntary
segregation and, 77–78
recreational facilities, 77; racism and,
52; reform and, 148–49

recruitment, 35–36; after World War I, 5; and all-volunteer army, 110–11
reenlistment rates, xxi, 9, 111; and casualty rates, 49; disillusionment and, 75
reform. *See* race reforms in military
refusal of orders: for combat duty, 106; for riot duty, 74–75
religion, and nonjudicial punishment, 56–57
Reorganization Act, 2
Reserve Officer Training Corps (ROTC), xiv, 94, 111
return from war, 106–13
reverse discrimination, claims of, 78, 82
Ribicoff, Abraham, 11
Ridgeway, Matthew, 8
right to fight, xviii, xix, 3
riot duty, refusal of, 74–75
Rivers, L. Mendel, 32
Roberson, Joe, Jr., 46
Robinson, Bill, 109
Robinson, Jackie, 31
Rodriguez, Carlos, 137–38
Rogers, Charles Calvin, 128–29
Roosevelt, Franklin D., xii, xviii, 5–6, 22
ROTC. *See* Reserve Officer Training Corps
Russell, Richard B., 48

salute, black power, 76, 88
Savage, Phillip, 84
Schaub, John, 92
schooling. *See* education
SCLC. *See* Southern Christian Leadership Conference
Scott, James H., 69
Seale, Bobby, xiii, 24, 70, 144
segregation in military: and veterans' organizations, 109; voluntary, 76–78, 82; in World War II, 6
selective service, 21–36
Selective Service Act of 1940, xii, 22

Selective Service Act of 1948, 22–23
Sellers, Cleveland, xiii, 25, 28, 33, 113
Seneff, George, 142–43
Sengstacke, John, 124
seniority, racism and, 45
Sepia, 53–54
Shoffer, George, 47–48
shopping: racism and, 53–54; reform and, 102, 152
short-timer's disease, 106
slave bracelets, xx, 56, 76
Smedley, Jack, 78
Smith, Billy Dean, 57, 61
Smith, Casper, 108
Smith, James Webster, xi
SNCC. *See* Student Nonviolent Coordinating Committee
Soul Alley, 75, 77
Southern Christian Leadership Conference (SCLC), 63, 66
Spring Mobilization for Peace, 64
Stanley, Clifford L., 111
stereotypes. *See* racial stereotypes
Stimson, Henry, 6
Stokes, Louis, 141–43; report of, 155–60
Student Nonviolent Coordinating Committee (SNCC), xiii, 24–25; and draft, 32–33; and Vietnam War, 63–65, 68
Students for a Democratic Society, 65
Sumpter, 92

Tapp, William B., 10
Tenth Cavalry Regiment, xi, 2
Terry, Bill, 107–8
Terry, Wallace, 69, 75
Tet Offensive, xiv, xix, 72–73
Thomas, Allen, Jr.; and civil rights movement, 68; interview with, 131–34; on King assassination, 73–74; and promotion, 40; on race relations, 110; record of, 51–52; on risk, 47; and segregation, 10; and

shopping, 54; and veterans'
    organizations, 109
369th Regiment, 4
Townsend, M. W., 91
Truman, Harry S, xii, xix, 7, 19, 122–23
Tuck, Thomas, 61
Turner, John, 64
Tuskegee University, 66
Twenty-fifth Infantry Regiment, xi, 2
Twenty-fourth Infantry Regiment, xi, 2

undesirable discharge, 60
unemployment, African Americans
    and, 9, 108
uniforms, reform and, 148–49
United States Colored Troops, xi, 2
United States v. Seeger, 29

Vance, Cyrus, 13
Veterans' organizations, and African
    Americans, 109
Vietminh, xviii–xix, 18–19; term, 17
Vietnamization, 105–13; and draft, 26–27
Vietnam War: African American
    military experience in, 39–62;
    demographics of troops in, xix–xx,
    21, 105, *119–120*; disillusionment
    with, 63–79, 137–40; origins of,
    xviii–xix, 17–37; public support for,
    72–73; Thomas on, 131
violence. *See* racial violence
Virginia Union University, 65
Vollmerhaus, Wilfried, 14
volunteers, in Vietnam, 50–51
Vo Nguyen Giap, 17, 19
Voter Education Project, 112
Voting Rights Act, xiii, 63

Waggoner, Lawrence E., 50, 69
Walker, Thomas F., 139–40
walking point, 47
Wallace, George, 105
Ward, J. D., 92
Warren, James C., 50

Washington, George, 21
Watkins, Willie, 71
Watts riots, xiii, 24
Weathermen, 65
Webster, Taft, 88, 111
West, Philip D., 53
Westbrook, Arthur, 47
Westmoreland, William C.: and antiwar
    movement, 73; on casualty rates, 49;
    and housing, 14; on race issues, 41,
    50–51, 81, 95, 100; and reform, 97
West Point, 2, 5, 94
Wheeler, Earle G., 48
White, John R., 46
White, Milton, xv, 69, 72, 95
white officers: and black commanders,
    3; and race reforms, 99–100; and
    racial violence, 89; Thomas on, 132
whites: and black militants, 82; and
    institutional racism, 46–47; Thomas
    on, 131–32
Whitmore, Terry, 71, 112
Williams, Jimmy, 107–8
Williams, John Bell, 28
Wilson, John, 65
Wilson, Wesley C., 10–11
women, African American, in Vietnam,
    50, 77, 87–88, 95, 152
World War I, xviii, 3–5, 21–22
World War II, xviii–xix, 5–7
Wright, Alfonza, 95, 109
Wright, J. M., 53–54

X, Malcolm, 24, 68–69, 134

Yale demonstration, 65
Young, Charles, xi, 2–3
Young, Whitney M., xiv, 67–68, 93, 124;
    on casualty rates, 49; on racism, 50

Zumwalt, Elmo R., Jr., xv, 90, 96, 98,
    100; reputation of, 110–11;
    telegrams by, 147–54

~

About the Author

James E. Westheider is associate professor of American history and interim chair of the Humanities Division at the University of Cincinnati–Clermont College where he has been a faculty member since 1998. He is the author of *Fighting on Two Fronts: African-Americans and the Vietnam War*. He and his wife Virginia, a college administrator, live with their golden retriever, Sam, and three cats, Clio, Josh, and Tucker.